THE
LAST
GOOD
YEAR

THE
LAST
GOOD
YEAR

SEVEN GAMES THAT ENDED AN ERA

DAMIEN COX

VIKING

VIKING
an imprint of Penguin Canada,
a division of Penguin Random House Canada Limited

Canada • USA • UK • Ireland • Australia •
New Zealand • India • South Africa • China

First published 2018

LIBRARY AND ARCHIVES CANADA CATALOGUING IN PUBLICATION

Cox, Damien, 1961-, author
The last good year : seven games that ended an era / Damien Cox.

Issued in print and electronic formats.
ISBN 978-0-7352-3476-5 (hardcover).—ISBN 978-0-7352-3477-2 (electronic)

1. National Hockey League—History. 2. Toronto Maple Leafs
(Hockey team)—History. 3. Los Angeles Kings (Hockey team)—History.
I. Title.

GV847.8.N3C69 2018   796.962'64   C2018-902389-9
                                                          C2018-902390-2

Jacket and interior design by Kelly Hill
Jacket photos: Graig Abel / Contributor / Getty Images;
(ice) MagicDogWorkshop / Shutterstock

Printed and bound in Canada

10 9 8 7 6 5 4 3 2 1

Penguin
Random House
VIKING CANADA

To VW
My compass, my muse.

CONTENTS

PROLOGUE

A QUARTER CENTURY AGO, the NHL was chaotic and lively. A beautiful mess. An absence of order defined the league, combined with a charming informality. It was a gold mine for a newspaper reporter with ambition and curiosity. For me, it was my fourth year covering the NHL and the Toronto Maple Leafs as a beat reporter for Canada's largest newspaper, the *Toronto Star*. At that time, being with the Leafs on a daily basis was to be in the middle of an intensely competitive newspaper battle for stories and scoops, and the Leafs were never far from controversy and headlines. Some editors insisted it was the most important beat at the paper. It was old-style, kick-the-other-guy's butt journalism. You woke up every day wondering what the competition had, and you went to sleep every night hoping against hope you had something they didn't. News wasn't tightly managed or controlled. It could come from any angle and a multitude of sources. Everybody was willing to talk, and there were no repercussions for talking out of turn. Reporters and media members mingled with players and coaches at airports, taxi stands, bars and hotels. We flew on the same flights they did, sometimes sitting beside them. We had their home phone numbers. We met their families. The Leafs hadn't been very good for a long time, but they were wonderfully rich copy and they were still at the epicentre of the hockey world, despite years of losing. The self-destructive Harold Ballard era was over, and the arrival of Cliff Fletcher, Pat Burns and Doug Gilmour created excitement and intrigue around the team. There were a lot of people involved with the team that were easy to like and interesting to cover. The '92–93 Leafs were, in many ways, an open book.

They were a reflection of a league that was in many ways anything but sophisticated. Or even well managed. Some teams were rich in history and success, others were disorganized and poorly run. There was an unevenness to the NHL's structure, and sometimes there was no structure at all. The players, once almost exclusively Canadian, were coming from the US and Europe in steadily increasing numbers, bringing new ideas and sensibilities about how the game should be played, coached and organized. At the same time, traditional forces dominated, insisting that certain elements of the game, particularly the most violent, needed to be retained at all costs. This produced a clashing and blending of hockey styles, and a variety of different competitive approaches by different teams.

No two players skated the same. Arenas smelled different from one another, and felt different. The lights might go out in the middle of the Stanley Cup final. The league president might go AWOL in the middle of the playoffs, sparking a wildcat officials strike. Teams went broke, owners transgressed unwritten rules (and written ones). Players were exploited, important problems were swept under the rug in infuriating fashion. The game was filled with secret deals and hush-hush agreements. The owners lied about the size of their profits, unwilling to see the players as anything more than employees. Or pawns.

Wide-open offensive hockey ruled and goalies were normal-sized men wearing normal-sized gear. The 1992–93 season was the last NHL campaign with an average of more than seven goals per game. News filtered slowly from outpost to outpost in the last days before the World Wide Web. The barriers between players and reporters were paper-thin. A player like Al Iafrate would chat while working on his sticks, lighting cigarettes with a blowtorch as he sought the perfect curve. You didn't need an appointment for an interview, or to go through public relations staff. Just pull up a chair, and hope you don't mind the smoke. The biggest name in the game, Wayne Gretzky, would conduct interviews in his car outside his team's practice facility. The game oozed characters, and those characters were easily accessible.

The NHL was a confusing and compelling cornucopia of stars, goons, goals, fights, corruption, rumours, egos, tradition, scoundrels, fierce competition, raw ambition, intrigue, blood, brilliance and greed.

Was the 1992–93 NHL better than the NHL of today? It was a better story, for damn sure.

For fourteen days in May, 1993, the Toronto Maple Leafs and Los Angeles Kings, two teams oozing personality and style, captivated the hockey world. The memories of that playoff series remain vivid and lasting. It still breathes, almost as if there is something more to give, answers yet to be unearthed.

Filled with colourful characters, superb athletes, rugged competitors and controversial incidents, the series serves as a snapshot of a certain time and place in NHL history. It produced indelible moments, some that can still cause arguments over exactly what transpired. The memories of that series can still bring grown men to tears a quarter century later. Some can't even bring themselves to talk about it at all. Others can't watch the final games, still frustrated by the mistakes they made. One game is remembered mostly for the identity of the referee, and the infamous decision he made.

The competition literally pitted blood against blood, cousin against cousin. Players received death threats in their hotel rooms. Accusations still fly across the benches over some of the uglier moments. "It was intense, man," recalls Barry Melrose, coach of the '93 Kings. "There was a lot of stuff said and done that probably a lot of people wish hadn't happened."

Seven games in fourteen days in two very different North American cities. The Leafs were a famous hockey club that had forgotten what winning even felt like. They had started the '93 postseason as though, as usual, they wouldn't be around long, losing two one-sided games to a high-octane Detroit team that had scored more goals than any other NHL club that season and shredded the Toronto defence in the first two games. This wasn't a surprise. The Leafs, after all, had only won two playoff series in a decade, and they hadn't made the playoffs at all the previous two seasons. But this team somehow absorbed the early setbacks and ultimately outlasted the favoured Red Wings in seven games, winning the series in Motown on Nikolai Borschevsky's thrilling tip-in goal in Game 7. The city of Toronto reacted with an impromptu combination of excitement and delight. In a city where there hadn't been a Stanley Cup parade in twenty-six years, fans took to the streets to register their enthusiastic approval. It was only a first-round playoff victory, but fans danced in the streets, chanting "Go Leafs Go" as if a championship had been won. Cars drove up and down Yonge Street, the city's main thoroughfare, honking horns. They'd seen Blue Jays fans celebrate a World Series triumph months earlier, and if this party appeared a little over-the-top for a relatively moderate accomplishment, if it caused hockey fans in other towns to mock Toronto, Leafs fans didn't mind looking a little silly. Instead of throwing team jerseys on the ice in disgust, they were wearing them proudly for the first time in years.

When the Leafs then defeated St. Louis in another tough seven-game series, with Wendel Clark's thundering slapshot off the mask of Blues goalie Curtis Joseph as the punctuation point, fans celebrated again. More fans. This was gaining momentum. It was all so unexpected, and fans of the team were thrust into an unfamiliar state of being.

Was this really happening? Could the Stanley Cup, a memory in black-and-white, really be a possibility?

The next opponent hailed from Hollywood, long a destination for Canadians with big dreams of fame and riches. The Kings, the most expensive team money could buy at that time, arrived on their luxurious private jet with one of Canada's greatest hockey heroes, Gretzky, as their leader. They were a hardnosed band of veterans and ruffians, big-money stars and rookies, a team that loved to score and fight and was just as determined to end their franchise's reputation as a loser as the Leafs were determined to stop being a punchline to every hockey joke.

The clash between the Leafs and Kings turned into a riveting, unforgettable hockey play told in seven acts, and it came down to the final minutes of the third period of the seventh act before anything was decided. Even then, only a winner was decided. Many other things were left unresolved.

When it was over, it seemed as if the two teams had taken the history of the NHL, packed all the traditions, contradictions and gut appeal of the sport into seven raucous, unforgettable games, and then moved on to a new era.

It was in that playoff series, with one foot in the past and a toe moving into an uncertain future, that the NHL seemed to hit its sweet spot.

Just enough order, and just enough chaos.

Today, the NHL has improved in every way. The athletes are wealthier, stronger, healthier and more skilled. The game is faster and far less violent. The benefits and protections for the players have been massively enhanced. The owners have a far more profitable venture, and can sell new franchises for $650 million, more than twelve times what they could a quarter century ago.

There is now a high level of quality control, creating a league of parity, of sameness. The NHL, once a collection of idiosyncratic franchises run with relative independence, has become a single unit devoted to the manufacturing of hockey as a product. As Andy Warhol once said of the modern consumer culture, "all the cokes are the same and all the cokes are good." That's the NHL today. All the hockey is good. And all the hockey is the same. Las Vegas joined the league as an expansion franchise for the 2017–18 season and immediately became one of the best teams. The Golden Knights were instantly just as good as everyone else. Just the same.

Games are now staged in massive football and baseball

stadiums, packaged as hockey returning to its outdoor roots. You can read all about it on NHL.com, public relations disguised as journalism. Or watch it on the NHL Network. Every day is sunny and breezy. Today, the NHL is organized and unrelenting in its message.

With change has come undeniable progress. No longer are the official game summaries hand-written in ink like they were back in '93, different in every town. You get the same NHL standard wherever you go. But something has also been lost. Like when the corner coffee shop that's been there for years gives way to a Starbucks. Or when something that was once handcrafted becomes mass-produced. You might get consistency, reliability and even affordability, but without the quirks, oddities and enduring uniqueness. "It was always a business," says Clark, the former Leafs captain. "Now it's only a business."

So it's easy to be drawn once again to the powerful embers of '93, to a time when the game offered something you felt in your gut and produced more of a visceral reaction.

It feels good to go back to that time, those arenas, those players who we seemed to know better because we might see them walking to their car after practice. There is a danger, sure, in wiping away the cobwebs from all that has transpired, in drinking too deeply of the nostalgia. But there were important things about the game that have been mislaid along the way. Things that made our pulse quicken. "You had guys on your team who would go through the end boards for anyone who sat next to them," says Tony Granato, a winger on that LA team. "I know I'd like to have that back in our game. That competitiveness, that brotherhood, that willingness to do anything for a teammate."

For fourteen days in May, the Leafs and the Kings controlled the attention of the hockey world. Much has changed in hockey since. But the tale those teams wove remains as entertaining, compelling and meaningful as it ever was. It's a joy to revisit.

Damien Cox
June, 2018

ACT ONE

"It was always the seventh game of the Stanley Cup final."

That was hockey for Marty McSorley. Every game—whether it was as a boy on a frigid winter day rushing to get his skates on and hustle down to play on the canal that cut through his family's three-hundred-acre farm or any one of the 1,076 National Hockey League games in which he was a participant—was Game 7. Always Game 7. You competed every day like the Cup was on the line. He was the fifth of ten children, and the fourth son, born to Bill and Anne McSorley. "There was no crying," he remembers. McSorley men were tough. His blessed mother was tougher. "I remember her up in the haymow with a baby on one hip, dragging bales." He shed no tears and avoided no battles in the NHL either, accumulating 3,755 penalty minutes along with 225 official fights. He was a kid who fought his way to professional hockey, became a well-known bodyguard to one of the all-time greats and evolved into a quality NHL defenceman. He became a Stanley Cup champion. For all of that, he paid a price, a fearsome price, one he breathes and feels every day.

At fifty-four, still with a full head of hair, he looks good decked out head-to-toe in black, just like in his Los Angeles Kings days after the team had dumped its traditional purple-and-gold for something more menacing. He has the same wide, mischievous smile and the same excited earnestness that makes him an effective debater when it comes to causes or ideas he believes in. He oozes personality, just like a lot of players who earned reputations as tough guys during their NHL careers. Often the enforcers were the most quotable players on their teams, the most engaging, and McSorley certainly was always that. They had a hard, frightening job, and many were insecure about how they were perceived as hockey players. It was as if, by being participants in the daily hockey conversation, they could feel more a part of it. Or they just had more to say about it.

McSorley has arrived ten minutes late at a stylish restaurant in Manhattan Beach. He orders two glasses of a favourite California Pinot. "But only if it's been opened today," he says, also asking if the tomatoes on his swordfish are fresh. The Cayuga, Ontario farm boy with a touch of LA style. He's been at his nine-year-old daughter's basketball game near Hermosa Beach, where he and his family live. Did she score any points? "A lot," he says. "You know, this is a crazy gene pool here. There are all kinds of former NHL players, NFL players, the best volley-ball players in the world, they all live here. The kids' sports are amazing." He's married to a former professional volleyball player himself, and they have three children under the age of ten.

Life is mostly good. He's in touch with lots of old hockey friends, helps organize alumni games, and gets to relive the old battles and victories. But getting up from a chair is often difficult. Painful. Remembering things, like this appointment, can be a challenge. "I had to leave two Post-it notes and get my wife to remind me," he says, "or I would have been sitting at home when you called wondering where I was." The conversation leads to his physical well-being, to all the injuries he incurred in years of playing in the NHL, wearing a helmet that offered little protection and shoulder pads that were designed for quickly sliding off after the gloves were dropped. He suffers from severe arthritis in his right wrist. The fist that mashed the cartilage in many a nose now has barely any grip strength. The left wrist pops freakily out of joint. Both hips are untrustworthy, which means when he rides his bike, as he did tonight, he needs to use the curb to get on and off. His left arm, badly dislocated at the shoulder once, can't be lifted above his armpit, and he has to sleep every night on his right side. He pays $30,000 a year in health insurance but can't get the brain scan he wants to give him confidence he's going to be okay in the years to come. He's been fighting an ongoing battle over workers' compensation.

All this takes time, patience and energy, and some days McSorley just doesn't have enough of any of those commodities. He likes to get up at 5 A.M., go for coffee and try to play Sudoku or do a crossword puzzle. Sometimes he can; sometimes he can't. Through all the challenges, he still remains upbeat and articulate, loves to talk hockey and remember the big games and the big fights, loves to talk about when he was one of the best big men in the game. "I loved to play," he says. "I'm proud that I was a hockey player. I played with the best players in the world for seventeen years. I got to play with the best player in the game."

Today, what McSorley was, the role he played, no longer exists in the NHL. He is now, in effect, a fossil from an old world that used to be the NHL, one in which a player capable with his fists and willing to fight every night, and sometimes more than once, could get drafted, signed and gradually develop the skills necessary to play either a regular shift or even become a star. For his entire career, fighting was accepted not only as a feature of hockey but something integral to the sport. It mattered, the players always insisted it mattered, even as critics suggested it shouldn't be part of the game, and players who did it well could be part of very good teams and earn a very good living.

Teams actively sought that kind of player regardless of what other skills they might have, and many became household names. It came fairly naturally to McSorley. It was in his blood. He had a grandfather nicknamed "Box" because he liked to scrap. He had brothers, and they solved their disputes on their own. He was essentially a big, raw-boned tough without refined hockey skills when he entered the league with Pittsburgh in 1983.

He was so raw, he wasn't even drafted. But five years later, after having moved on to Edmonton, he was included in the famous trade that sent Wayne Gretzky to Los Angeles specifically to make sure Number 99 had adequate protection as he spread the gospel of the NHL in Southern California. Hollywood happily embraced a new, colourful sheriff in town. From there, McSorley developed into a very good defenceman, with offensive flair and boldness, albeit one who still earned hundreds of minutes in penalties every season. His years in Edmonton with the high-flying Oilers had helped him acquire skills that many players with his job description never had an opportunity to develop. He grew to the point where he could dominate a game with his talent, not just his fists, a player with offensive confidence and patience who could collaborate with the very best hockey players on the planet.

Today, the type of prospect he was when he started wouldn't even get his foot in the door. The enforcers of yesterday have all been replaced by faster, more skilled players in the faster, more skilled NHL. Fights rarely occur in the modern NHL. The game moves too fast for those who need it to stop before their real skills kick in. "We don't fight in hockey anymore," says Gretzky. "And I think that's a good thing."

McSorley and others who played the role of NHL "policeman" were themselves a product of the NHL's evolution. For the first four decades of NHL competition, there was lots of fighting, but players usually fought their own battles when avenging a perceived grievance. There were tough customers and dirty players, players you'd best steer clear of, but no designated enforcers. Gordie Howe and Rocket Richard didn't need their teammates to fight their battles, so teams saw no need to employ such one-dimensional types. By the 1970s, however, the Boston Bruins had developed a tough team with multiple fighters to surround Bobby Orr and Phil Esposito. Part of Boston's game plan became intimidation, daring other teams to stand up to the "Big Bad Bruins." Orr could handle himself, but he also had many teammates willing to fight each other's battles and start trouble if it needed starting. It became a group thing. The Philadelphia Flyers took it to a whole other level, using fighting, goonery and intimidation as tactics to help win the Stanley Cup. They didn't have the stars the Bruins had, but they had even more muscle, players who otherwise wouldn't be in the NHL. They dared the league to call even one-quarter of the fouls they committed. Dave "the Hammer" Schultz was the first specialized, high-profile enforcer. Schultz had been a scorer in junior hockey with Swift Current, but he all but abandoned that element of the game once he turned professional. He could fight, and did so with great enthusiasm, and he would seek out the best players on the other team and terrorize them. When Borje Salming arrived in the NHL with Toronto in 1973 as one of the first European players, Schultz sought out the highly skilled Swede in one of his first NHL games and gleefully pounded him with his fists. Salming learned how to fight back, but his fellow Swede Inge Hammarstrom was less inclined to do so and was mocked by his own owner, Harold Ballard, as a player who could go into a corner with a pocketful of eggs and come out without a single one broken. Schultz and other Flyers—Don Saleski, Bob Kelly, Mel Bridgman, Andre Dupont—protected Philadelphia's best player, Bobby Clarke, and other teams had to find similar players to protect their stars.

All teams eventually had one enforcer. Then two. Sometimes three. Massive players, players with cement hands less useful for scoring goals than for delivering a concussion, even punching a player's head into the ice as he lay on his back. That might not exactly have been accepted as fair or honest, but it happened. As the NHL grew and then faced competition from the World Hockey Association, there was even more call for such players. That was the professional world McSorley stepped into as a nineteen-year-old in 1983. Fighters had become a necessary element on any successful team, and McSorley had the skill set to thrive.

When McSorley played, when he was in his prime, the role of enforcer mattered. A lot. Those who did it well were celebrated. They became enormously popular and sometimes were given colourful nicknames. Dave "Charlie" Manson. Dave "Tiger" Williams. Stu "the Grim Reaper" Grimson. Ken "Bomber" Baumgartner. Tie Domi. Bob Probert. Mick Vukota. Those with enough skills to score goals or play regularly, like Williams, Manson, Probert and McSorley, were extremely valuable. In the 1980–81 season, Dave Williams led the NHL with 343 penalty minutes and was fifth in the league with sixteen fighting majors, but he also scored thirty-five goals for the Vancouver Canucks. Only twenty-seven NHL players scored more that season. Probert was the NHL's heavyweight champion and also played on Detroit's power play. Manson and McSorley could kill penalties, play the power play and take regular shifts. They could be trusted to be on the ice in the final minute of a game or wear a letter for their team and also to fight the toughest player on the other team.

The game was structured in such a way that even less talented tough guys could be difference-makers because of their muscle, not liabilities limited to playing only a few minutes a night because they couldn't keep up. Violent, illegal play was either punished lightly or not punished at all. To a significant degree, the league left it to the players to maintain order. Suspensions were rare. Bench-clearing brawls were frequent. Most games had at least one fight, and many had three, four or more. Enforcers and tough guys could abuse opposition players unwilling to pay the same physical price. Meanness was a valued commodity. All fighters were useful in that environment, but fighters who could contribute in other ways were doubly useful. Long before concerns emerged about concussions, chronic traumatic encephalopathy and the dangerous self-medication of NHL fighters, these players were glorified, and there was no broad debate over whether what they did was "good" for the game.

Many hockey fans adored them, thought these policemen were what was best about the game. Many fans believed they injected a sense of manliness into hockey, and also personal honour. People didn't see them as bullies, particularly if they played for their team. They saw them as proud, brave gladiators who would do what others lacked the guts to do. In a split second, these players could change a game, and often did. If a game was lost, they could still inflict pain or injury on the opposing players to soften them up for the next game. Intimidation did play a role, mostly because it was a tradition, but also because hockey—including the NHL—permitted it to be that way. The menacing presence of enforcers also created an undeniable dramatic tension.

McSorley was a classic member of this fraternity. At his very best, he could carry a team, even one with Gretzky, on his broad shoulders. He could change a game, and he was happy to pay the physical price to do it. "Yeah, it was worth it," says McSorley. "My only regret was playing through injuries when sometimes I shouldn't have. But there's no crying in hockey."

MAY 1993 HAD BEEN a steamy month in Toronto, with temperatures as high as 28°C pushing the limits of sixty-two-year-old Maple Leaf Gardens, which had no air conditioning. Just blocks away was the state-of-the-art SkyDome with its revolutionary retractable roof. By comparison, the Gardens, at the corner of Church and Carlton Streets, was a quaint relic of a bygone era. The yellow-brick building, built in a hurry during the Depression, was unremarkable, even ugly. The marquee at the front seemed old-fashioned. Yonge Street, to the west, once seedy and crime infested, had been cleaned up by the cops years earlier after the awful murder of a twelve-year-old shoeshine boy. Jarvis Street, to the east, was home to streetwalkers, and another block farther, well, there was trouble there if you were looking for it and sometimes even if you weren't. But the Gardens sat safely and comfortably enough in the downtown core, surrounded by parking lots that suggested the real estate around the famous arena wasn't as valuable as you might think. You could walk to Bigliardi's for a postgame meal and maybe run into a hockey celebrity or two. One of Canada's most famous musicians, Gordon Lightfoot, often ate there. He was a huge Leafs fan. Meanwhile, the favourite watering hole for players, P.M. Toronto, was across the street. Leafs players were known and protected there. They could mingle, or they could retreat to an area behind a velvet rope.

It was a time when many arenas still oozed history and personality. Leafs captain Wendel Clark believed he could identify a rink just by standing at centre ice with his eyes closed, because each had its particular smell. The Montreal Forum. Boston Garden. Chicago Stadium. They didn't have corporate names or luxury boxes. The revenue they generated came from selling seats, and organizations would try to build a team that fit their home rink. The Bruins, with a rink that held only 14,500 spectators and ice that measured nine feet shorter and two feet narrower than the NHL standard, realized there was no point trying to be overly fancy. In a rink originally constructed with professional boxing in mind, the press box hung over the ice, making reporters feel they were looking straight down at the players, and fans seemed to be on top of the action. Sure you needed a few stars, but a team dominated by bangers and grinders could create a hostile atmosphere for any opposing side. By contrast, when Edmonton entered the NHL in 1979, their Northlands Coliseum was a large, expansive arena with the best ice in the league. Speed and skill made sense there and became Oiler trademarks. The next generation of NHL arenas, which would be more generic in design, was years away. Maple Leaf Gardens, at least the ice surface, didn't have distinguishing features like the Boston Garden. The place was more of a shrine to the sport, the scene of past glories. It was a hockey museum that represented tradition. NHL players, coaches and executives, particularly those who had grown up in Toronto or Southern Ontario, had a special connection with the Gardens, either from watching on television or playing there.

As the Toronto Maple Leafs and Los Angeles Kings prepared to contest the 1993 Clarence Campbell Conference final, many on both sides felt the Gardens was a unique and special place. "I thought it was the greatest arena. Ever," says Gretzky. He'd gone there as a six-year-old with his grandmother, sitting in the last row of greys to watch the Leafs beat the Oakland Seals, and played there as a peewee when his team from Brantford, Ontario, was invited to use the rink before a Toronto Marlboros junior game. Later, as a teenager playing minor hockey, he lived in Toronto for two years and would go down to watch Marlies junior games on Saturday afternoons with a buddy from West Humber Collegiate. "It was one dollar for standing room, and there was an old gentleman who would always save me a spot," he recalls. "I did that pretty much every Saturday for two years." He played his first NHL game at

Maple Leaf Gardens on November 21, 1979, registering two goals and two assists for Edmonton in a 4–4 tie. Later that season, on March 29, he came to the Gardens again as an Oiler and had two goals and four assists in an 8–5 victory. The rink, not to mention the competitive state of the bedraggled home team, fit his game. Going into the series against the Leafs in the spring of '93, Gretzky had played twenty-one NHL games at the Gardens and recorded an incredible twenty-five goals and thirty-five assists. Over the course of his NHL career, the only visiting rink he scored more goals at was the Winnipeg Arena. "Maple Leaf Gardens was definitely an arena, other than my home arenas, that gave me more enthusiasm than any arena in the league," he says. "The atmosphere and the history behind it was matched only by the Montreal Forum. It was really a special place for me."

On the Leafs side, assistant coach Mike Murphy had grown up in the west end of the city and attended his first game at the Gardens in 1957. "We went with my dad. Ed Chadwick was in goal, and I shared a seat with my older sister, Patricia. They let us both in on one ticket. They were playing the Rangers," Murphy says. "My dad always had season's seats, so I was a regular. I would wear dress pants and a nice shirt, and my dad would often wear a tie. My dad had a parking spot three blocks away where he could park for free." Murphy went on to play there regularly as a member of the Marlboros, the junior team Gretzky would later watch on Saturday afternoons. "It was hallowed ground. Almost like a sanctuary. It was a place you revered," says Murphy. "I dreamed about playing for the Leafs there. It was a magnificent place for me. The slanted hallways, all the little cubbyholes, the different ways you get around the building, the small dressing rooms. In time, I came to know everybody there."

In the spring of '93, the fabled Gardens looked much as it had for years, with old blue-and-white tiled floors, painted cinder-block walls and black-and-white photos on the walls of Leafs heroes and famous athletes from bygone eras. The photos were cheaply mounted, and over the years they had faded and their surfaces had bubbled. It was cleaner than the Boston Garden or the Chicago Stadium, though. Fewer rats, too. But lots of closed doors led to dark places. It was a rink filled with hidden secrets. The door to the coach's office, just past the corridor that led to the rink itself between the two benches, was heavily lacquered, shiny wood, like it had been covered and re-covered many times over the years as the inhabitant of the office changed, something that had happened with alarming frequency over the previous twenty-five years as the Leafs regressed from Cup winners to losers to national laughingstock. A turnstile might have been better than a door.

Change, however, had started to arrive at the Gardens by the fall of '93. Smoking, for example, was no longer allowed in the rink. After years of cigarette and cigar smoke so thick in the corridors you could chip a tooth visiting one of the crowded washrooms between periods, the air now stank only of mildew, faded memories and regret. For the first time, beer was being sold in the building, $4.25 for a fourteen-ounce plastic cup, a welcome change now that the early heat and humidity of May had engulfed Toronto. Baseball fans in the city had been able to drink beer at games for fifteen years, but arcane provincial alcohol regulations had prevented hockey fans from doing so. Shortly after legalizing Sunday shopping in Ontario the previous summer, however, the provincial government also announced it would permit beer sales at all professional sports stadiums, including the Gardens. "Toronto the Good" was being allowed to let down its hair, although not so much that Mayor June Rowlands could refrain from banning an act called the Barenaked Ladies from playing at City Hall. She deemed the band's name offensive to women.

Being able to sell beer came at a perfect time for the Leafs. Two years after the death of long-time owner Harold Ballard, who had been adamantly opposed to selling beer in the Gardens, the Leafs had put together the biggest payroll in team history, and they needed ways to pay for it. The Gardens had been called the "Carlton Street Cashbox" for years, but in reality very little had been done in the Ballard era to maximize potential streams of revenue. Ending the tradition of a dry Gardens was one way to increase proceeds, perhaps by as much as $3 million a season. Back then, that was only about $1 million less than the entire payroll of the Ottawa Senators. The price of tickets for Leafs games had also been jacked up by 25 percent. The Leafs and the Gardens were a sleeping financial giant, and local millionaire Steve Stavro, with one eye on history and the other on winning a battle for control of the famous hockey team, had already aggressively started the awakening as the new man in charge. This wasn't the personal toy of a crazy old man anymore. Three years had passed since Ballard had been declared mentally incompetent and unable to run the hockey team, igniting a bitter legal battle between his three children and his long-time companion, Yolanda. But those days were long over. Maple Leaf Gardens was going to be a money-maker, and the new owner was going to cash in.

By the time the Maple Leafs and Kings stepped on the ice for Game 1 of their best-of-seven playoff series on May 17, the temperature had eased somewhat but not the sense of anticipation. Outside on Carlton Street, as the streetcars of the Toronto Transit Commission squealed past, scalpers hawked tickets at inflated prices and the delicious odour of chestnuts being roasted by street vendors hung in the air.

In Toronto, the playoff season had started with very modest expectations, but now anything, even a Stanley Cup, seemed possible. The city crackled with hockey talk, even as the Toronto Blue Jays, 1992 World Series champions, shook off a so-so start to take two of three from the New York Yankees at Yankee Stadium. The Jays were the hottest ticket in town, selling out the fifty-thousand-seat SkyDome for each and every home game. But the Leafs were coming to life after two decades of ruinous Ballard ownership. With a new star in Doug Gilmour and a new head coach in Pat Burns, the disciplined, hard-hitting Leafs had surged to a ninety-nine-point season, good enough for third place in the Norris Division, known to many as the "Chuck Norris Division."

Nicknaming the division after a famous martial arts expert and film star was a good fit, for the division had earned a reputation more for brawling and bench-clearing fights than for superb hockey. That fancy-dan stuff was left to the Alberta teams in the Smythe Division or the Pittsburgh Penguins of the Patrick Division. In the Norris, you manned up. You might find a degree of success without much skill in the lineup, but you couldn't survive without being tough. If you were tough enough, the division allowed you to make the playoffs by winning only twenty-five of eighty games, as the Leafs had done seven years earlier. Teams wore membership in the division like a badge of honour even though Cup contenders only occasionally emerged from that group. Priorities were a little different in the Norris.

As recently as two years earlier, the Leafs had been one of the worst clubs in hockey, seemingly sentenced indefinitely to be a punch line in the annals of Canadian sports even if they were a Norris Division member in good standing. But with Burns at the helm and general manager Cliff Fletcher pulling off blockbuster trades, the Leafs had won more games than they'd lost for the first time since the 1978–79 season. A run all the way to the '93 Stanley Cup final still looked somewhat over-ambitious. Unthinkable, really. This was a hockey team used to being made fun of by other cities and called the "Laffs." Just a few seasons earlier, fans had worn bags over their heads and thrown team jerseys on the ice in protest. Yet here, apparently out of nowhere, were the '92–93 Leafs, just four wins away from getting to the final, a gritty team of personality and, perhaps, destiny.

The Kings rolled into town for the series opener with their own compelling story to tell. With the peerless Gretzky, they had become one of the NHL's biggest attractions over the previous five seasons, with a host of high-profile stars acquired by team owner Bruce McNall. The Kings had never gone beyond the second round of the playoffs, before Gretzky or after. But finally they were in the conference final against the Leafs. Toronto was trying to regain the hockey world's respect. The Kings had never really had it. They had certainly never earned it. They were led by a rookie coach, Barry Melrose, who looked like a character out of a Hollywood screenplay, with a

16   THE LAST GOOD YEAR

carefully groomed mullet, a gold watch, fancy ties and $2,000 suits. The costume seemed designed to dress up a more basic, hardnosed, take-no-prisoners hockey mentality rooted on Canada's Prairies. Melrose, like his cousin Wendel Clark of the Leafs, was from Kelvington, Saskatchewan, a place where referees were there to drop pucks and get out of the way while hockey players kept the peace. Or created the mayhem, if necessary. The Kings had surrounded Gretzky with a crew of tough hombres led by McSorley, hockey's Darth Vader in his black helmet and uniform. They were the NHL's most penalized team and would have been a good fit in the Chuck Norris Division. Few teams fought more than the Kings. McSorley had led the league with 399 minutes, but his teammate Warren Rychel actually fought more often. If the Kings couldn't beat you, well, they had other options.

The Leafs, once English Canada's team, had emerged again as a club worth respecting after being quickly remodelled by Fletcher, one of hockey's most respected executives. They now had a chance to get back to the Stanley Cup final after a twenty-six-year absence. It seemed disrespectful, almost impertinent, that the cocky Kings had arrived with Gretzky, Canada's national treasure, to block Toronto's path. So it was Hollywood versus *Hockey Night in Canada*, even though the Leafs were the team with the better script—Gilmour played by Tom Cruise?—and Gretzky had been a featured performer on Canada's traditional Saturday night hockey broadcast for years. There were good guys in this scenario, and they weren't the boys who had flown in from California wearing black. "I was from Ontario, and I couldn't believe how much the people in Toronto hated us," recalls Kings forward Dave Taylor.

The Leafs had sentiment on their side, but otherwise the series looked even, a collision between two teams that didn't have a lot of history, friendly or otherwise, between them. Toronto had the better regular season record and had Burns at the helm, surely with a decided advantage over the younger, less experienced Melrose. LA did have Gretzky, who looked sharp, having put up twenty-three points in twelve playoff games. Only Gilmour had more. Gretzky was thirty-two years old, but the numbers suggested he was still a dominant force in any series and still could lead a team to the Stanley Cup.

Montreal had already earned a 1–0 series lead on the New York Islanders in the Prince of Wales Conference final, but the Canadiens-Isles series was almost an afterthought to many hockey fans in Canada and the United States. Goaltender Glenn Healy, the hero of the Islanders' second-round upset of the two-time Stanley Cup champion Pittsburgh Penguins, confessed that many of the combatants in the New York–Montreal series were transfixed by the Toronto-LA series. "We made sure we watched it, because it was riveting," says Healy. "It was must-see TV for the players. The Leafs. Gretzky. That series had everything."

Gretzky understood many fans were already looking ahead to a historic showdown for the Cup. "Everyone was hoping for a Toronto-Montreal final. That was the talk of the country," he says. Montreal needed three more wins to hold up their end of the bargain, while the Leafs were just getting started. They needed four.

The beer, still a novelty for hockey fans in Toronto, was flowing as Game 1 got under way. With no air conditioning, the Gardens was a sweatbox, much hotter on the ice under the heat of the bright television lights. It was the most anticipated play-off game at the Gardens since the Leafs had faced the Canadiens in the NHL semifinals fifteen years earlier. That Montreal team was a powerhouse, and it swept Toronto. This looked much more winnable to Leafs fans. It almost seemed like the hardest part of the job was already done. Their team was no longer the plucky underdog it had been in the first round against Detroit. Now, against an LA team with a poorer regular season record, they just needed to keep playing well.

The Leafs dressed twelve forwards and six defencemen, using centre John Cullen and defenceman Dmitri Mironov sparingly. LA went with eleven forwards and seven defence-men, employing veteran rearguard Tim Watters mostly to kill penalties. Michael Burgess, the Canadian star of the stage musical *Les Misérables*, sang the anthems. During "O Canada," Gretzky, showing a faint goatee, sang the words. Clark, with a thick, dark beard, glared upwards at the Canadian flag waving electronically on the video screen. His face betrayed neither nervousness nor fatigue. He'd learned over the years his body wasn't as stout as his heart. Now, he just wanted them to drop the puck. Gilmour's eyes darted around as if he were looking for friends, or sizing up the situation. Leafs rookie goalie Felix Potvin took his mask off; Kings goalie Kelly Hrudey kept his on. Other players grimaced, shifting in their skates. When Burgess was done, fireworks exploded over top of the score clock. Broadcaster Bob Cole, calling the game from the gondola that Foster Hewitt had made famous, pronounced it an "unlikely matchup." "But here they are," he said. "A high-scoring Kings team, and a Leafs team that looks to defence. Something has to break, right?" Cole said he had walked into the Gardens before the game with Gretzky, and the star player "looked as good as he ever has."

FROM THE START OF THE GAME, Melrose set the tone by scrambling his forward lines as if he were using a blender. Gretzky started the game between fourth-liners Pat Conacher and Dave Taylor, but during the first period skated on eight different units as the LA coach sought to prevent Burns from matching either Gilmour or his checking line of Bill Berg, Peter Zezel and Mark Osborne against Number 99. Gretzky's old Edmonton teammate Jari Kurri had been shifted to centre during the season, and he started there against the Leafs. Gilmour started the game between Clark and another ex-Oiler, Glenn Anderson. Both teams were anxious to get a sense of how the series would be played. Winning Game 1 could be huge, but neither team had been given much time to prepare. Toronto had finished off St. Louis only forty-eight hours earlier. There was some familiarity from the regular season, and the rest they'd have to figure out on the fly.

On the first shift, Clark took a run at Gretzky around the red line, but Gretzky twisted away, as he almost always did. It had always been difficult to get solid body contact on Number 99. In an era of violent hockey, he seemed to have a sixth sense of how to avoid trouble, and the presence of a watchful McSorley helped deter many. Clark, the Leafs captain, wasn't easily put off. By charging at Gretzky, he was sending an early message that he was aiming to get a body on his Kings counterpart. Unfazed by his miss, Clark set his sights on LA rookie rear-guard Alexei Zhitnik and decked him with a monstrous hit, losing his own helmet in the process. It was the first of many hits the young Russian would absorb in that game, and the series. Clark had started the '93 playoffs slowly, but he had gotten stronger and stronger with every game. Right from the start against the Kings, he looked like a hungry grizzly demolishing a campsite in search of food. Clark had two scoring chances before Burns even had an opportunity to make his first line change of the night.

McSorley, naturally, took the first penalty of the series. He was tied up with Berg as the linesmen blew the play dead for an icing call. Berg, as was his way, yapped something at the big LA blueliner. Zezel skated behind McSorley, chirping as well. As Osborne skated past, he changed his route slightly to brush past McSorley's shoulder. McSorley lifted his right glove and stuck it in the veteran winger's face. It was a nothing moment thirteen minutes into the game, hardly worth a penalty, particularly compared to the hooking and interference already going on in every shift. But referee Dan Marouelli called one anyway. McSorley looked disgusted as he sat down in the box. He pointed to the number 33 on his left bicep as if to suggest Marouelli was punishing the reputation, not the actual act.

The visitors killed that penalty off, but they were back on their heels. The pace was frenetic, with, by today's standards, shocking amounts of interference and stickwork. "I had started wearing padded things underneath my elbow pads, like a sleeve," recalls Berg, a hardnosed checker. "Literally, you'd have track marks from sticks down your forearms. You'd rope and ride. You'd be riding the gauntlet if you had the puck, but they'd always get you. The blade of their stick would tear your skin. That's how it was. That's how you played. Wooden sticks, man. They hurt. I'd rather give than get, but I got a lot too."

The goalies, Hrudey for the Kings and Potvin for the Leafs, wore relatively slender upper body padding which exposed them to bruises and welts over the course of a season. Potvin was a lean, unimposing goalie, and his equipment roughly reflected his body type. He liked to play deep in his crease, almost hiding under the crossbar, an expression of his shy personality, the confidence he had in his reflexes and the new style of NHL goalkeeping. Only twenty-one, he was just a few months removed from playing for Toronto's farm club before a few thousand fans in Newfoundland. Hrudey wore tiny thirty-two-inch goalie pads, cut down from the thirty-four-inch pads he received from the manufacturer to give him more mobility. They came to just above his knee. He wore a black Jofa helmet, one favoured by European skaters, and slightly more protective than the flimsy Jofas Gretzky and McSorley wore. Hrudey wore his with a wire cage attached. A blue bandana, which was really a strip of fabric torn from a hockey undershirt, stuck out the back. He wore a mismatched set of gloves, a white blocker and a black catching mitt, and loved to roam outside his crease to challenge shooters or play the puck. Like their teams, Potvin and Hrudey looked starkly different from each other, and played differently.

The first goal came at 17:19 of the first period, and not surprisingly it came off the stick of Gilmour, who had been brilliant in the first two rounds of the playoffs after a career-best 127-point regular season. The puck skimmed up the left boards in the LA zone, past Gretzky to Leafs blueliner Bob Rouse at the right point. Rouse's shot went towards the front of the Kings net. Gilmour worked himself around the big body of defenceman Rob Blake and redirected the puck past Hrudey for a 1–0 Toronto lead with less than three minutes left in the period. The marquee matchup was Gilmour against Gretzky, and Gilmour had fired the opening salvo.

The Kings had scored fifty-nine goals in twelve previous playoff games. They figured to get at least one on this night, so giving up the first one didn't seem decisive. For the Leafs, it was the start they wanted. The Toronto fans leapt to their feet. Following the Game 7 triumph over St. Louis two nights earlier, it was the seventh consecutive Leafs goal they'd cheered without having seen one from the opposing team. If there was any doubt that this magical spring could continue against Los Angeles, that goal dispelled it.

The Kings came out in the second period with greater confidence, and the game turned in LA's favour. Melrose got momentum-swinging shifts from the small, speedy line of Tony Granato, Mike Donnelly and Corey Millen. At one point, Donnelly and Granato had a two-man break on Potvin after Rouse whiffed on a bouncing puck at the LA blueline, but Potvin shut that opportunity down with a sprawling poke check that kept the visitors from tying the game.

With just over five minutes left before the second intermission, Potvin made another series of stops but then was finally beaten with the line of Gilmour, Dave Andreychuk and Nikolai Borschevsky trapped well up ice in the Kings zone. It was the kind of mistake that would make the positionally conscious Burns fume. The puck was flipped out to Gretzky, who was moving through the neutral zone, and Gretzky made a delicate backhand saucer pass to Pat Conacher that was so perfectly timed it allowed the speedy winger to slice between Rouse and Dave Ellett. Conacher wasn't a prolific scorer. He had managed only nine goals in eighty-one regular season games that year, but the Alberta native deftly lifted a backhand off the right post behind Potvin to deadlock the game 1–1. The assist extended Gretzky's playoff streak to nine games with at least one point. As the Kings surged on the mushy Gardens ice, the Leafs wilted. The Gardens had never been known as a particularly noisy rink, and Toronto fans were often criticized for sitting on their hands rather than getting behind the home team. When the Leafs weren't playing well, they got quiet, almost pensive, and they'd done it again tonight.

When the game resumed for the third period, it appeared that the Kings would not give up the momentum they'd established. Melrose's team kept pushing and pushing, forcing the Leafs to ice the puck. The game seemed to have temporarily lost the breathless speed with which it had started. LA's young defence was holding up well. Blake and Zhitnik were usually paired together. Darryl Sydor, who had won a Memorial Cup junior championship the year before with the Kamloops Blazers of the Western Hockey League, had turned twenty just four days earlier, but he had the poise of a veteran. It was his more seasoned partner, Charlie Huddy, who whiffed on a hip check attempt that allowed Anderson, his former Edmonton teammate, to spring free for a good scoring chance. Hrudey then blocked a Clark blast, standing up and squeezing his pads together, a goaltending technique that was soon to become extinct.

All over the ice, players committed infractions without being penalized, dragging each other to the ice, elbowing each other in the face, raking their sticks across their opponents' hands. McSorley and Blake, both bigger than any defenceman for the Leafs, used their sticks and bodies to mete out punishment in the LA zone. "There were no fucking rules," says

Gilmour. "Nobody knew what penalties were. My boys watch it now, and they die laughing." In the 1980s, coaches had actually started to teach players to use their sticks to lock on to opposition players and not let go, and that had created a different type of game. Using the stick to hook and hack at the puck-carrier was just accepted as part of the sport, as the gauntlet skilled players had to walk to score goals. If you wanted to score, you had to put up with it. The area in front of the net, meanwhile, was viewed as a place where the rule book didn't apply. It was the game's no-holds-barred zone, where you could do things that weren't allowed anywhere else on the ice. "To clear out the front of the net, you were pretty much allowed to do anything unless someone was decapitated," says Rouse. "You wanted to play right up to the line without drawing a penalty."

This was the kind of contest Game 1 was until, suddenly, it changed into something else entirely. And so did the series. In the ninth minute of the third period, Gilmour came in low with what replays showed was a clean hip check on Zhitnik. Perhaps, if you were a Kings fan, you would have thought it was a half-steamboat late. The Russian rookie flipped into the air, rolled and landed heavily on his head. He'd taken the Clark hit in the first without much problem. Now, he left the ice clutching his left knee. Apparently his head could take anything.

Less than a minute later, with the fans still murmuring over the hit on Zhitnik, the Leafs jumped ahead 2–1 on a goal by Anderson from Gilmour. While being pitchforked to the ice by Sydor, Gilmour put a pass from behind the Kings goal to a wide-open Anderson cruising into the slot. The Kings had been playing an erratic defensive game all season, very different from the Leafs, a team built on the defensive tactics Burns had relied on as head coach in Montreal. "We weren't playing defence," recalls Hrudey. "We were trying to out-score the other team, and I was cool with it. I found it fun. I found it enjoyable." On this play, the LA defensive shell split wide open. Both Gretzky and left winger Luc Robitaille were turning away from the LA net as the puck came to Anderson, and both of LA's defencemen were behind the end line. Anderson ambled in untouched and beat Hrudey with a backhand. All that work the Kings had done to deadlock the game after giving up an early goal and then earn the edge in play on the road had vanished in one careless sequence.

Just sixty-six seconds after that, the Leafs jumped ahead by two. It was Gilmour again. His second goal of the game concluded a wild sequence in the Kings zone as the game lost all semblance of orderliness or predictability. It looked more like professional wrestling, a feature Sunday night attraction at the Gardens for decades. Zhitnik, back into the fray, tripped Gilmour, then kicked Borschevsky's skates out from under him. In front of the LA net, Blake grabbed Andreychuk by the front of the jersey and yanked him to the ice. McSorley might have had the bigger reputation, but Blake was serving notice he could be just as mean, and even dirtier. The absence of any effort by Marouelli to enforce the NHL rulebook was almost farcical. As they did in those days, he seemed to decide that because it was the third period he wasn't going to call penalties unless absolutely forced to. As bodies littered the Kings zone, the puck skittered back to Leafs defenceman Jamie Macoun at the left point. Gretzky was behind him, having leaked out into the neutral zone looking for a cherry-picking opportunity. Macoun's low shot was stopped by Hrudey, but Gilmour, back on his feet, corralled the rebound, spun and fired the puck home to give the Leafs a 3–1 lead.

As soon as the Leafs had their third goal, they surged forward in search of a fourth. For seven minutes, they roared, ultimately building a 22–1 shots-on-goal advantage. Berg stuck his foot out on Granato to take a penalty at 13:12 but then jumped out of the penalty box to accept a brilliant no-look pass from Gilmour, who had stolen Millen's errant pass in the LA zone. Just as Gilmour fed the puck back to Berg, he was hit in the head by a flying elbow from Zhitnik, eager to avenge the hit of earlier in the period. Berg partially fanned on his shot, but the puck still eluded Hrudey, and the Leafs had a 4–1 lead.

With more than five minutes left in the third, the game was clearly in Toronto's control. In those days, that often meant trouble. The philosophy was that if a game was out of reach, it was important to "set the tone" for the next one, which frequently meant starting fights, usually by the team that was losing. In this case, not satisfied with just winning the game, the Leafs decided they wanted to inflict some pain on their opponents and possibly generate some casualties. Clark was like a wrecking ball looking for Kings to hit. He would miss one, then find another and connect. This was classic Clark, showing the spirit and recklessness which had long endeared him to Leafs fans. It was one of those nights when he had one setting: full speed ahead.

LA, HOWEVER, WAS IN no mood to accept what the Leafs were shoving down their throats. It was enough that they had already lost the game. Granato delivered a flying elbow into the side of Rouse's head along the glass in the Leafs zone, and an enraged Rouse set off in hot pursuit. He grabbed the nearest King, which happened to be Donnelly, and started pummelling him. A massive pileup of ten players ensued at the red line. Neither team was going to be deterred by the fact that new NHL commissioner Gary Bettman, just three weeks earlier, had appeared to establish a new draconian approach to NHL violence by hitting Washington's Dale Hunter with a twenty-one-game suspension for his late hit on Pierre Turgeon of the New York Islanders. It was abundantly clear that the potential was in the air for something similarly ugly to happen between the Kings and Leafs.

McSorley had been relatively quiet most of the night, partially because no Leaf had been able to lay a glove on Gretzky. The game had been rough, but McSorley had teammates capable of handling themselves. Now, with the game out of reach, the big LA bruiser had seen enough. Quietly finishing the game wasn't an option. His DNA wouldn't allow it. Meekly surrendering just wasn't the way you'd do it back on the farm in Cayuga. His team wasn't playing well, and he detected that the heat, the noise of the building, the Leafs' surge and the hostility of the Toronto crowd were getting to some of his teammates. Not all the Kings had experienced the kind of on-ice mayhem he had, particularly during his days in Edmonton, when the "Battle of Alberta" against Calgary wasn't for the faint of heart. McSorley was keenly aware that many players on the Kings roster hadn't been this far in the playoffs before and faced this kind of difficult situation, and he believed the game had become so one-sided it threatened to carry over into Game 2. "It was 4–1 for the Leafs, and our young guys were intimidated," he says. "In a lot of ways, I was a leader on that team. Charlie Huddy led in his way. Wayne led in his way. But in that game, we had to push back. We couldn't accept the way that game was going. We really hadn't played well. I was on our bench, and I thought, Well, it's time to kick the hornet's nest. I wasn't going to leave that game quietly."

With 2:35 left in the third, Gilmour crossed the LA line at the right boards, dropped the puck for Anderson and swerved into the middle of the ice, the proverbial "trolley tracks," as veteran NHL observers still call that route to open ice. The idea is that once you get locked into that path, there is no escape route. Most of the time, cutting into the middle is perfectly safe. But when a player gets it wrong, it's like steering right into the path of an oncoming train.

After a half second, Gilmour quickly looked up as if realizing his mistake. He knew he'd momentarily lost his concentration and put himself in jeopardy. Sure enough, the six-foot-three, 235-pound McSorley was bearing down, with gloves and stick and elbows high. McSorley's right elbow crashed into the right side of Gilmour's face as he turned away, lifting his helmet up. Gilmour always wore his chinstrap loose, and the force of the collision yanked it up hard against his throat. His stick went flying twenty feet away as if it had been ripped from his arms. Marouelli, who had watched the nastiness increase over the course of the game, shot his right arm upwards to call a penalty. But as Gilmour writhed in pain on his hands and knees, it was immediately clear this was out of the referee's hands. No one familiar with the NHL game had any doubt what was coming. You could almost feel the crowd flinch as one before it roared in outrage. McSorley knew exactly what he'd done and what was going to happen next. He wanted it to happen.

Clark saw the hit, glanced over his right shoulder to see if there had been a call, and then made a beeline for the much bigger McSorley. Call or no call, he had business to conduct. His gloves were off before he arrived. That's how he fought. He didn't wait. He wanted to land the first punch, and he wanted it to hurt. In the first round of the playoffs against Detroit, Clark had been specifically told he could not fight Bob Probert, one of the NHL's nastiest heavyweights. But he'd received no such instructions for the Kings. "By the time the McSorley thing happened, nobody could tell me I couldn't fight him," Clark says now. McSorley wore a wide-sleeved jersey like those worn by goaltenders. As was his style, he started to shake off his jersey, shoulder pads and elbow pads as the fight began, to the delighted screams of the Gardens crowd. Clark continued to fire away at him in fury. One, two, three. McSorley absorbed them all, then started to gain an edge. He'd taken Clark's best shots, and now it was his turn. The crowd came to its feet. Their gladiator was fighting for justice against a formidable opponent. Just as it appeared Clark was in trouble, that McSorley would get all his gear off and begin to assert his physical superiority, linesmen Ray Scapinello and Swede Knox, who had been circling a few feet away, intervened.

The scrap lasted thirty-eight seconds, less than half the length of McSorley's longer bouts, although many remember it as a marathon. "Once I got my jersey off, they broke up the fight," recalls McSorley. "Wendel gave up twenty pounds to me, but he was a good fighter. I was trying to get my arm loose and get my jersey off. You can look at my longer fights against guys like Sandy McCarthy and Stu Grimson that went much longer. I have long arms. I didn't wear big shoulder pads. Getting my jersey off was my whole strategy. Why did they break it up? It wasn't a good fight! It didn't last long enough! They had no business breaking that fight up." Clark had a different interpretation. "Marty was the kind of fighter who wants it to go all day. Wants a war of attrition. That's his MO. My MO was the other way. I don't think there was a winner. But it started the whole series off at another level."

Afterwards, Clark confided in assistant coach Mike Kitchen. "Clarkie said to me, 'When I hit him with that first punch and he didn't go down, I knew I was in trouble,'" says Kitchen. Clark says he could have taken a different approach after McSorley had decked Gilmour. "They went after our best player. What if I'd just gone over and one-punched Wayne? Then there would have been a bench-clearing brawl! Can you imagine? But I wouldn't do that." McSorley, however, had been more than willing to do to Gilmour what Clark would never do to Gretzky. The LA defenceman's brazen assault on Toronto's best player, and his fight with Clark, had dramatically revved up the level of emotion. "It's heated up to a boil already!" said *Hockey Night in Canada* commentator Harry Neale.

The drama wasn't over. As the fight between McSorley and Clark ended, Gilmour, cut over the bridge of his nose, was standing in front of the LA bench in a challenging stance. He was the new darling of the Leafs, of *Hockey Night in Canada*'s broadcasts and particularly of iconic commentator Don Cherry, who was from Gilmour's hometown of Kingston, Ontario. But the Kings weren't about to give Gilmour special treatment. Tomas Sandstrom and Luc Robitaille leaned over the boards barking insults, while Sydor jabbed at Gilmour's legs with his stick. It was getting personal, and the two teams had progressed to this point in the playoffs because they were filled with players unlikely to back down. The hit on Zhitnik and the three quick Leafs goals had been the kindling and the logs, and McSorley's thunderous hit on Gilmour and subsequent fight with Clark had been the lighter fluid and match.

McSorley got five minutes for elbowing and a fighting major, and as he left the ice surface he put his hand over the television camera trained on him, still annoyed that the fight had been, in his opinion, interrupted prematurely. Clark got an instigator minor and a fighting major. As they sorted out the penalties, the TV mic caught Gilmour saying very clearly to Marouelli, "That's fucking bullshit." Years later, his point of view was very different. "My fault," he says. "Absolutely. I always cut into the middle. But I knew the guys I had to worry about. McSorley was one of them. I was watching my pass. You don't do that. Clean hit. He got me. But it didn't feel good." McSorley's intent was clear. "Was I trying to take Gilmour's head off? No. Was I trying to stir it up? Yes."

While all this was going on and players milled around the ice, Hrudey was trying to find shelter under his net as cups of soda and beer rained down. He knew something important had just happened. "We weren't fully committed to Game 1 until then," he recalls. "We had just won against Vancouver and were feeling pretty good. But we were not fully engaged with the Toronto series yet, and we were getting kicked squarely in the teeth. Marty knew that. He had to change that, and he did."

For Barry Melrose, it was a slightly awkward, if familiar, situation. Clark, after all, was his cousin. Clark's grandfather and his grandmother and were brother and sister. They'd grown up together in the same small town, although the older Melrose was closer to Clark's brother Donn. They'd all played baseball on the local squad during the summer, along with other NHLers like Trent Yawney, Kevin Kaminski and Kelly Chase. Melrose was a prodigious home run hitter. Clark's dad, Les, ran the local ice rink, and Melrose's dad, Jim, later took on the job. Melrose knew his cousin could handle himself. "I'd seen Wendel fight enough." Actually, he also knew it from personal experience. Clark and Melrose had played against each other in the NHL and had been at the centre of a bench-clearing brawl at the Gardens seven years earlier, when Melrose was playing for Detroit. "Barry and I started it," says Clark. It had been a fight-filled game, and late in the third Clark flattened Melrose with a high hit as his cousin came to bodycheck him. Leafs defence-men Gary Nylund and Bob McGill skated in from the blue-line to join the fray, then Lane Lambert led the Wings off the bench, ostensibly under orders from Detroit coach Brad Park. It was a bizarre scene, with seven fights going on at once. Little Leafs forward Miroslav Ihnacak fought Wings goalie Eddie Mio. Probert dropped the gloves with McGill, and after McGill's helmet came off, Probert viciously head-butted him. "I probably saved somebody's life that night," says Melrose. "I stayed with Wendel and we just hung on, or he would have killed someone."

Seven years later, here were the cousins again involved in a situation that threatened to get out of hand. This time, someone else had started it. Somebody threw a crutch, of all things, onto the ice near the Kings bench, adding to the mayhem. There were arguments in the stands near the LA bench. Burns looked over at Melrose. Melrose looked back and decided to throw a little more kerosene on the fire. He inflated his cheeks like a blowfish. "Pat was a little chunky then," he says. At the Gardens, the distance between one team bench and the other was literally five steps, no Plexiglas between them. It was a clear path separated only by a short row of seats. Scratched or injured players might watch from there. The medical staff might stand there. A police officer or two, perhaps. But there was no physical barrier.

Burns came charging across the aisle and was intercepted by team doctor Simon McGrail and a police officer before assistant coach Mike Kitchen pulled him back. Melrose stared straight ahead. Burns never got close enough to throw a punch at Melrose, not like he had with Ron Lapointe in a memorable junior hockey dustup one night, not like that time back in '78 when Eddie Johnston, coaching Moncton's AHL team, and Pat Quinn, coaching the Mariners, actually went out on the ice and exchanged punches. This seemed a little more comical than actually threatening, like Burns was saying, "Let me at him!" while being restrained, knowing he couldn't actually reach the LA coach. Melrose was a younger, bigger man only six years removed from his playing career. But Burns was an ex-cop. He knew how to fight, and fight dirty if necessary. It was great theatre, and fans and media saw it as evidence that there was simmering bad blood between the coaches. Maybe it had to do with Burns's contention, repeated many times to the Toronto media, that the Kings' first choice as coach the previous summer had been him, not Melrose. Leafs general manager Cliff Fletcher went down between the benches to keep the peace. Neale, providing the commentary, observed, "Cliff Fletcher's down between the benches, I'm sure to talk Burns out of going behind the LA bench. It was last year when he was offered the job. They don't want to give it to him this year!"

After a long delay while the penalties were sorted out, the Leafs were handed a four-on-three power play, and Gilmour was right back out there. Obviously, the McSorley hit hadn't shaken him up too badly, but the Leafs and Burns were determined to make the Kings pay for standing up for themselves in the way they, and their coach, had. With the fans chanting "*nah-nah-nah-nah, nah-nah-nah-nah, hey-hey-hey, goodbye!*" McSorley was fuming in the Kings dressing room, but other LA players could still express their frustration and a few Leafs still had scores to settle. Hrudey viciously chopped at Kent Manderville's legs twice in front of the net. In the dying seconds of the game, Rouse took a run at Granato at centre, trying to get even for the earlier elbow. By modern standards, at least two and possibly three of the hits in that game would have been deemed head shots worthy of possible suspension. Back then, they were just hits that created a thirst for revenge. "I think we're in for a long, bitterly fought series," said Neale on the game broadcast.

The Leafs had won the opener 4–1, but the Kings' vigorous response in the third had diminished the victory, or at least reduced the tone of Toronto's victory celebration. LA was a tough team with one of the greatest players in NHL history, and the Kings had demonstrated they weren't going to be cowed by the hostile environment, by *Hockey Night in Canada*, by historic Maple Leaf Gardens or by the sense of fate in some quarters that the Leafs were destined for a collision in the Stanley Cup final with the Canadiens. The McSorley hit altered the narrative of the series and became the headline from

Game 1. He had done what enforcer types could do, take a game that was lost and make it seem like less of a defeat. To hell with sportsmanship or accepting defeat gracefully. This was the NHL, and that was how things were done. The Kings also realized that their priorities had to change. "At the start, the game plan was to stop Gilmour," says Melrose now. "But five minutes into the first game it became evident that Wendel was the key. Wendel was virtually unstoppable. He was physical. He was just awesome. We had to stop him or we weren't going to win the series. I don't think Wendel ever played better than he did in that series."

In just sixty minutes, expectations for the series had already been exceeded. New plot lines had been established. Newspaper columnists had more than enough fodder to feed the beast. The stars had their names on the scoreboard, the hockey had been ferocious, violent and explosive, and all the main characters on both sides had interjected themselves early into the story. After just three periods, this already felt like a series to remember.

McSORLEY ORDERS A CUP of tea and the restaurant's "bark" dessert: toffee and chocolate on a graham cracker. But he doesn't touch it. He has it boxed up. "For the kids," he says, smiling. He hardly seems the villain who intentionally delivered a head shot to Gilmour and had a bare-knuckle scrap with Clark that people still talk about twenty-five years later. He's quiet and reserved. There's still a fire there, but it's tempered by maturity and the fact that his body is breaking down and wouldn't allow him to be that character today, on or off the ice, even if he wanted to be. He's still articulate, likeable and funny, but these days he's worried, apprehensive about what the future has in store. He fondly remembers the 1992–93 season as his best NHL campaign, when all his body parts worked and he could talk the talk and walk the walk, when his combination of skill, courage and pugilistic talent made him an impact player and one of the most colourful characters in hockey. "I think we had the ability to have a lot more personality back then," he says. He had won two Stanley Cup rings with Edmonton, but LA gave him a new audience and the chance to grow and become not only one of the best-known players in the league but a player who could alter the course of a game at its most important juncture. "For me, LA was a little different than my years in Edmonton. In Edmonton, they didn't need me to be front and centre. In LA, I felt like I needed to be front and centre. It was time for me to lead."

He can't tell you how many concussions he accumulated in his long NHL career. Hundreds, he imagines. He knows they have taken their toll. "I've been driving and had to pull over and call my wife because I can't remember where I'm going," he says. "Sometimes, I have trouble remembering the plot of a children's movie, or remembering the story after fifteen pages of a kids' book." But he remembers the hockey battles. Most of them anyway. Of all the fights in his career, he's asked about that thirty-eight-second bout with Clark the most. "People come up to me and say, 'Boy, Wendel really gave it to you.' And I say, 'Did you watch that fight?'" The fireworks he initiated late in Game 1 showed the impact players of his type could have in those days if they were willing to push hard enough. "Did it work? Absolutely," says McSorley. "Look what happened in Game 2."

ACT TWO

All roads have always led back to Kingston, Ontario, for Doug Gilmour. Back to the head of the great Saint Lawrence River. Back to the site of the penitentiary that held some of Canada's most notorious criminals, where his father worked for decades. Back to his formative years in hockey, starting at Calvin Park Public School and playing with the Church Athletic Team. Back to being the smallest player, to being doubted. The belief and the confidence had to come from a place deep within. A dark place within. Other than his parents, Don and Dolly, his older brother, Dave, and maybe his best buddy, Ian MacInnis, there weren't many in Kingston who imagined Gilmour would one day grow into one of the NHL's biggest stars. Most just thought he had the wrong attitude. Or maybe the right one, the one a small player had to have. "There was a sportscaster, growing up in Kingston, named Max Jackson," recalls Gilmour. "He would say, 'If you can't play a sport, be one.' That was his line. Well, I was a poor sport. I fucking hated losing more than anything." Everybody was the enemy, trying to keep him down.

It's fifteen years since he retired as an NHL player, and Gilmour doesn't compete like that anymore. He can't. He has a chronically sore neck, evidence of those days when he was right at a comfortable cross-check level for bigger NHL defencemen. He takes it easy in Leafs alumni games. This night, he strolls casually into his new hockey kingdom fashionably late. The entrance to Kingston's K-Rock Centre at the corner of Ontario Street and The Tragically Hip Way brings him into the arena behind the home team's net just as the national anthem is starting. In a stylish short leather jacket and casual pants, he looks more like a hip hedge fund manager than a traditional hockey man. His team, the major junior Kingston Frontenacs of the Ontario Hockey League, quickly builds a lead in their playoff game. The building is only about one-third full. Gilmour has been involved in the operation of the team for a decade, either as coach or general manager or something else, sometimes happily, sometimes not so happily. At one point, he hired, then fired, his former Leafs teammate Todd Gill as head coach. They haven't spoken since. He drafted Max Domi, son of former teammate Tie Domi, then was told the Domi family wanted Max to be traded to a better team. Ugh. The politics of the junior game were no fun at all. Everybody had an agenda.

Gilmour came back to Kingston to join the Frontenacs when his dad got sick, leaving a job as assistant coach with the Leafs' top farm club, one that probably would have led him back to the NHL. He has stayed on for a decade, commuting from his home in Burlington, just outside of Hamilton. He worked with the "Fronts" during his father's final days, and for years he continued making the drive to visit his mother, who suffered from dementia and didn't remember that he'd been to see her. Being with the Frontenacs kept him close to his family. He lost his mother in the fall of 2017.

For two periods, as he watches his Frontenacs, Gilmour sits in the press box, jokes and tells stories. Some are about his dad coaching him as a boy, some are about the NHL. He laughs about playing in Chicago for Bob Pulford and that day in practice when Pulford didn't notice one of the lenses in his glasses was missing. There was also the year he played a half season for Rapperswil of the Swiss elite league and, as the team's leading scorer, had to wear a helmet painted a gaudy metallic gold, part of a league sponsorship deal with a Swiss bank. He's still in touch with friends from that team.

Gilmour also tells the story about that day in 1996 when, as the very popular captain of the Toronto Maple Leafs, he met with Cliff Fletcher and offered to surrender his captaincy to Wayne Gretzky. Fletcher summoned him to his Maple Leaf Gardens office and told him there was a deal in the offing to bring Gretzky to the Leafs as an unrestricted free agent. Gretzky had been dealt to St. Louis by the Los Angeles Kings the previous season but was looking elsewhere. Vancouver and the New York Rangers were possibilities, but Fletcher was convinced he had the inside track. "I said, 'No problem. He can take the captaincy.' That's how much I respected Wayne," Gilmour recalls. It was more than that. Gilmour might have been less than a good sport as a youngster, but he had his role models. He grew up first admiring Bobby Orr, and then, when he was playing junior down the highway in Cornwall, Ontario, admiring Gretzky. Adoring Gretzky, more like it. Wanting to be Gretzky. Tucking his sweater into his hockey pants like

Gretzky. Using a straight stick like Gretzky. "I copycatted everything from him," says Gilmour. "Making plays from behind the net, everything." There were only three years between the two, but because Gretzky was a legend at such a young age and had started his professional career as a seventeen-year-old in the World Hockey Association, Gilmour didn't view him as a contemporary. So when it seemed Gretzky might become his teammate, his immediate reflex was to take a back seat to his hero and let Gretzky wear the C with the Leafs.

Gretzky as a Leaf never happened. Leafs owner Steve Stavro, confronted with financial problems, refused to approve the funds to pay for Fletcher's plan. Gretzky says if he had signed with Toronto, which he would have done at a bargain basement price, he would never have accepted the C from Gilmour (although he did accept the captaincy in LA when Dave Taylor insisted he take it). "Dougie was without question the captain of that team with what he had done," says Gretzky. "I would never have gone in that direction. Ever." The respect was apparently mutual.

Gretzky, if he had joined the Leafs, would have attracted much of the attention that for Gilmour had become a heavy burden. The missed opportunity came a little more than three years after the two had gone head-to-head in the 1993 Clarence Campbell Conference final as the star centres of the two highest-profile teams in hockey at the time. That occasion wasn't billed just as Toronto versus LA but as Gilmour versus Gretzky, for the first time putting Gilmour on the same marquee as the player he'd modelled himself after. As a Leaf, he'd blossomed into a dynamic, must-see player, a player who got the big minutes of playing time that stars demanded, a player who moved the crowd to the edge of their seats when he grabbed the puck and burst towards the other team's net, capable of either making a perfect pass to a teammate or scoring himself. This series would be the biggest challenge of Gilmour's career, the biggest conundrum. How did you compete against your idol, a player you had always deferred to? How did you refuse to lose and be the best you could while not making your idol look bad or second best? Letting Gretzky be better wasn't an option. But beating him would not only be difficult, it would almost be disrespectful. If it had to be done, it had to be done the right way. And if the right way got a little crooked, well, he'd never listened to Max Jackson anyway.

THERE WAS NO WAY the NHL was going to allow Game 2 of the '93 Campbell Conference final to pick up where Game 1 had left off. Gary Bettman had taken over the leadership of the NHL three months earlier, and if there was to be further mayhem, by gosh it had to at least appear that the league was trying to contain it. Back in 1976, Toronto fans remembered, the league had lost control of what was happening on the ice to such a degree that Ontario attorney general Roy McMurtry issued arrest warrants for three Philadelphia players—Don Saleski, Mel Bridgman and Joe Watson—after a playoff game between the Flyers and Leafs. Given the events that had transpired between the Leafs and Kings in Game 1, one might have wondered if this series was headed down the same path. There were surely enough good citizens of Toronto who would support the arrest and imprisonment of the outlaw Marty McSorley. Someone just had to print up the WANTED posters and they'd be plastered all over town.

"A McSorry Incident!" screamed the headline in the *Toronto Star*, Canada's largest newspaper, commenting on McSorley's hit on Gilmour in Game 1 and his fight with Wendel Clark. The accompanying picture showed McSorley looking as if he'd been captured on a perp walk after being arrested. "That was a real cheap shot," Leafs GM Cliff Fletcher was quoted as saying. "The intent was to put [Gilmour] out. Fortunately, [McSorley] didn't." The nature of the news cycle at that time allowed the story to gather steam on the off-day between games.

The game had ended just before 11 P.M. on Monday night and then would have been reported on the late evening sports shows. Toronto was just getting the beginning of twenty-four-hour talk radio. There were no internet chat rooms—there was no internet—no iPhone interviews, no "wheel" showing the same TV highlights through the early hours of the morning. The morning papers, three of them in Toronto, would land on doorsteps and in hotel lobbies at dawn, and by the time the teams arrived for practice at the Gardens, the debate on what had happened the night before would be cranked up again, providing another day of theatre and lively quotes.

A particularly sensational or critical story might get pinned up in somebody's dressing room stall. Players didn't receive media training, and team officials weren't eavesdropping on every interview to interrupt if the questions or answers got too provocative. There were more notebooks than television cameras, and no podiums or formal interview areas. A reporter might just catch a player in the hallway, or walking to the team bus. Off-days were often entertaining, a chance for coaches to set the stage and players to get their opinions in the paper. "Dougie's just gone back to his planet to rest," quipped Leafs head coach Pat Burns on being asked about the health of his star centre when Gilmour didn't show for practice. There were lots of threats, implied or otherwise. The Leafs talked about inserting their own enforcer, Ken Baumgartner, who had been a healthy scratch for twelve consecutive games. Baumgartner confirmed he had chatted with Burns but did not reveal the subject matter. "It's classified information," he said.

Kings head coach Barry Melrose, meanwhile, said he thought Gilmour's hip check on Alexei Zhitnik in the third period was a much dirtier hit than McSorley's. "They were knocking us all over hell's half acre," said Melrose. "We hit one guy and Canada wants to send out the militia." McSorley received more than one hundred threatening messages in his hotel room, all intercepted by his brother. Fletcher predicted there wouldn't be any more assaults on Gilmour. He declined to provide details. "Ever play in the NHL? Go ask someone who has," said Fletcher. That had been part of hockey for as long as the game had been played, the dark suggestion after an ugly incident that revenge would be on the menu in the next game. Truth was, it rarely happened that way. The next game was often quiet. Retaliation, if it ever happened, would come further down the road. Served cold.

Still, a sense of order was important, or at least it had to be implied. That was the NHL in those days: often it produced ugly violence but then acted embarrassed by it, or pretended to be surprised and horrified. Don Koharski was officially handed the job of ensuring order was restored in Game 2. Koharski was a veteran NHL referee, and he knew what he was expected to do. He would clamp down on the Leafs and Kings early and often in the second game, sending a steady stream of players to the penalty box. Many were called for misdemeanours that hadn't been called in the series opener. It was like the NHL rule book had been reviewed and revised between games.

MCSORLEY, LIKE A BRUISED survivor of single combat, skated out for Game 2 with a grotesquely blackened right eye courtesy of a Clark punch. "What else could a guy from Hamilton expect after mugging Doug Gilmour, the Gardens' Sirius, the brightest of night stars, and fist-fighting with Wendel Clark, the Leafs esteemed captain from the wheat belt? He got exactly what he expected—a shiner," wrote legendary *Star* columnist Milt Dunnell. Clark didn't anticipate McSorley would be looking for him in Game 2. "Truth is, we play a lot alike," said the Leafs captain. "This time, he got the black eye. Next time, I'll probably get one."

Both teams had made lineup changes for Game 2, and not to add finesse. The Kings inserted winger Warren Rychel, who had led the NHL in fighting majors during the season. The Leafs replaced smallish centre John Cullen with six-foot-three pivot Mike Eastwood, although Eastwood was not regarded as a player who sought out physical confrontations. Koharski had his eye on Rychel from the start, and at the forty-five-second mark he sent him to the penalty box for a high-sticking minor on his first shift of the series, an early sign that the referee intended to assert his authority. As the Leafs went to the power play, McSorley stood up Gilmour with a punishing hit at the LA blueline, clearly not backing off an inch despite all the controversy after the first game. Gilmour didn't respond, but moments later he carried the puck into the LA zone at the right boards and cut into the middle, just like he had in Game 1 before being nailed by McSorley. He wasn't backing off either. This time, however, it was he and winger Nikolai Borschevsky going two-on-two versus the LA defence pairing of Rob Blake and Tim Watters, and because the Kings were short-handed, Blake was not as free to come across aggressively as McSorley had. Blake and Watters miscommunicated slightly as Gilmour and Borschevsky criss-crossed and worked a give-and-go play. Gilmour finished it off with a backhand move for his third goal of the series at 2:25 to give the Leafs a swift 1–0 lead. It was a shocking start. The Kings had been outshot 22–1 in the third period of Game 1, and now the Leafs had stunned them with an early goal in Game 2.

That made it three goals for Gilmour in just over three periods of competition against the Kings, a dream start to the series for him and for the Leafs. It also continued the dreamlike narrative that had dominated the Leafs' playoff run and their regular season. Clark was Toronto's heart and soul, of that there was no question. But Gilmour's acquisition from Calgary on January 2, 1992, had breathed life into a moribund franchise that had once been the pride of all of English Canada. It had changed the Leafs just as much as Gretzky's trade from Edmonton to Los Angeles four years earlier—one of the most famous deals in hockey history—had changed the Kings.

THE GILMOUR TRADE WAS crucial for a number of reasons. For starters, it had at least temporarily bailed Fletcher out of a very awkward position. He'd been hired in the summer of 1991 by then Leafs president Don Giffin but had little confidence he'd be able to stay in his new job for long. Giffin and Stavro, both wealthy Toronto businessmen, had been two of the three executors named to handle the estate of Leafs owner Harold Ballard, who had died in April 1990. For more than two decades, Ballard had been the biggest mouth in hockey. He had bought into the Leafs in 1961 with Stafford Smythe—son of Leafs founder Conn Smythe—and John Bassett, and was part of the club's ownership during the glorious 1960s as the team won four Cups, although he had little to do with the actual team.

Ballard outlasted both of his business partners and took control of the Leafs and the Gardens in late 1971. The following year, he went on trial on forty-nine counts of theft, fraud and tax evasion. He was convicted and sentenced to nine years in prison. His first stop was the maximum security Millhaven Institute, in Bath, Ontario. While incarcerated there, he called Red Kelly to ask if he might be interested in coaching the Leafs. Later, Ballard was moved to a nearby minimum security facility, and was paroled in October 1973. For years, members of the Toronto media referred to Ballard as "Millhaven Fats." Instead of being permanently banished from the NHL lodge, he simply returned to run the team and resumed his place on the NHL board of governors. Four years later, he was inducted into the Hockey Hall of Fame, an outrage that was evidence of that institution's corrupt nature in those days and the manner in which NHL business could be steered to suit the whim of powerful owners.

As the sole owner of the Leafs, Ballard was charitable with his money but also crass, sexist and often vulgar. There had been no NHL owner quite like him before, and there hasn't been one since. He told CBC Radio host Barbara Frum to "keep quiet" during an interview and suggested that women were only good in the bedroom and the kitchen. After reconsidering his decision to fire head coach Roger Neilson, he wanted Neilson to show up for the next game with a paper bag over his head. To protest the shooting down of a Korean jetliner by a Soviet fighter jet, he flashed the message "REMEMBER KOREAN AIRLINES FLIGHT 007 SHOT DOWN BY THE RUSSIANS. DON'T CHEER. JUST BOO" on the video scoreboard at the Gardens during an exhibition hockey game between Canada and a Soviet team. He refused to trade legendary Leaf Dave Keon in the latter stages of his career, then lost him to the World Hockey Association for nothing. He all but drove star centre Darryl Sittler out of town. Ballard was part provocateur, part carny. He said what he wanted when he wanted. But he wasn't a successful hockey man. He never produced a winning team. From 1971 until his death, the Leafs won eight playoff series and made it past the second round of the Stanley Cup playoffs once. In his final years, with his eccentric partner, Yolanda Babic, by his side, the team slipped further and further from the mainstream. Other clubs started acquiring Russian players as they became available, but Ballard wouldn't allow it. The Leafs became more a subject for tabloid gossip than a contender for the Stanley Cup. Giffin and Stavro, both on the Gardens board of directors, each quietly had his own ambitions of succeeding Ballard and running the famous hockey club when he died. They soon became rivals.

Fletcher watched from afar as the Leafs organization spun into chaos and uncertainty following Ballard's death. He quit as GM of the Flames after the '91 playoffs, then considered an offer from the New York Rangers before agreeing to join the Leafs as GM after being courted by Giffin in his capacity as team president. He was given a long-term contract and a large salary, the kind of salary Ballard never would have approved. "I was assured absolutely, categorically, Steve [Stavro] would never get the team," Fletcher says now. The assurances turned out to be empty.

The night before he was to be introduced as Toronto's new GM in June 1991, Fletcher was invited to meet Stavro for dinner at the Palace Restaurant in Toronto's Greektown. It wasn't a congratulatory meeting. It was a dismissal. "Steve wanted to meet me," says Fletcher. "Everybody told me not to go. But I thought, I'll go. Stavro had his lawyer there with him. We had a talk. He said, 'I like you. But you're going to be a casualty of war. If you're smart, you'll get right back on that plane tomorrow and head back to Calgary. Because when I take over, you're gone.'" Stavro's preferred choice as GM was local businessman Lyman MacInnis, who had once tried to organize a sale of the Leafs from Ballard to iconic Canadian singer Anne Murray. But Stavro was powerless to remove Fletcher immediately, because Fletcher had an iron-clad, five-year, $4-million contract, and Stavro didn't yet have controlling interest in the hockey club. "I just played it out," Fletcher says.

But he didn't have a lot of time with which to work. Stavro was hovering, determined to make the Leafs and the Gardens his own. Fletcher needed to do something dramatic to turn the hockey team around, to provide evidence that he could make the Leafs a winner and help make them a money-maker. The team was in terrible shape, and Fletcher knew there was no time for gradual rebuilding plans. After twenty years of running NHL teams, he was an experienced trader. He knew how to make big deals, and he needed to make some. Quickly.

The initial situation was dire. At his initial training camp workout in the fall of 1991, Fletcher watched briefly from the stands then walked down to the ice surface and called over his assistant coaches Mike Murphy and Mike Kitchen. "Can't you get them to skate faster?" he pleaded. It's not like Fletcher had imagined it would be much better. "I'd been coming in here with Calgary for years and walking out with eight-goal victories. I knew exactly what the team was," he says now. But there was perception and there was brutal reality. On Boxing Day, Toronto went into Pittsburgh and surrendered the first goal of the game to winger Joe Mullen. Leafs winger Kevin Maguire tied the game 1–1. Then the Penguins scored eleven consecutive goals, with Leafs goaltender Grant Fuhr, acquired a few weeks earlier in Fletcher's first big deal as Toronto GM, left in for all the Pittsburgh goals. Mullen ended up with four goals, and the embarrassed Leafs fell to 10-23-5 on the season, the third worst record in the NHL. Fletcher's first months as saviour of the Leafs were not going well. "Cliff was flipping out," recalls Bob Stellick, then a public relations aide. Fletcher understood the rebuilding task at hand, but losing to the Penguins like that was humiliating to the proud hockey lifer. "It was like . . . hide the rope," he says grimly.

With Fletcher's old team in Calgary, the situation was very different. The powerful Flames had won the Stanley Cup two years earlier with a payroll of $4 million, and they were struggling to come to grips with the fact that their payroll was about to get a lot bigger, probably well over $10 million, if they wanted to stay at the top. Stars such as Gilmour, Joe Nieuwendyk, Gary Roberts, Al MacInnis, Gary Suter, Sergei Makarov and goalie Mike Vernon were all going to have to get paid. It was a tricky situation for GM Doug Risebrough, who had played with some of those players—but not Gilmour—during his own five-year playing stint in Calgary before retiring. Risebrough and Gilmour had bickered about a new contract for the veteran centre for months, and it had turned personal. Really personal. Gilmour had made about $411,000 the previous season. The battle over a new contract had ended in arbitration, quite often a messy process for NHL players. The team offered $550,000 at the August arbitration hearing. Gilmour asked for $1.2 million, and arbitrator Gary Schreider decided on $750,000. That enraged Gilmour, who felt that because the league got to pick the arbitrators, the system was rigged against players.

Risebrough wasn't all that pleased with the result either as he contemplated his payroll challenges. Youngster Theoren Fleury, making only $251,000, was good enough to supplant Gilmour as the team's number-two centre behind Nieuwendyk. Risebrough started looking for other NHL clubs who might want Gilmour in a trade, something Gilmour learned quite by accident. In early October, with the Flames in San Francisco before a game with the San Jose Sharks, Gilmour woke early to hear a loud voice from the adjoining hotel room. It was Risebrough on the phone, clearly unaware Gilmour was in the room next door. Gilmour got out of bed and lay by the door to Risebrough's room, listening. "What the fuck are you doing?" said Tim Sweeney, who had woken to find his roommate on the floor. "Come here," Gilmour hissed, waving him over. The sight of two NHL players lying on the carpet to eavesdrop on their neighbour must have been hilarious. But to Gilmour it was no joke. He heard Risebrough talking in cold, businesslike tones to someone at the other end about why he was going to have to trade Gilmour, and soon. That just made the already strained relationship between GM and player worse.

Gilmour hung in for thirty-three games knowing Risebrough was trying to trade him. A number of teams had expressed interest. Los Angeles, for one. Gretzky had spoken to Gilmour about his fight for more money, and the Kings were the highest-spending team in hockey. Hartford, perhaps, could be convinced to part with the original Little Ball of Hate, winger Pat Verbeek. Then there was poor, downtrodden Toronto, an easy mark for many teams over the years. The Leafs had traditionally been a team desperate to do anything to get better, like four years earlier when they traded their first-round pick in the 1990 draft to New Jersey for veteran blueliner Tom Kurvers, who initially refused to join the awful Leafs organization. The pick had turned into the third selection overall for the Devils and landed them future Hall of Fame defenceman Scott Niedermayer.

Risebrough had apprenticed under Fletcher. They had a close relationship, and talks commenced. Then, after a New Year's Eve victory over Montreal, Gilmour decided he'd had enough and left the Flames. Less than twenty-four hours later, Fletcher and Risebrough agreed on a trade that sent Gilmour and four other players—defencemen Jamie Macoun and Ric Nattress, goalie Rick Wamsley and young winger Kent Manderville—to Toronto from the Flames. In exchange, Calgary received star winger Gary Leeman, enforcer Craig Berube, defenceman Michel Petit, young blueliner Alexander Godynyuk and backup goalie Jeff Reese. It was, to a great extent, a money deal. Toronto was taking on salary; Calgary was dumping it. Stavro may have wanted to fire him, but until that happened, Fletcher had a free hand to spend on players. He'd already added Fuhr's $1.247-million contract for the '92–93 season in a deal with Edmonton, but this trade with Calgary was going to cost the Leafs a great deal more, starting with the understanding they'd have to re-do Gilmour's contract. Within a year, they'd double his earnings. Not only did Gilmour want more money, so did Macoun and Nattress, while Wamsley was looking for more playing time in order to secure another contract.

For the Flames, not only did the trade relieve financial pressures, Leeman was also a potential replacement at right wing for Brett Hull, who had been traded by Fletcher to St. Louis several years earlier as the Flames tried to win the Cup. Calgary did win it all in '89, but the deal had become an embarrassing one for the Flames. Hull had scored seventy-two and eighty-six goals for the Blues the previous two seasons and was on his way to seventy goals in '91–92. Leeman wasn't Hull, but he had scored fifty-one goals two seasons earlier, and that was after back-to-back thirty-goal seasons. With better players in Calgary, he might score even more.

But he was a bust in Calgary. Indeed, the trade with Toronto so weakened the Flames they missed the playoffs, and then, with a less powerful club the next season, they were the first-round victims of the Kings in the '93 playoffs. The Gilmour deal, then, helped set the stage for the classic '93 playoff confrontation between the Leafs and Kings. Gone forever were the days when the road to the Stanley Cup went through Alberta. The trade strengthened the Leafs immeasurably and also cleared the way for LA to make the playoff run they hadn't been able to gain since acquiring Gretzky.

"We were so bad," says Fletcher, recalling the trade. "So how could things get worse? I knew the players I was getting better than the ones I had given up. I didn't know how Leeman was going to play when he went to Calgary. He could be a fifty-goal scorer. They loved Leeman. I don't know why he didn't play well when he got there. But he never played anywhere near the level he did with Toronto. I knew we were getting three solid guys, and the young kid in Manderville, and with Gilmour, we had to do it." He remembers the trade wistfully, evidence of a bygone era in the game. "Today, there's no trades like that. Today, I really feel for the general managers. Everybody makes mistakes in this business. At least when I was a general manager you had a much better chance to recover from a mistake. You could spend a little money. You could go out and get another player. Today, these poor guys, they commit to a player and they commit to the money you're giving him, they're screwed. Twenty-five years ago, there were a lot of teams that were sloppy, a lot of teams that couldn't spend money to hire personnel, a lot of teams that weren't up to snuff. Today, it's a level playing field. Everybody wants to get an edge. But today, it's almost impossible. How do you get an edge? You can't." Fletcher insists he didn't set out to fleece Risebrough, his former student, out of anger or bitterness with his former team. "I wanted to win the deal, but I didn't want to see Calgary killed like that," he says. "I'd run the team for nineteen years! But I never asked for anything. All I did was say yes to every proposal they made."

The deal was one-sided from the start, an enormous windfall for the Leafs and a major victory for Fletcher, known as the "Silver Fox." Stavro, at least for the time being, couldn't possibly make a move to fire him. For Gilmour, nicknamed "Killer," it was the opportunity he craved, a chance to be the focal point of an NHL team for the first time in his pro career and a chance at a larger pay cheque. He was twenty-eight years old and already had registered a hundred-point season in the NHL. He was ready for a bigger role, and the Leafs were a team desperate for stars and firepower. When Gilmour arrived in Toronto, expectations were tragically low. The stink from the Ballard years was still in the air. Gilmour was a highly respected player, but how much could one player possibly do? As it turned out, it was more than anyone would have predicted.

A plus for Gilmour was that Toronto was closer to Kingston, which meant family members were able to visit more easily and watch him play. His marriage had dissolved in Calgary, and now he could start over nearer to home. Over the course of five seasons as a Leaf, he would change his address six times, constantly searching for a home he could retreat to and feel comfortable in while learning to embrace life as a hockey superstar. He was wealthy and single but unable to find a place to rest his head. At the beginning, he moved into an apartment building on Wood Street, adjacent to Maple Leaf Gardens, where many incoming players often stayed temporarily. He rented a two-bedroom apartment for $2,000 a month—very expensive in those days—and stayed for more than a year.

The World Wide Web had only just been invented, so what existed of internet access for most people, including sports writers, was extremely limited. Social media was a long way off, while Bell Canada was just starting to advertise its exciting new "call waiting" feature on *Hockey Night in Canada* broadcasts. Hockey players in Toronto, while famous and recognized on the street, could live a life of privilege while existing in relative privacy. P.M. Toronto was a lively and very public bar across the street from the Gardens, and while Gilmour lived on Wood

Street it was a go-to place. His teammates unwound there, local entrepreneurs interested in making connections with NHL players came by, and there were all kinds of new friends available. It was a place where Leafs players knew the owner and could enjoy a slice of privacy. Gilmour's teammates called him "Backdoor Gilmour" for the way he would sneak out the back door of the bar and go home early. One second he was there in the middle of the party, the next he was gone.

He struggled to find a more permanent home. "In my second year, I moved to the west end, to a warehouse condo," he recalls. "After a game one night, I went over to Mr. Sub. A guy says, 'Hey, Doug Gilmour! How you doing? You smoke crack?' I said, 'No, I'm good.' So then I moved again. Mostly, I didn't go out. People think I went out all the time. I didn't. I was in my little pad. I had my daughter Maddison with me on the weekends. I had my parents there on the weekends. During the week, Monday nights we all went out to the Phoenix [nightclub]. That was about it. I didn't really go anywhere. My security blanket was having friends on the outside. We did things people didn't talk about. We went to shelters, gave out Christmas presents, sleeping bags, jackets."

Gilmour cut a very different public figure than Clark, the simple farm boy with straightforward farm attitudes in the big city. Gilmour was a walking contradiction, a conundrum. He seemed secretive, but he could also be open and trusting, and his generosity knew no bounds. He would take sportswriters into his confidence, but never to rip a teammate or a coach. He talked the talk of the traditional hockey player, but you quickly got the sense he had seen a lot of things in his career and his life. He'd been married young, and it hadn't worked out, but he loved to talk about his daughter and spend time with her. Soon, he started a new, very public romance with Amy Cable, a Gardens usher, and eventually married her. He was a complicated character who had been around the block, and he wasn't a hypocrite; he didn't pretend to be Mr. Clean, or even a clean hockey player.

He was also a refreshing change on the Toronto sports scene, a Leaf who wasn't tarnished by years of losing. Fuhr and Glenn Anderson had been acquired from the Oilers to add a winning edge, but Gilmour was immediately a much greater presence and seemed to breathe confidence into an organization that had little. Always small for his age, and eventually small for the NHL, he had succeeded by overcoming his lack of size and brought that same "no fear" attitude to the Leafs dressing room. He also became the biggest practical joker on the team and dealt with the new inconveniences of fame in his own mischievous way. "One day we had an open practice for the public," he recalls. "Outside the arena, it was jammed. I thought, How am I going to get in there? So I put my Leafs jersey on, put on a ball cap and walked in with the crowd."

Hockey-wise, Toronto was a perfect fit. In his first forty games in Maple Leafs blue and white, Gilmour managed forty-nine points playing as a true number-one centre for the first time in his career. The Leafs caught fire in the second half of the '91–92 season after getting Gilmour from the Flames, but they couldn't quite catch the North Stars for the final playoff berth. After the season, Fletcher dismissed head coach Tom Watt and hired Burns to replace him. Burns and Gilmour held their first one-on-one meeting at Filmores, a famous Toronto striptease joint. "That was Pat Burns," chuckles Gilmour. It wasn't exactly a place Gilmour would find uncomfortable either.

Gilmour would be not only Burns's best offensive player but also his most conscientious defensive player as well. It was the perfect marriage between coach and player and, by early in Game 2 of the '93 conference, a relationship that looked like it might take the Leafs to their first Stanley Cup final in twenty-six years.

The confrontation in the conference final with Gretzky, Gilmour's role model as a junior, seemed nearly poetic, but it was also awkward. Some of the nastier tactics Gilmour used against other opponents were inappropriate against Gretzky. At the same time, this was another chance to prove himself, and to prove again that the Flames—and Risebrough—had made a tragic mistake by underestimating him, like people had been underestimating him since he was a boy with big hockey dreams.

He'd played against Gretzky many times, but this was a much bigger stage, and unlike in Calgary, he wasn't supported by other elite centres in Toronto. "There was a lot of respect there for Wayne," says Gilmour. "A lot of guys I'd chirp at. Wayne was one guy I wouldn't chirp at. So I played different against him. But I wanted to play hard against him. I tried to hit him, but clean. You think I didn't want to beat him? That was my challenge. Beat him." With a 1–0 lead in Game 2, Gilmour seemed well on his way to meeting that objective. The Leafs were dominating the Western Conference champions just as they had during the regular season, and celebrations of a possible Toronto-Montreal Cup final were already under way.

There wasn't much recent history between the teams, but there was some. The Leafs and Kings had met four times during the regular season, and the only game that ended in an LA victory, on November 21, had contained an incident that foreshadowed the bad blood that would surface in the conference final.

Gilmour assisted on three of the four Leafs goals in that game, but he also picked up a high-sticking minor for hacking Kings winger Tomas Sandstrom. Afterwards, it was revealed that Sandstrom's arm was broken. It takes a heck of a chop with a stick to break an NHL player's arm. The league, with long-time NHL counsel Gil Stein temporarily at the helm after the resignation of president John Ziegler, took action. Stein had invented the concept of suspending players for non-game days, and he suspended Gilmour for eight. He could play, but not practise. "It was an accident. It was not intentional," Gilmour said at the time. "I get ten whacks like that a game. But because I injured a guy, I get crucified."

It cost Gilmour $28,984 in pay plus a $500 fine. Burns was predictably outraged on behalf of his most important player. "Guys get whacked all the time. Guys get broken arms," he said. "The Kings are always crying about something. . . . LA or Pittsburgh, you can't touch them without getting a suspension. . . . I looked at the tape and didn't see anything. We're too quick to condemn Doug Gilmour. Why does everyone want to hang Doug Gilmour by a rope?" Don Cherry chimed in from his *Hockey Night in Canada* bully pulpit, calling Sandstrom a "backstabbing, cheap-shotting, mask-wearing Swede and he got exactly what he deserved."

Gilmour's peculiar status during his ban mystified newcomer Bill Berg when he was picked up on waivers from the New York Islanders. "I said, 'Doesn't he practise? Does he just play games?'" Berg recalls. Sandstrom missed twenty-four games after the Gilmour slash, and some had suggested that the

McSorley hit in Game 1 could be traced back to that incident. Hockey players could carry grudges for weeks, months or years, either for themselves or on behalf of teammates.

THE 1–0 LEAD EARLY IN Game 2 had the Leafs on a roll, much to the glee of the Gardens crowd and the twenty-five thousand Leafs fans watching on a huge video screen a few blocks away at SkyDome. But the Leafs couldn't make that early lead last. Burns usually liked to start his prized checking line of Bill Berg, centre Peter Zezel and winger Mark Osborne after goals either for or against the Leafs. He felt that trio could either build on momentum, or stop any momentum the opposition had going. This time, however, he went with two inexperienced forwards, Eastwood and Manderville, alongside veteran winger Mike Foligno. That curious decision backfired. With the Leafs forwards uncertain of their checking assignments, LA defenceman Charlie Huddy fired a high shot that produced a big rebound, and speedy Mike Donnelly slammed the puck past Felix Potvin at 2:56 to tie the game 1–1. So much of the talk before the series had been about LA stars like Gretzky, Jari Kurri and Luc Robitaille. But Donnelly, along with his linemates Corey Millen and Tony Granato, would prove to be a much more significant factors in the series than anyone initially believed.

Two goals in the first three minutes of a Stanley Cup play-off game was highly unusual. The Leafs made it even more surprising by scoring again before the game was four minutes old. Clark didn't appear to have much speed as he lugged the puck through the neutral zone, moved around Sandstrom on the right boards and skated in on Watters. The Leafs captain spun towards the boards and attracted the attention of three LA checkers, leaving Anderson, with a reputation as one of the best playoff scorers in NHL history, to cruise untouched into the Los Angeles slot just like he had in scoring a goal in Game 1. The veteran winger coolly redirected Clark's centring feed past Hrudey. The goal came just sixty-three seconds after Donnelly's, and it meant that between the two games the Leafs had scored five times on Hrudey in less than fifteen minutes of action. They were picking the veteran goalie apart.

Koharski kept calling penalties, trying to keep a lid on the game. Melrose chewed gum furiously on the LA bench, clearly concerned his team hadn't been able to contain Toronto's best players. Towards the end of the period, McSorley and Gilmour came together again along the boards, and McSorley delivered a sneaky punch to the much smaller man's jaw. No Leaf—no NHL player, probably—would dare do the same to Gretzky.

But for McSorley, Gilmour was fair game. Koharski either didn't see the punch or didn't acknowledge it. It was the kind of bullying from bigger players that Gilmour had endured his entire career, and he wasn't about to start accepting it now. He never, ever backed down. Seconds later, after the whistle, Gilmour shoved McSorley at the side of the LA net, and McSorley shoved him back. Gilmour then clearly leaned in and head-butted the Kings defenceman in the face. Head-butting, like kicking, was supposed to be out of bounds for honest hockey players. But Gilmour, no hypocrite, never said he was honest all the time on the ice. "You know, I wasn't all there sometimes when I played," he recalls. "These were the days when you had to survive, and I was 170 pounds. It was survival.

I had to get people to think, Hey, this guy's not all there. After the game, after I took my helmet off, I would often go home thinking, Are you stupid? But when I put the helmet back on, I wanted them to think I was crazy." Years earlier, while playing in St. Louis, Gilmour's older teammate Brian Sutter had been shocked at how vicious Gilmour could be when antagonized. He nicknamed Gilmour "Charlie," as in Charlie Manson, the murderous California cult leader. "That's where my nickname 'Killer' later came from. It started with 'Charlie,'" says Gilmour.

Koharski was standing less than five feet away when the Leafs star lowered his helmet into McSorley's face. He saw the head-butt. He'd probably also seen McSorley's punch. Koharski could have thrown Gilmour out of the game, and probably should have. Instead, he gave both players roughing penalties. In those days, that's what they called "managing" the game by veteran referees. "Gilmour cut my lip with the head-butt," recalls McSorley. "It was right in front of Koharski. I said, 'You gonna call that?' He said, 'Get away from me.' He wasn't going to call it." Gilmour never denied he'd done it. "One hundred percent, I did it," he says now. "Oh, yeah, I got away with it. I did it on purpose. I was pissed."

Gilmour escaped a more serious penalty for the head-butt, but the Kings and McSorley were clearly getting under his skin, distracting him from scoring and setting up his teammates. The more time he spent trying to get even with McSorley or defending his honour like he'd always done, the better it was for LA in a best-of-seven series. The Kings wanted him to react . It would sap his energy, make him less dangerous offensively. The respect Gilmour had for Gretzky was not being extended to him just because he was Toronto's biggest star. He was fair game for any

Kings player who had the urge to give him a whack. But there wasn't a Leaf who would even think about skating over to Gretzky during a scrum and punching him in the face.

Of course, Gretzky also wasn't inclined to do the things Gilmour would do. Partway through the second period, Koharski gave Gilmour a roughing penalty for skating over and taking a poke at Granato as he sat on the LA bench. All the Kings were now out to irritate Gilmour, and it was working. The momentum the Leafs had generated by blowing the Kings out of the Gardens in the third period of Game 1 and scoring two quick goals early in Game 2 was slowly vanishing. The game bogged down. The home team took penalty after penalty, including one by usually placid winger Dave Andreychuk.

Andreychuk had come over in a deal with Buffalo during the season and scored twenty-five goals in thirty-one games playing mostly with Gilmour as his centre. Suddenly, he was being paired with other linemates and wasn't nearly as effective, which seemed to frustrate him. He was sent off for knocking down Hrudey beside the Los Angeles net. "Boy, oh boy, Mr. Koharski is in the hair-splitting business tonight," said *Hockey Night in Canada* commentator Harry Neale. With Andreychuk in the box, Granato tied the game on LA's third straight power play. Granato took a pass from the speedy Millen, wheeled in front and fired a shot through Potvin's legs to make it 2–2. Granato had become an opponent half the Toronto team wanted to kill, and now he'd been the one to score.

Before the period was over, Clark took a charging penalty for decking Granato after he hit Gilmour. The LA strategies were working; Clark had been drawn into defending Gilmour again. The Leafs had clearly lost the plot, or at least any sense of what the objective was. During the second intermission, Melrose refused to let any Kings players go on the *Hockey Night in Canada* show. After Game 1, Gilmour had gone on the show, and Don Cherry, a fellow Kingston boy, had given him a big kiss on the cheek. Melrose either interpreted that as a bias against his team or just wanted to get his players to think that was the case. He was looking for any edge, and creating an us-against-the-world atmosphere for his team might give him one. He wanted to get his Canadian-born players in particular to believe the hockey broadcast they'd all grown up watching had turned against them.

The game stayed close past the halfway mark in the third. With Macoun and Kings winger Pat Conacher sent off for hacking at each other with their sticks, there was suddenly some room for offence, with four skaters out for each club. The Leafs sent out Gilmour and Anderson, with Todd Gill and Dave Ellett on defence. The Kings countered with Gretzky and Sandstrom, backed up by Blake and rookie Darryl Sydor. From inside the LA blueline, Sandstrom passed the puck to Gretzky at the right boards on the far side of the Gardens surface. Gretzky, in trademark fashion, pulled up. Several Toronto checkers paused for just an instant, which was all Gretzky ever needed.

The moment others hesitated, he saw openings no other players saw. He hit Sandstrom in stride with a tape-to-tape pass just outside the Leafs blueline. The Swedish winger wasn't quite in the clear. He had Anderson over his left shoulder and Gill in front of him to his right. But he had just enough room. A strong, skilled winger, Sandstrom turned to his left, shrugged off a weak stick check by Anderson and fired a snap shot that may have caught Potvin by surprise. The shot beat him high to the glove side inside the right post. It was a soft goal, Sandstrom's seventh of the playoffs, and partial revenge for the Gilmour slash that had broken his arm during the regular season. Gilmour was on the ice, but too far away to stop the Kings' scoring play. The Kings had their first lead of the series, 3–2, with less than eight minutes to play in the third period.

Even though the visitors were up by one, they had a problem, albeit one of which very few of the Kings players were aware. Hrudey, unbeknownst to everyone else on the ice, could barely stand up in the LA crease. He was a zombie. He was no longer sweating profusely, as he usually did. He had a case of the cold sweats, uncomfortable for any athlete. "I had hit a wall. I couldn't move," he says. Clark, proving to be the force the Kings feared he would be, tried one bull rush after another to even the game. With two minutes left, he had a glorious chance in the slot but fired wide of the left post, sending the puck whizzing past the dazed Hrudey's left ear. "Luckily for me, they didn't get another great chance," recalls Hrudey. "I don't think I could have stopped it."

With thirty-four seconds left, there was a faceoff in the Kings zone to the right of Hrudey with Potvin out of the Leafs net for an extra attacker. Gilmour wasn't conceding anything. He won the draw over Conacher, but a Macoun point shot went wide. With three seconds left, the Leafs iced the puck, and Gilmour took McSorley heavily into the end boards. Another confrontation seemed momentarily possible, but McSorley just skated away. He wasn't about to let LA's hard-fought road victory be tainted by a late-game brouhaha. The Kings had stolen home-ice advantage, and the series was tied 1-1.

Gilmour had scored half of the Leafs' goals so far. Gretzky, meanwhile, had two assists but had generally been quiet. Having the edge in the Gilmour-Gretzky matchup, however, hadn't been enough for the Leafs in the second game. It was the other players on the LA bench, players willing to do the dirty work, who had done most of the damage in Game 2, either by scoring or making Gilmour see red. The Leafs had allowed LA nine power plays in Game 2 with a succession of penalties, killing their chances of getting an early stranglehold on the series.

Sandstrom's winner was symbolic, the first indication in the series that the dream sequence of the Leafs' season might be interrupted. Gilmour seemed bothered by the opposing team for the first time in these playoffs, a storyline Toronto would need to change as the series moved to California.

The Kings were back in the series at least partly because they were willing to abuse and antagonize Gilmour in a way the Leafs were unwilling to abuse or antagonize Gretzky. It was apparently acceptable for any player on the Kings to take a shot at Killer, but no Leafs player seemed to believe it was acceptable to do the same to "The Great One." McSorley hadn't hesitated to deliver a nasty head shot in Game 1, but Gretzky was unlikely to receive anything similar. Certainly, no one was willing to deliver a destructive hit like Gary Suter had laid on Gretzky two years earlier, knocking him out of the '91 Canada Cup. A slash like the one from Adam Graves that had broken Mario Lemieux's hand in the '92 Stanley Cup playoffs? Unthinkable. Gretzky simply existed in a different category.

The easy explanation for years had been that with players like McSorley and Dave Semenko riding shotgun for Gretzky over the years, opposition players were unwilling to pay the price of taking "liberties" with Number 99. Now, however, the Leafs clearly weren't afraid of McSorley or what he might do.

Clark had already fought him and left him with a shiner. Gilmour had hit him, as had Berg, Osborne and others. It wasn't out of fear of McSorley that the Leafs weren't being as nasty to Gretzky as they could be. It was out of deference. Nobody had told them to behave that way. It was just understood. Gilmour and Gretzky were the stars of each team, but one had a little more freedom to operate than the other.

GILMOUR'S GOT ANOTHER story to tell as he watches his Frontenacs play. He called a few days earlier to renew his Maple Leafs season tickets, and the woman at the other end of the line didn't recognize his name. He laughs about it, not insulted. He takes it for what it is. Not everybody remembers. Not everybody was there back in '93 when he and Gretzky went head-to-head, winner-take-all. Back then, it seemed unlikely he'd ever have to buy a drink in a Toronto bar, let alone buy his own Leafs tickets. But time rumbles along. Other stars have worn the Leafs uniform with distinction since he did. Mats Sundin. Gary Roberts. Curtis Joseph. These days, it's Auston Matthews, Mitch Marner, William Nylander. Gilmour and Clark often do promotions together wearing their old jerseys. They're the old-timers now, the alumni, just like Johnny Bower and George Armstrong were when Number 93 and Number 17 were the headliners on the ice.

For Gilmour, long gone are the days of the $4-million mansion in one of Toronto's most prestigious neighbourhoods. He talks about scaling down his lifestyle, selling his remaining property in Kingston. His mom and dad are gone now. Fewer ties hold him to his hometown. He talks about making life simpler, daydreams of a time when he won't be in hockey anymore. Maybe he'll buy used classic furniture and refinish it in his garage. He's a trim 182 pounds, and there's still a full head of hair, but it's greying. There are deep creases in his face. He lives with his partner, Sonya, and their preteen daughter, Victoria, his fourth child from three different unions. He's also a grandfather now. Maddison, the youngster who once would visit him in that Wood Street apartment, is married to a professional hockey player, Evan McGrath. They live in Austria with the couple's infant daughter. Gilmour also has two boys with Amy Cable. His oldest son, Jake, was drafted by the Frontenacs, and at one point Gilmour traded Jake's rights to another OHL team. That's junior hockey. Sometimes you trade your own kid. Jake attends Brock University, while his younger brother, Tyson, forged a reputation as a high-scoring winger with the Powassan Voodoos of the Northern Ontario Junior Hockey League. There's a chance he might land a scholarship at a US university.

It was only for that brief time, for two weeks in the spring of '93, that Gilmour and Gretzky were the two main characters on the same stage, occupying the same space. These days, Gretzky is back squarely in the hockey limelight as an executive with the Edmonton Oilers. He was the NHL's ambassador during its centennial season. His number is retired, not just by the teams he played for during his career but by every NHL club. Gilmour's jersey was retired by the Leafs. Otherwise, he's more removed from that stage now, and that's where he wants to be. He wrote a book and did a promotional tour for it, but he doesn't yearn to be back in the NHL mainstream. He's done with that. When he first joined the Frontenacs, they weren't a well-respected OHL team. Top prospects wouldn't play there.

Domi's kid was just one of them. Over time, Gilmour has helped change that, slowly making Kingston a place where elite players play, where future NHLers get their start. He's no longer officially the team's GM, but he's involved in an unspecified capacity and frequently makes the seven-hundred-kilometre round trip from his home to Kingston and back during the season in his BMW X5. It's not the NHL, but it's enough. It's comfortable.

Back in '93, it was about him and Gretzky, the two top scorers not just of their teams but the entire playoffs. For that one series, they were more than opponents; they were equals, although Gilmour chafes at that characterization. "No, no, I wouldn't say I was his equal. I wouldn't say that," says Gilmour. He's not sure who had the edge in that famous one-on-one confrontation. "To this day, I think he's great," he says of Gretzky. "He's awesome. When I turned fifty, they had a quiet party for me at a small bar in Toronto. He came. Brought Theo Fleury with him." When they met in '93, Gilmour afforded Gretzky a level of courtesy he afforded few others in the NHL. No insults, no trash talk. No stickwork. Others might get the Killer treatment, but not Gretzky. "I couldn't play his game, although I tried to play it sometimes," says Gilmour. "But I could beat him in a different way. I had to be a little crazier. I had to run someone. But I loved playing against Wayne. It was a challenge. Do I think I beat him in that series? Did I give everything I had? Yeah, I think I did okay."

ACT THREE

Bruce McNall loves to tell stories, sometimes for the joy of the telling, often to represent himself as something he is not. Or to please his audience. This day, just weeks after Donald Trump had been inaugurated as the forty-fifth president of the United States, McNall has a Trump story. "Donald came to a Kings game in 2014," he says. "I'd known Trump over the years. I took him to a box with a bunch of lawyer friends of mine. And he says, 'Bruce really screwed up.' Yeah, of course I did, I think to myself. Then Trump says, 'He should have borrowed the kind of money I borrow. Banks don't screw with you then. He didn't borrow enough money! When you borrow what I have, you own the bank. Not the other way around.'"

McNall laughs. He's in his office in downtown Santa Monica, not far from the wealth, poverty, beautiful blondes, buff dudes, sadness, ambition, filth, tourists, drugs, sunburns and surfers of Palisades Park. All LA worlds converge in Santa Monica. It's also not far from the elegant Loews Santa Monica Beach Hotel, where the Toronto Maple Leafs lived, rested, healed and imagined themselves possible Stanley Cup finalists as they took on McNall's Los Angeles Kings in May of '93. A quarter century later, this is the part of LA where McNall is playing out the final chapters of his sensational and ethically questionable career in business.

A half mile from the Loews, he works out of a small, relatively spartan office with no view on the second floor of a ten-floor glass building at Wilshire and Third that has For Lease signs on the front lawn. Outside, there are panhandlers on every corner. His hair, once stylishly silver, is now thinner and totally black. He walks with short, tentative steps. "If I'd known I was going to live this long," he says, "I would have taken better care of myself."

He remains friendly and charming, just as he's always been. Impossible not to like, really, which in many ways was both the source of his power and his undoing. Sixteen years after being released from federal prison, he rents a modest home in Malibu, a far cry from the $10-million mansion in Holmby Hills he once owned, where he held parties for Hollywood stars and sports celebrities. Once, he would have been driven home by limousine or taken one of his fleet of private cars, perhaps the Aston Martin. Now, he drives himself home in a leased BMW. There are no more $100-million deals, no more rare baseball cards to show, no billionaire sports owners knocking on his door.

He sometimes goes to Kings games when he's invited and admires the team and its success under its current owners, including two Stanley Cups and investments in local minor hockey that have seen Southern California start to produce NHL quality players, unthinkable when McNall bought the team in 1988. He is still close with some of his former players, including Wayne Gretzky. He tells a story about how he, Wayne and Janet Gretzky and Caitlyn Jenner (formerly Bruce Jenner) all recently attended a funeral for the comedian Alan Thicke. The story comes with a punchline about Jenner playing from the ladies' tees at the Sherwood Country Club.

He admits to all of his past sins and offers no excuses. He admitted it all in a book. There's no pretence of innocence here. In terms of his hockey past, McNall understands he operated the Kings in a completely different era, when it was possible to do things it is no longer possible to do, when there were fewer rules and plenty of people willing to look the other way. So McNall did what he wanted and became the most powerful man in hockey. Back then, the NHL was a much smaller business. You bought a team, you pretty much ran it the way you wanted.

McNall bought the Kings for $16 million, mere pennies compared to the $650 million the league now demands for an expansion franchise. He rose to become chairman of the NHL board of governors. He handpicked Gary Bettman to run the league. He brought Anaheim and Florida into the NHL family. He was a one-man show making up the rules as he went along. Today, he is a living example of the contrast between the way the NHL did business then and the way it does it now. Now, NHL headquarters runs the league and has specific guidelines for everything, including which owners can talk to the media and what they can say. Back then, it was sometimes a free-for-all, with flamboyant individual owners free to cut deals, move franchises, speak their minds, rip the league office and trade hockey players for cold, hard cash if they needed, or just wanted, the money. When he bought the Kings, McNall stumbled into a world that would let him do pretty much whatever he wanted to do. So he did.

BY THE TIME THE 1993 Campbell Conference final series switched to a new stage in Southern California, it already felt like a unique piece of theatre was unfolding. The series was tied 1–1 after two bruising, controversial games at Maple Leaf Gardens. After the ugliness late in Game 1 that made Marty McSorley look like a bully and Wendel Clark a Good Samaritan, Kings officials lobbied strenuously, but unsuccessfully, to have star Leafs centre Doug Gilmour suspended for his unpenalized head-butt on McSorley in Game 2. The gamesmanship in the series was already intense. The Kings had received a hostile reception in Toronto, but now the two teams were in Los Angeles at the Great Western Forum for Game 3.

The action away from the rink was just as dramatic, although hidden from the eyes of fans and media, not to mention the players on both teams. As his team prepared for its first home game of the series after stealing home-ice advantage in Game 2, McNall was looking every bit the flamboyant sports owner. The NHL had never attracted a personality quite like him before, and in remarkably short time he had gained immense power across the league. He wore expensive suits and was surrounded by executives and lawyers. He had a broad smile and a big laugh that communicated confidence. But looks were deceiving. Inside, he was churning, his mind constantly racing as he looked for ways out of the corner into which he had painted himself. He knew he was in big, big trouble. He had acquired his immense wealth largely through fraud. For a decade, he had been generating phony financial statements to make it appear he was a much wealthier man. He had become involved in rare coins as a teenager, and by the late 1970s he was seen as an expert, travelling the world to conduct all kinds of murky transactions. Over time, he created phony inventories of those coins and used them to secure massive loans from six different banks. The amounts involved were staggering, an estimated $267 million. He had used some of those millions to get involved in the movie business and some to buy the Kings five years earlier. He had diverted money from the gate receipts of Kings games, the only revenue he had from the team, to prop up his other schemes.

As the Toronto-LA series was taking place, he cut the figure of a major hockey power broker with immense personal resources. In reality, he was madly trying to pay his bills, avoid his creditors, stay one step ahead of the law and sell his hockey team. He was so close to disaster, he could barely sleep at night.

Steve Stavro, by contrast, had become a multi-millionaire by legitimate means, principally through his grocery chain, Knob Hill Farms. He dabbled in expensive race horses and owned glamorous homes in Toronto and Florida. That was all in good shape. Now, however, he was also attempting to complete his acquisition of the Maple Leafs and Maple Leaf Gardens, and was using more questionable business methods to do so. Harold Ballard had died three years earlier, and Stavro was furiously trying to finish the process of getting his hands on Ballard's hockey empire, even if it meant lying about the true value of the club so he could buy it at a bargain basement price.

So McNall had effectively stolen millions and used the proceeds to buy the Kings legally, while Stavro had made his money legally and was trying to steal the Leafs, the most valuable sports franchise in Canada.

The two men were not friendly. "Stavro and that gang liked Wayne, but they didn't like McNall," says Toronto sports consultant Brian Cooper, who worked for McNall. "Stavro didn't like his style. Bruce was brash. I would literally see Stavro cringing when they were talking." McNall and Stavro, the two impresarios who bankrolled the theatre of the Kings-Leafs series, were opposites in demeanour and public personality but similar in their willingness to look beyond the limits of the law, or at least the laws that limited others, to get what they craved. Both sought public acceptance, respectability, awards and affection. McNall, born in LA, was nonetheless an outsider, a self-professed geek who sought fame and perks by purchasing a unpopular sports team and making that team cool. Stavro was also an outsider, an immigrant whose father had run a fruit stand. He was drawn to more traditional and conservative corridors of power in Toronto and coveted the Leafs, the very essence of Toronto tradition, a team with legions of fans not only in the city but across the world.

As the series switched to LA for Game 3, the walls were starting to close in on both men. The authorities were sniffing around McNall's business practices, while Stavro was being hotly pursued by Gardens investors who believed he was trying to rip them off. The investors were becoming increasingly public with their unhappiness, which was embarrassing to Stavro, an intensely private man.

McNall was extraordinarily popular with his players and other Kings employees. He was the fan who had bought his favourite team and wanted everybody to be just as happy cheering or working for the team as he was. The most noteworthy evidence of his largesse was the Boeing 727 he had bought for $5 million for the private use of the Kings. After years of tiring commercial travel, where a trip to Quebec City or Winnipeg could take a full day, the players looked at the plane as a complete luxury. Painted black and silver, it had first-class seats and television screens, plus a table at the back where the team masseur could work on players. No other NHL team had such a plane.

Stavro kept some distance from the Leafs and was publicity shy. He did buy all the players blue leather jackets with a commemorative patch for "winning" the NHL's Norris Division by beating Detroit and St. Louis in the first two rounds of the '93 playoffs even though there was no official title for accomplishing that feat. "We didn't really know [Stavro]," says Gilmour. "He came in, took over the team, but we never saw him." Stavro, Donald Crump, director Terry Kelly and other Leafs officials arrived at LAX on a charter flight for Game 3 with the kind of entourage Ballard never would have countenanced. They were enjoying the ride and the notoriety that came with running the Leafs.

Outside the Leafs dressing room, assistant coach Mike Murphy paced the hallway and conferred with head coach Pat Burns and fellow assistant Mike Kitchen. They were looking for ways to get the team rolling again. That was the job of NHL coaches. The players knew, for the most part, how to play, or they would never have made it to the world's top hockey league. They could skate, pass, shoot. They could deal with the punishment of being bodychecked. They usually had a specific position they had trained to play for years. But that didn't always mean they were collectively focused or organized in the best possible way, and that could change from day to day. As much as coaching in the NHL was about teaching and developing skills, it was more about staring at the same roster of athletes day after day, and then coming up with new ways to align them, motivate them and send them charging into the fray with the best possible chance to win. Line changes. Taking players who hadn't played the game before and putting them into the lineup while yanking other players out. Trying to find ways to get certain players out on the ice against certain players from the other team, and avoiding getting your worst players out against their best. By the time NHL teams got to the final stages of the Stanley Cup playoffs, that was all coaches could do. So every day, they examined those options. When they won, they'd go with the same combinations. When they lost, they'd shuffle the deck.

For Murphy, a lot more was on the line in a personal sense than for either Burns or Kitchen, and he was surprised how emotional he had become about the series. Perhaps he shouldn't have been surprised. For fifteen years, he had given the Kings his best as a committed hockey man, first as a player, then captain, then assistant coach, then head coach. He'd raised his four children in Southern California. But twenty-seven games into the 1987–88 season, Murphy had been fired unceremoniously as the team's head coach. "My LA years ended on a sour note," he says. The way in which he was fired would have left anyone bitter. The team was on the road in Washington, and when he went up to his suite at the downtown Hyatt hotel he found the key didn't work. He went down to the front desk and was directed to the concierge, where he found his luggage all packed. He was told to go to the room of general manager Rogie Vachon. "We've decided to make a change," said the Kings GM. Murphy was stunned.

Now, five years later, he was with the Leafs, locked in an intense playoff battle with the Kings. "I wanted to beat them so bad," says Murphy. "I was a good player for them, a captain, a coach, and when it was over I was dismissed and kicked out of town. It hurt. Then you add to that I was working with the Leafs, my childhood team, well, I couldn't believe it. There was a lot of emotion for me in that series."

Murphy was the link between the Leafs and Kings, part of the history between Toronto and Los Angeles that had existed decades before men like McNall and Stavro tried to buy it all and call it their own.

Bill Barilko of Timmins, Ontario, one of the great legends of Maple Leafs history for scoring the Cup-winning goal in 1951 then disappearing in a plane crash, made the first plane ride of his life to California in the fall of 1945 to rent a room in a three-bedroom house at 265 South St. Andrews Place near Hancock Park, south of Hollywood. He was there to play for the Hollywood Wolves, who had a loose affiliation with Conn Smythe's Maple Leafs. "Because the Wolves games were on TV, a bit of a fan base grew around Bill," says author Kevin Shea, who wrote *Barilko: Without a Trace*. "He began to be seen in photo shoots with various Hollywood starlets. He became 'Hollywood' Bill Barilko."

When the Kings joined the NHL in 1967 with five other US teams—Philadelphia, Minnesota, Pittsburgh, St. Louis and Oakland—the league was almost exclusively populated by Canadian-born players. Players from the great Leafs teams of the 1960s that had won four Cups suddenly found themselves headed to California. Red Kelly became the first coach of the Kings, and Terry Sawchuk was one of his goalies. Bob Pulford, Dick Duff, Pete Stemkowski and Eddie Shack would follow them.

Kings owner Jack Kent Cooke was born in Hamilton, Ontario, before his family moved to the Beaches area of Toronto. In 1945, with the help of financier J.P. Bickell, who had at one time helped Smythe build Maple Leaf Gardens, Cooke bought a Toronto radio station, then six years later branched out into sports by purchasing Toronto's minor pro baseball team. Eventually, he moved south, went into business in California and became a US citizen. In 1966, having been unable to buy into big-league baseball, he sought and ultimately bought an NHL expansion franchise for $2 million, named it the Kings and began building the Forum.

In 1972, Pulford became LA's new head coach. While a Leaf, he'd played golf at Toronto's Lambton Golf and Country Club with John Murphy, whose son Mike was a high-profile NHL prospect. In those days, if you were a star bantam hockey player in Toronto, you were a star NHL prospect. Mike Murphy came from an Irish Catholic family, learned to skate on a backyard rink and played peewee hockey for his local parish. After two seasons of Junior A hockey skating for the OHL Toronto Marlboros, Murphy was selected in the second round of the 1970 NHL draft by the New York Rangers, twenty-fifth overall.

Pulford followed the progress of his golf buddy's son and convinced the Kings to trade for the right winger in the fall of 1973. Murphy was dealt to Los Angeles along with defenceman Sheldon Kannegiesser and forward Tom Williams. Murphy remembers flying out of Kennedy Airport on a drizzly, cold New York day and landing in bright sunshine at LAX. "LA is tired now, but back then it was literally lotus land, a beautiful place. Everything was fresh and new, and things were booming. Everything was casual," he says. "The sun was shining, and life suddenly became easy. It was a much different scene than I had left." Another Ontario boy was headed to Hollywood.

This was also around the time McNall, a young man growing up in Arcadia, California, became a lifelong fan of the Kings. The team had drawn poorly in the first few seasons, but now it was improving and fans like McNall at least had something to cheer for. "They were a secret that about eight to nine thousand people shared," says Bob Borgen, who was born and raised in LA and later went on to become the producer of televised Kings games. McNall was a student at UCLA when a friend convinced him to attend a game. "Nobody was there," McNall recalls. "You could buy twenty-dollar tickets for three dollars. I got caught up with it. I loved a lot of the players, like Vachon and Butch Goring. I just enjoyed the sport a lot." The 1972–73 season marked the first time the club drew more than ten thousand fans on average to games.

Murphy became the team's captain in 1977. He had married a Californian named Yvonne Horvat, who sang the national anthems at Kings games once or twice a season for several years. (Yvonne had an older sister, Connie, who married Kings forward Vic Venasky, and a younger sister, Sandra, who later married another Kings player, Daryl Evans. Three Sisters for Three Kings, as it were.) Life in LA in the '70s was intoxicating for young people, including young athletes, with easy access to parties, drugs and alcohol. Alongside Gene Carr, his more adventurous Kings teammate, Murphy would go to Dan Tana's restaurant, a favourite haunt of actor Jack Nicholson, and then to the famous Troubadour nightclub to mingle with celebrity musicians like Glenn Frey, Jackson Browne, J.D. Souther and Linda Ronstadt. Carr was good friends with the musical types and got into the lifestyle. Frey called him "Hockey Hollywood" and sometimes wore a Kings jersey with Carr's number 12 on stage with his band, The Eagles. Some believe Frey helped write the hit "New Kid in Town" with Carr in mind. "Once we left the rink, nobody knew who we were. We weren't celebrities. But life was really good," says Murphy.

The same year Murphy became captain, Dave Taylor, the son of a Scottish immigrant and a Quebecois mother from the Northern Ontario mining town of Levack, population three thousand, joined the Kings. He signed for $40,000 a year and a $15,000 bonus, another Ontario hockey player looking for fame and fortune in Los Angeles. "I remember my dad saying, 'If you don't want to work in the mines, you better skate faster,'" says Taylor. As Murphy's days as a front-line right winger for the Kings were fading, Taylor jumped past him on the depth chart and became part of the Triple Crown Line with Marcel Dionne and Charlie Simmer. In the 1980–81 season, all three players managed one hundred or more points, the first time that had happened in hockey history. In 1983, with Murphy's career effectively over, GM George Maguire offered him a job as assistant to the GM, and then he became an assistant coach to ex-Leafs bench boss Roger Neilson during his short stint with the Kings. Then the Kings hired Pat Quinn, who kept Murphy as an assistant and made Taylor, not Dionne, his captain.

In December 1986, Quinn was suspended by NHL president John Ziegler for negotiating a contract and accepting a $100,000 bonus cheque to become president and general manager of the Vancouver Canucks while still under contract to the Kings. Murphy, with little experience, became LA's new head coach for the final thirty-eight games of the '86–87 season, and then, after the first few months of the following season, he was fired. Jerry Buss was still theoretically in control of the Kings, but McNall, a minority owner, was becoming increasingly involved in the day-to-day operations. By the spring of '88, McNall had bought out Buss, and soon after he swung the blockbuster trade that brought Gretzky to the Kings. McNall quickly became front and centre, quoted everywhere and anywhere, and wanted his players to be front and centre with him. He wished to be friends with his players, and he was. He liked to hang out with them, buy them things, do business deals with them. Early in his tenure, before the Kings got their plane, he would fly his private jet to away games then fly a select number of players, usually seven, back to LA while the rest flew commercial. The players who got picked were called the "Magnificent Seven," and the unlucky ones were the "Dirty Dozen." "I loved him," says goalie Glenn Healy. "I loved his stories about coins. I looked at him as an awesome person who was a great owner. He was a player's guy through and through. That said, I still don't know what was real. That's part of the legend."

McNall's generosity, albeit expressed using other people's money, knew few bounds. "We're in Vancouver one day, so myself, Gretz and Kelly Hrudey, we were walking down the street, and there was a Versace store," recalls McNall. "We walked in there and looked around, and there was this really great leather jacket. Kelly kept looking at it. The price was twenty-five thousand dollars for this jacket. So I said, 'Hey, Kelly, how many shutouts are you going to get for this?' And I bought him the jacket." Hrudey's recollection is slightly different. He remembers the jacket costing around $6,000. It was black, hip length, with gemstones all along the arms and body.

"It was something a rock star like George Michael at that time would wear," says Hrudey. That was the kind of owner McNall wanted to be. "In today's NHL culture, you couldn't do that," says McNall. "But I didn't just watch the game like it was robots on ice. These were people who I got to know and care about."

The Kings had changed from an NHL outpost to a preferred destination for players. Tony Granato and Tomas Sandstrom arrived in a trade for popular Bernie Nicholls in 1990. Granato became Gretzky's roommate on the road and his linemate, and he found himself enthralled with the attention showered upon the Kings. When Granato went to join the Kings in Vancouver after the trade, he was surprised to learn he was rooming with "W. Douglas" at the team hotel. He ran into broadcaster Bob Miller on the elevator and asked Miller who this Douglas fellow was. "That's Wayne's pseudonym on the road," Miller told him. It was evidence of the new world Granato was entering. "Everybody, including everybody in Hollywood, wanted to be a part of the LA Kings when we were on our run," Granato says. "There was only one person who could have made that possible. That was the excitement, the presence, of Wayne, that everyone just wanted to be a part of it. The rest of us were fortunate to be there and experience that excitement. It's hard to explain, to be in LA, to watch people who knew nothing about hockey suddenly want to be part of it. The people that would come into the locker room just to shake Wayne's hand. It really was a heckuva ride for all of us."

It was all flashy and exciting, but it was largely built on a foundation of lies. The media estimated McNall's worth at $100 million, which was nowhere close to reality. He had multiple homes and nine cars, but also massive debt underwritten by phony financial statements. His hockey business couldn't pay its bills. "Economically, I had made a huge mistake when I got Wayne in '88. It wasn't about getting Wayne. It was the business around it," says McNall. "I didn't own the building. I didn't own the parking. I didn't own the television. I didn't own the radio. I didn't own the food services. All the ancillary things that make franchises profitable today, I got none of it. I just got ticket revenue, basically."

The Kings built the highest payroll in hockey without the revenue streams to pay for it, and McNall also promised Gretzky he would always be the highest paid player in the NHL. "Then, I could do that. I could manoeuvre around," McNall says. "We could do whatever we wanted to do. I guess I could have gone to the other [NHL] owners and said, 'Guess what, if you want Wayne to play in your building and hope he doesn't happen to get sick that day, I want half your revenue.' I could have played some extortion game, I guess. But that's not real ethical within the sport itself, so I really couldn't pull that off." Amidst the razzle-dazzle and circus atmosphere, not to mention McNall's uncanny ability to get people to like him, nobody inside or outside the Kings organization understood that what seemed too good to be true really was too good to be true. Everyone wanted to believe McNall really was the man who had figured out how to make the NHL popular and profitable in Los Angeles.

For years, scribes and broadcasters from traditional hockey regions like Canada, the northeastern US and Minnesota had been coming to LA to see the Kings, often as much for a warm winter vacation as to see anything noteworthy. The Triple Crown Line generated a lot of attention. But for most of the 1980s, the important hockey stories were taking place on Long

Island or in Montreal or in Alberta and being broadcasted on *Hockey Night in Canada* from the show's Toronto studios, far from Hollywood. Then Oilers owner Peter Pocklington sold Gretzky to the Kings, and suddenly playoff encounters with Edmonton and Calgary brought more attention from the hockey establishment to 3900 West Manchester Boulevard in Inglewood, California, home of Cooke's "Fabulous Forum." This was not one of LA's most glamorous communities, nor was it a hockey community in any real sense. Inglewood had been slow to integrate over the decades, but by the early 1990s it was split roughly equally between African-American and Hispanic residents. LA's economic boom of the mid-1980s hadn't benefited places like Inglewood or South Central LA, which became hard hit by street gangs and the crack cocaine epidemic of the 1980s. Here, there was more economic despair and racial tension than affluence and progress. This was the hardscrabble place the Kings called home.

In the 1970s, during training camp, the team would have two-a-day practices and the players would live at the Airport Park Hotel across the street from the Forum. That stopped happening as the community changed and struggled, and players were more careful as crime became more of a concern. The Forum was where they played and practised, and then they quickly drove to tonier areas of the city where they lived and raised families. Visiting NHL clubs wouldn't stay anywhere near the arena, and there were few appropriate hotels. They would stay in Santa Monica or near Los Angeles International Airport, then bus in and out. Postgame watering holes like Harry O's in Manhattan Beach, owned by former Kings for-ward Billy Harris, were destinations more than staying in

Inglewood or going to downtown LA. Hockey players got frequent reminders that LA came with unique safety challenges. In November 1991, for instance, three Leafs players—Jeff Reese, Claude Loiselle and Bob Halkidis—were robbed at gunpoint after a game against the Kings not far from their LAX hotel. They lost about $1,000 in cash and jewellery, including Reese's wedding ring.

On April 29, 1992, four LA police officers were acquitted of assault in connection with a sensational incident in which local resident Rodney King had been beaten after a high speed car chase. The acquittals sparked race riots in South Central LA that then spread to areas across Los Angeles County including not far from the Forum. There was looting and widespread assaults as a horrified America looked on from afar at the mayhem. More than 3,600 fires were set, and the National Guard was called in. When it was over, fifty-five people had been killed and two thousand injured.

Bruce Springsteen was recording in East Hollywood as word of the violence spread. "I stopped for a moment near the Hollywood Bowl where my windshield was filled with city-wide fury," he wrote in his 2017 autobiography. "It was a fiery, smoking panorama from a bad Hollywood disaster picture. . . . Unlike the Watts riots of 1965, the fire this time looked as if it might spread out beyond the ghetto of those afflicted. Fear, and plenty of it, was in the air."

For Kings players, who had been eliminated in the first round of the playoffs by Edmonton the day before the Rodney King verdict, this was a brand new reality, a new danger surrounding their daily workplace. Hrudey was at the end of his third full season in LA, living with his wife and young family in Redondo Beach. "I remember the day the verdict came down, and [truck driver] Reginald Denny getting beaten up at that intersection. We were quite a ways from there, but from our second floor balcony you could see the fires in the distance," he says. "What I remember most about that day is, living right across from us, there was a young guy. His dad was a police officer on the Redondo Beach police force. The son comes over around four o'clock in the afternoon and he's got a gun, a .357 Magnum. He says, 'My dad wants you to have a gun.' And I said, 'No, I'm not interested. I've never held a gun in my life. I don't really believe in guns.' He said, 'Okay, but we're going to keep watching what happens.' About six thirty, his dad comes back over and says, 'You're gonna take this fucking gun. And you're gonna protect your family at all costs.' He would not accept no. I'll never forget that."

Playing for McNall, and getting the chance to play with Gretzky, still made players happy to be in Los Angeles. They saw themselves as playing for the most generous, warm-hearted owner in hockey. When the NHL Players' Association chose to strike briefly in the spring of 1992, Hrudey remembers the Kings voting with the rest of the players to strike but also feeling like he had betrayed McNall. "I know he took our vote personally, and why wouldn't he? But we weren't voting to go on strike that day because of the way we were being treated. We were voting to go on strike because of the way the rest of the players were being treated by some of their organizations." They didn't know yet about McNall's financial shell game.

In 1991, McNall added to his collection of sports toys by purchasing the Toronto Argonauts of the Canadian Football League from Harry Ornest, the former owner of the St. Louis

Blues and the Hollywood Park racetrack, across the street from the Fabulous Forum, and also one of the largest shareholders in Maple Leaf Gardens and the Leafs. Gretzky and actor/comedian John Candy were McNall's partners in the Argo purchase. The price was $5 million, and suddenly McNall was a significant presence in Toronto, home of the Blue Jays, a growing powerhouse, and the awful Maple Leafs. Jack Kent Cooke had left Toronto twenty-five years earlier to become a high-profile sports owner in Southern California, and now LA hockey money and a hint of Hollywood glamour were coming to influence the Toronto sports scene.

Like most McNall deals, the Argo transaction was heavily financed. McNall believed that the Argos might also give him the inside track if the National Football League ever decided to put a team in Toronto. Gretzky had a relationship with Brian Cooper dating back several years from the Wayne Gretzky Celebrity Sports Classic, held annually in Brantford, Ontario, Gretzky's hometown. He convinced Cooper to come aboard with the Argos, first as executive vice-president, then eventually as chief operating officer.

At the time, Cooper didn't know McNall or Candy. He met McNall at a party at Gretzky's Balboa Drive home in Los Angeles. "Bruce drives up in a Bentley," says Cooper, "and he's dropping names left, right and centre. Don Henley, Sylvester Stallone. . . . His company had just done *The Fabulous Baker Boys*. I thought, This is impressive. Money was nothing. We go out to dinner, and they're ordering bottles of six-hundred-dollar wine, talking about his investments with Merrill Lynch on coins. He's blowing me away. Later, we go to a Kings game. Before the game, there's dinner at the Forum with celebrities. Elton John, Rob

Lowe. And we start talking about the Argos." The football team had traditionally lost money. McNall made a splash by signing University of Notre Dame star Raghib "the Rocket" Ismail, but the Argos had to pay Ismail $4 million up front, completely outrageous by the standards of the small nine-team league. Indeed, the $18-million, four-year personal service contract was more than he would have made in the much larger NFL. The vision was that Ismail would do for the Argos what Gretzky had done for the Kings. But just as the Kings couldn't actually support those types of contracts, Ismail certainly didn't make financial sense for the Argos.

The Argonauts organized a spectacular opening night, with Dan Aykroyd and Jim Belushi performing as the Blues Brothers at halftime and celebrities like Mariel Hemingway on hand. It was different from anything the Leafs or Blue Jays had ever produced, and very different from anything the Argos or the CFL had ever seen. The spectacular evening made waves in Toronto, and attendance increased. "What made it fun was that John [Candy] loved it," says Gretzky now. "If John hadn't been involved, I don't know if I'd have been willing to jump in. But John truly loved it." With Ismail, quarterback Matt Dunigan, running back Michael "Pinball" Clemons and a host of stars, the Argos went 13–5 and captured the Grey Cup. Ismail had been a disappointment, but he scored on a thrilling kickoff return to win the title game. The dollars behind the project made no sense, however, and McNall's Argos left unpaid bills all over town.

THE LEAFS, MEANWHILE, had been in a state of paralysis after the death of Ballard in April 1990. Nobody knew who was going to buy the team. "We just don't know. I can see a lot of lawsuits flying around here," said Paul McNamara, chairman of the Maple Leaf Gardens board of directors. McNall and Ballard had crossed paths at NHL governors meetings. "I liked him in some ways, although he was not a likeable human being for the most part," says McNall. "We were distant. We'd say hello, we'd talk. He'd disagree with everything I wanted to do, and I'd disagree with everything he wanted to do. We were not buddy-buddy, nor from a business standpoint did we agree on many issues. They were traditionalists, very much, in what they were doing. And I was not. I'm sure they viewed me as some kind of alien." Having McNall show up in town and start generating flashy headlines with the Argos just made the Leafs look old, tired and broken.

When Ballard died, the organization owned several ancillary businesses that were losing money. Selling the major junior Toronto Marlboros, the CFL Hamilton Tiger-Cats and Davis Printing, which printed Leafs tickets, freed the team from $5.5 million in losses annually, and moving the team's American Hockey League affiliate from St. Catharines, Ontario, to St. John's, Newfoundland, saved another $1 million. The team's business operations were outdated and messy. There were no budgets or financial records, and very little security around the building. Ballard himself had been scalping Leafs tickets for years, and his estate was left to deal with a trail of debts and liabilities. "By the end, people were exhausted with the Harold regime," said Bob Stellick, who worked in the team's front office. "We were barely a franchise. We knew we had no chance of success."

Bill Ballard, one of Harold's sons, angled for control after his father's death. Many thought one of the major Canadian breweries, always active in the sport, would emerge as a majority owner. Then there was Stavro. A Toronto businessman of Greek-Macedonian heritage, Stavro, born Manoli Stavroff Sholdas, immigrated to Canada with his parents when he was seven years old. He was reserved and publicity shy, a product of Toronto when it was, as once described by famed literary critic Northrop Frye, "a good place to mind your own business."

After Ballard's death, few believed the sixty-two-year-old Stavro would be the one to take over. "He was not a confidante of Mr. Ballard," says Bob Stellick. "He was never around." Stavro also had only a passing financial interest in the team. Long-time Detroit Red Wings executive Jimmy Devellano owned 32,375 shares in Maple Leaf Gardens (MLG) Ltd., making him the third largest non-controlling shareholder in the company. Don Giffin, who had been named chief executive officer of MLG Ltd. the previous January, owned 60,000 shares, while Harry Ornest, the same man who had sold the Argos to McNall, owned 90,000, about 3.5 percent. "Stavro had only five hundred shares. Five hundred! That's how interested he was," says Devellano. "I think I was closer to Harold Ballard than Stavro was."

But Stavro had known Ballard for decades and had been appointed to the board of the Gardens in 1981. He told Theresa Tedesco, author of *Offside: The Battle for Control of Maple Leaf Gardens*, that he believed Ballard wanted him to own the Leafs. "I figured he believed in me and I could do something with the club," Stavro told Tedesco. That belief was apparently strong enough for Stavro that he was able to convince himself that angling for control of the Leafs wasn't a violation of the trust Ballard had placed in him by making him a co-executor of his will.

The scramble for control of the Leafs and MLG Ltd. began within months of Ballard's death. Harold E. Ballard Ltd. (HEBL), a holding company, controlled 80 percent of Gardens shares. Ballard willed control of HEBL to a three-man trust of Stavro, Giffin and Donald Crump, who were also named executors of his estate. The trustees were to "retain and vote" the HEBL shares for no more than twenty-one years and direct any proceeds from the sale of those shares to the Harold E. Ballard Foundation, a charitable organization. Ballard's intentions as expressed by his will seemed clear; he wanted charities to benefit from the sale of the Leafs, not his friends, and not the trustees. It was thought Giffin and Crump, who had been named commissioner of the CFL while Ballard owned the Tiger-Cats, would be allies in getting the best deal for the club and the arena. Giffin had helped Ballard get the loan with the TD Bank he needed to buy control of the Leafs when Stafford Smythe had died in 1971. But he ended up being outflanked by Stavro, with Crump's help. The grocery magnate wanted the team for himself. Stavro "seized an opportunity," according to Devellano. "The other executors didn't have the money to finance it," he says. "Stavro was able to do it."

The chase to own the Leafs shifted in October 1991 when Stavro became chairman, gaining a foothold he hadn't had. He paid off a $20-million loan Molson Breweries had made to Ballard in 1980, and in so doing purchased the right to buy Gardens shares from Ballard's estate. Molson also sold its MLG shares to Stavro. There was no doubt he was now in it not to safeguard Ballard's interests but to further his own. It was no longer about selling the team to the highest bidder via a public auction to benefit Ballard's favoured charities. Stavro never believed he was in a conflict of interest as an executor or trustee. He convinced himself that Ballard wanted him to own the Leafs, and he was determined to pay the least amount of money possible for the team, even if it meant Ballard's charities might end up getting less. Or nothing. When Giffin died on March 20, 1992, it removed the final obstacle for Stavro to take over the Leafs. Rather than maximize share value to benefit the Harold E. Ballard Foundation as he was supposed to do, Stavro offered shareholders a lowball price of $34 a share. To substantiate that figure, he misrepresented the value of the team's television revenue. He just assumed he could strong-arm other Gardens investors into selling.

By the time the Leafs-Kings series opened on May 17, 1993, however, Stavro was having more and more trouble fending off disgruntled shareholders like Devellano and Ornest. His plan to use his position as an executor of Ballard's will to get his hands on the Leafs was running into new roadblocks with every passing day. Government agencies and financial regulators were starting to take notice. Devellano and Ornest refused to bend to his will. "I didn't like Stavro, because I thought he was arrogant," says Devellano. "He thought of me as a peon, thought he could just sort of get rid of those little guys. We fought, and we fought hard."

MCNALL HAD EVEN bigger problems. Increasingly stressed by his money woes, he wanted to build a new arena as a solution. Instead of paying off his debts, he figured making more money would solve his problems. He spent the '92–93 season furiously working on a complex deal organized with Sony Corporation and his friend Peter Guber to create Sony Sports, a deal that would net him about $100 million for the Kings and ease his cash flow problems while keeping him involved in a senior executive position with a good salary. It was another way to keep the shells moving in his daily shell game.

Guber attended many of the games of the Leafs-Kings series in the spring of '93. But that massive transaction fell apart, at least partly because McNall identified another potential investor, a telecommunications company called IDB Systems, he found more appealing. "We didn't really know what was going on," says Gretzky now. "Quite frankly, it wasn't our business to know. So it stayed out of the locker room. The only thing I knew, because Bruce and I had been friends from the day I got there, was that he was trying to sell the team and that he was close to making a deal, and they were going to revitalize the Forum and re-do it, and build a new [arena], etcetera, etcetera. But we didn't know what was going on in his business world. It was just people guessing. We had no facts to base it on other than he was trying to sell the team and that was all going on during that year."

Players and coaches started noticing something wasn't right. During the '93 second-round playoff series against Vancouver, the team didn't stay downtown as usual but out in the suburbs. "The talk was that the previous hotel bill hadn't been paid," says Hrudey. McSorley says at one point the GM told the players that a member of the training staff wasn't going to be travelling with them anymore even though he was the person primarily responsible for sharpening the players' skates. Melrose remembers having to bring certified cheques to hotels on the road and paying for buses in cash. He'd played in the World Hockey Association when budgets were lean and sometimes players didn't get paid.

He knew the telltale signs when ownership had a case of the shorts. "The stick companies were complaining about not getting paid. Things like that. You could tell," he says. "The day-to-day running of the team was being hampered, there was no doubt about that. I'd been in hockey long enough to know that any time you have to pay in cash, that's not a good sign."

Other NHL owners didn't seem to know about McNall's financial problems. He says he felt like an "imposter" at NHL meetings because his debts so outweighed his actual assets, but other owners still wanted him to continue as chairman of the league's board of governors. He wooed Disney boss Michael Eisner and Blockbuster Video owner Wayne Huizenga as new expansion partners for the league and pocketed half of Anaheim's $50-million expansion fee for getting the deal organized, temporarily solving some of his money problems. But only temporarily. His core company was still in debt to the tune of at least $200 million. Both he and Stavro were doomed to lose all they had won. It would just come crashing down earlier for McNall.

AFTER FLYING BACK FROM Toronto with the team on "Air McNall," the Kings owner took his usual seat on the glass for Game 3 of the '93 Clarence Campbell Conference final alongside celebrities like actor James Woods and *Entertainment Tonight* personality Mary Hart. Movie stars and superstar athletes had been enjoying McNall's generosity for years, and he had turned Kings games into who's-who gatherings of Hollywood names. Pregame meals at the owner's tables at the Forum Club were well-attended feasts that drew celebrities like Michael J. Fox and Andre Agassi.

Down at ice level, Murphy moved in behind the visitors bench below the spoked-wheel ceiling of the Forum. Only a Plexiglas barrier separated him from the Kings bench he had either stood behind as a coach or sat upon as a star player wearing number 7. His stomach was churning with anticipation. Lineup changes had always been the antidote for coaches after losing games, so the Leafs had yanked Kent Manderville, Mike Eastwood and veteran Mike Foligno out of the lineup and inserted young winger Rob Pearson, centre Dave McLlwain and defenceman Dmitri Mironov. A new line was created with Peter Zezel at centre between captain Wendel Clark and Pearson. Hopefully, if it worked out as Murphy and the rest of the Leafs staff planned, these new configurations would give the Leafs a much-needed blast of energy for the team's first trip to the West Coast in three months. On that trip, they'd beaten Vancouver 8–0, San Jose 5–0 and the Kings 5–2, so there were good memories.

Mark Osborne, playing with McLlwain and Bill Berg, had the best early scoring chance for either team. McSorley hooked McLlwain to the ice, but as the speedy centre lost his balance and spun around, he managed to move the puck to Osborne at the top of the right circle. Osborne fired, but Hrudey made a sprawling save moving to his left. At the other end, Felix Potvin played the puck behind the net, and as he was circling back in front to his crease, he lost his balance and fell on his backside. Potvin had given up a softie for the winning goal in Game 2, and now he was in a precarious position. Darryl Sydor jumped on the loose puck at the top of the left circle and hammered a slapshot. In a sitting position, Potvin somehow blocked it, although he looked around bewildered as though asking for an explanation of how he'd done it.

Nikolai Borschevsky made a rare early appearance for the Leafs, but he was nailed with a stiff check by Sydor along the side boards inside the LA zone and immediately went off, not to be heard from again this game. Clark absorbed a big bodycheck from McSorley inside the Leafs zone but moved the puck forward to Pearson, the kind of hit to make a play the Leafs needed after taking too many unnecessary penalties, some for retaliation, in Game 2. But as the play moved into the Kings zone, Tim Watters blocked a Clark shot and trapped the puck between his legs. As the whistle blew, Pearson charged into Watters, knocking him down. Referee Andy Van Hellemond didn't like that, and early in the game the Leafs were short-handed once again.

Potvin made big saves on Tomas Sandstrom and Tony Granato as the visitors killed off the penalty. But then the Kings scored to take a 1–0 lead. With the puck against the boards in the Leafs zone, defencemen Bob Rouse and Sylvain Lefebvre both went behind the net, a cardinal sin for a Burns-coached team. Burns wanted one defenceman guarding the area in front of his team's crease at all times. Sandstrom suddenly burst out of the pile with the puck and slipped a pass through Gilmour's skates to Rob Blake, who was cruising in from the right point. He was Clark's man, but Clark wasn't watching carefully enough. Looking like a trained goal-scorer, Blake patiently waited for Potvin to go down, then backhanded the puck over the fallen Leafs goalie at 8:49 to give the Kings the lead.

Gilmour seemed to take personal offence at that goal. He took at run at Alexei Zhitnik, just missing the LA defenceman, then stole the puck from Pat Conacher and set up Glenn Anderson for a great scoring chance that Hrudey turned away. The Kings, however, seemed to be demonstrating that they were a faster team than the Leafs, which most analysts had predicted going into the series. Toronto appeared always a step behind on a Forum ice surface that was less rutted and mushy than usual, because the NBA Lakers had already been eliminated from the playoffs and the rink no longer had to be covered in plywood between Kings games.

Within a span of a few minutes, the Leafs then lost two of their regulars up front. Tired of being the nail, Zhitnik became the hammer and nailed Zezel with a high hit behind the LA net. Zezel crumpled to the ice and had to be helped off. He didn't return and was later diagnosed with a neck strain. Dave Andreychuk, trying to compensate for his lack of scoring chances by hustling on the forecheck, tried to get around Charlie Huddy as Huddy set a moving pick in the Kings zone. The Leafs forward inadvertently wrapped his stick around the veteran defenceman's head and caught him in the face. Van Hellemond gave Andreychuk a high-sticking major and game misconduct. Burns, wearing a grey suit and a yellow tie with a cartoon character motif, shook his head as Andreychuk skated to the Leafs dressing room. Murphy blew his lips outward in exasperation. The Leafs were down to ten forwards, but at least they were able to kill off LA's five-minute power play without further incident.

In the second period, Warren Rychel hit Gilmour hard, continuing the theme from the first two games of physically abusing the Leafs captain while Gretzky, looking like he had a little more jump in Game 3, escaped similar treatment. "The Kings are zeroing in on Gilmour, and why wouldn't they? It got him off his game in Game 2," said broadcaster Harry Neale.

The Leafs got consecutive power plays when first Zhitnik went off, and then Blake. Instead of scoring, however, Toronto's extra-strength unit gave up a goal. Todd Gill got caught up ice, giving McSorley and Jari Kurri a two-on-one break against Mironov. The big Russian looked uncertain and rusty as he ped-alled backwards, not surprising, since he knew he didn't have the confidence of the coaching staff. He didn't take away either the shot from McSorley or the pass. After luring Potvin towards him, McSorley slid a pass to Kurri, who buried his hundredth playoff goal into the open side to make it 2–0 for the Kings.

The Leafs looked stunned. But their veteran poise quickly asserted itself, and they began to fight back. Gilmour scored his fourth goal in three games, a power play goal off a nifty pass from Anderson to make it 2–1. Ken Baumgartner, on only his third shift of the game, managed to redirect a centring pass from Clark past Hrudey to tie the game 2–2 less than two minutes later. It was exactly the kind of contribution from sup-port players the Leafs hadn't been getting. A good sign.

Before the second period was over, Zhitnik scored a power play goal on a feathery pass from Gretzky to make it 3–2. The Russian blueliner was again demonstrating he could take a hit and keep on ticking. The Kings had outplayed the Leafs, and took that one-goal lead into the third period. The Leafs knew they hadn't responded to all the lineup changes, but despite that, still had a chance to win Game 3. Sometimes road victories weren't pretty, and there was still a chance to capture this game by winning ugly.

Robitaille, oddly ineffective after scoring sixty-three goals during the regular season, took a slashing penalty with one second left in the second, allowing the Leafs to start the third period on the power play. Melrose sent out speedy Pat Conacher to kill the penalty, along with Dave Taylor, now a thirty-seven-year-old spare part on the fourth line, a far cry from his days as a member of the fabled Triple Crown Line. Taylor had seen it all as a King. He'd had his cheques signed at different times by Cooke, Buss and McNall and had never played for another team. He had been captain of the Kings when Gretzky arrived, but after one season he voluntarily gave it to Number 99. "He was the leader and the spokesman," Taylor says of Gretzky. "In my heart, it was the right thing to do."

Taylor had been a healthy scratch by Melrose in the first game of the 1992–93 season, a sign he didn't fit into the coach's plans. But he changed Melrose's mind. Injuries over the course of the season meant he dressed for only forty-eight games. A severe concussion suffered when he was hit from behind by Edmonton's Louie DeBrusk was a major setback, and he'd scored just six goals during the regular season. Once upon a time, when he played with Marcel Dionne and Charlie Simmer, that would have been a good two weeks work. But the Triple Crown Line was history, and Taylor wasn't that player any more. Still, he gradually gained Melrose's trust as a reliable fourth-liner and penalty killer. When Melrose was uncertain which cards he wanted to play, he often sent Taylor out as his favourite default option.

That trust paid off on this night. With the Leafs hoping to tie Game 3 with a power play goal, Gill carried the puck up ice but lost it to Conacher, who skated back over his own blueline, attracting four Leafs players. Conacher backhanded the puck off the right boards past Dave Ellett to Taylor, who found himself all alone with Gill scrambling to cover from the other side of the rink.

As he had so many times on so many highlight reels in his better days with Dionne and Simmer as his linemates, Taylor steamed down the right side. With a flash of white tape on his

Sherwood 3050 "featherlight" stick, he wound up and slapped a perfect shot over Potvin's right shoulder at 1:26 of the third, the second short-handed goal of the game for the Kings. Potvin "was a butterfly goalie, and I was just trying to go high. Every once in a while, you hit the target you were aiming at," says Taylor, who would later have a picture of himself celebrating the goal framed for his home. The goal restored LA's two-point margin, deflating his old Kings teammate Murphy and the rest of the Leafs bench. It was the last important goal Taylor would score for the Los Angeles franchise. He remembers it mostly as a sign that he was still pulling his weight. "Everybody likes to score. Everybody likes to contribute."

The Kings carried that margin the rest of the way, although once again there were shenanigans in the final minutes of the game. Clark cross-checked centre Jimmy Carson. The Leafs might not go after Gretzky, but the Kings' other skill players were fair game. LA, meanwhile, continued to focus on Gilmour. Winger Gary Shuchuk elbowed the Toronto centre, knocking his helmet off. Gilmour then had a breakaway chance, but he was hooked by Huddy from behind and then slashed twice across the hands. Van Hellemond kept his whistle silent. A frustrated Gilmour low-bridged Robitaille without the puck in sight. The two veterans continued their argument into the penalty box. With a faceoff and eight seconds left, Burns sent out Baumgartner with McSorley for the Kings. Melrose, however, quickly called McSorley back to the bench and put out another player. With the game won, he wasn't about to see his top defenceman embroiled in a pointless fight with the Leafs enforcer.

When the 4–2 score was in the books, with the Leafs managing only twenty-two shots in their worst performance of the series, the two teams had in just five days played three games and flown across the continent, a punishing pace. The Kings had consolidated the home-ice advantage won in Game 2, while the Leafs, now down in the series, had some soul-searching to do. They'd only delivered at best three quality periods of hockey in three games, were getting production from less than half of their forwards and their special teams weren't functioning effectively.

The Kings were just two wins away from bringing the Stanley Cup final to California for the first time in NHL history. That would mean more gate receipts for McNall, and he needed all the infusions of cash he could get. If he couldn't make the deal with Peter Guber happen, maybe he could at least pay the stick bills. The Kings owner was in big trouble away from the ice as his financial world, what he liked to call his world of "wobbly dominos," was starting to collapse. But he was also a long-time Kings fan, and hockey was his oasis away from the madness. For a few hours, he could just cheer on the team and players he loved.

EVEN IN THE DISTINGUISHED company of a wide variety of luminaries at the Mount Pleasant Cemetery in Toronto, Steve Stavro stands out. Before he died in 2006, he oversaw the construction of a mammoth monument to himself. His tomb stands twenty feet high, an ostentatious piece of over-the-top art befitting a man who saw himself as a titan of industry. It reveals a man of incredible ego with an oversized view of himself as part of Canadian history. Atop the monument, which is surrounded by three large, snarling lions, is a statue of Alexander the Great on a rearing horse, with both hoofs in the air, symbolic of a hero who had died in battle. Alexander the Great didn't, however, die in battle. Neither did Stavro. Below the ancient king are Hellenic scenes and symbols and logos from Stavro's life in business, including the emblem of the Toronto Maple Leafs. Stavro may have exhibited fairly conservative taste in life, but not in death. The tomb is a shrine to a man built to glorify himself.

The nature of Stavro's legacy depends on who is reviewing the history. His supporters portray him as a philanthropist and a sportsman. He was awarded the prestigious Order of Canada in 1992. Others argue his legacy is besmirched by the highly questionable manner in which he acquired the Leafs and took the organization private, the conflict of interest he had as an executor of Ballard's will and buyer of the famous hockey team and the way in which he deliberately hid from other public shareholders information regarding the true value of Maple Leaf Gardens Ltd.

After several years of litigation involving the Ontario Office of the Public Guardian and Trustee, Stavro was forced to pay $49.50 per share for the team, 46 percent more than the $34 he originally offered. It cost him millions of dollars, and was a public humiliation. Anyone who had followed the entire process understood what he had tried to get away with. His determined fight to own the Leafs left casualties. "When I sold, I got 1.6 million dollars on an investment of about three hundred thousand," says Devellano now. "That's the good news. The bad news is, if they had just let me stay in, those shares would be worth twenty million dollars today. Twenty million dollars! So you can see why I don't like Steve Stavro. As I sit here, I'd have twenty million dollars."

Forced to come up with millions more to buy the team, Stavro told management to sell off players and refused to allow Fletcher to sign Gretzky as a free agent in 1996. Three years after he was strutting like a peacock around the Leafs as they battled the Kings in the postseason, now he was selling off hockey assets because of his own financial challenges. An investigation by the Ontario Securities Commission into his purchase of the Leafs ended with the company agreeing to pay a $1.6-million fine on behalf of Stavro. Ultimately, Stavro lost control of the hockey club in 2003 and was also forced to shutter his grocery chain and sell off properties like his luxurious mansion in West Palm Beach. If he'd hoped to own the Leafs until his last breath, like Ballard, that hope was dashed. One Gardens insider compared the hockey franchise to the famous Hope Diamond, a glittering object of desire that was rumoured to be cursed.

Bruce McNall, by contrast, has lived with his mistakes since he was released from jail in 2001. He was sentenced to prison in 1997, when he was forty-six years old, on five counts of conspiracy and fraud and started his sentence at the minimum security federal prison at Lompoc, California. He was later shifted to Safford, Arizona, Oklahoma City and finally Milan, Michigan. He spent six months in solitary confinement, a punishment he says he incurred because guards were getting him to sign sports memorabilia and he refused to divulge their identities when prison authorities investigated. "I can tell you this much. When I walked into prison the first day, I thought, This is heaven! This is great! Wonderful!" He insists it was a relief after years of lies and juggling his financial commitments. The end came when he defaulted on a $90-million bank loan in December 1994. He was forced to sell the Argonauts and the Kings, as well as his various homes and luxury cars. Many of his friends and players, including Gretzky, stood by him and still vouch for him. They choose to remember his generosity and good nature, not his crimes. "Despite living in mansions, with jets and helicopters and teams and all that stuff, what came with that was enormous responsibility," says McNall. "I was responsible for not just myself and my immediate family. I was responsible to the teams, to all the employees I had, and, when you own a franchise, to the people in those cities. Which meant LA and Toronto. So all of a sudden I went from that to having no responsibilities. Zero! I couldn't fix anything, I couldn't help anybody. I couldn't do anything. So I thought, This is easy. This is cool."

McNall says his years in prison and the loss of his wealth, status and family changed him. "I feel much more peace of mind. I never want to get myself back in a situation where I have that many responsibilities, that hassle, that lifestyle. I've had it. If I hadn't, would I want it? Sure. But look, I've lived every dream of every guy in the world. I was in the movie business. There were movie stars I was dating, any girl I might want, two sports franchises that were hugely successful. My whole life was about acquiring stuff, whether it was teams or houses or whatever. Ever since [prison], the idea of ownership is not important to me. Because we all rent anyway. So don't obsess yourself with owning stuff."

ACT FOUR

I t's a cold but sunny day in early April, a few degrees chillier down by Lake Ontario, where Bill and Wendy Berg live on land that's been in Wendy's family for three hundred years. They built their house at the turn of the twenty-first century, and filled it with wooden furniture in simple farmhouse style. Today is a perfect day to set off on their bicycle made for two, custom fitted with disc brakes after an unfortunate braking incident some time ago. They laughingly call themselves "country bumpkins" and enjoy taking trips to Disney World in Florida, just the two of them. It's a simple, fun life, far from the madding crowd.

On most days, they can see across the lake to the city that once made Bill Berg one of hockey's household names. Twenty-five years ago, Berg was part of the most famous checking line in the world. He went from nobody to somebody just by being placed on waivers by the New York Islanders and getting picked up by the Toronto Maple Leafs at a time when Toronto was awakening from a long, deep sleep and again becoming the most important hockey city on the planet. For Berg, it was going from obscurity to fame in a heartbeat just because one NHL team didn't want him and the Leafs did.

But now, reviewing his roots in the game and the joy it once brought him is a little more complicated than peering across a frigid lake. The sport that gave him a career and a degree of fame has turned on him. It's ripped his family apart. He was a traditional grinder when he played. He was an everyman, the player non-NHLers could look at and imagine they could be, if only a coach had liked them, or they hadn't busted a shoulder at the wrong time. Berg was also a little more open-minded than most, a little more willing to question hockey orthodoxy. When he played, he accepted that orthodoxy to be a good team player, but that didn't mean he believed in it. On the ice, he was a valuable role-player. Off the ice, he was upbeat with a ready laugh, an NHL player without pretence who could laugh at himself, an athlete capable of introspection. Interviews would often stray into different topics. Life. Finance. Other sports. He remains that same person today. Still curious about things other than sticks and pucks. But now, to some, to the mob that sees any challenge to hockey's group-think as betrayal, he's an outlaw, the guy who wants to help wreck the game.

His son, Sam, is challenging the very foundations of hockey in Canada. Once a hockey player with dreams of following in his father's footsteps, Sam is the lead plaintiff in a controversial, high-profile class action suit against the Canadian Hockey League demanding minimum wage for major junior players in Canada. He was an aspiring prospect with the Niagara IceDogs of the Ontario Hockey League but now wants to change the system he feels did him wrong. Bill Berg, who played in that junior system, is fully behind his son's efforts, even though he knows former teammates and coaches shake their heads at Sam's attempt, as they see it, to bring down a system that has brought hockey fame—and wealth—to so many. A quarter century after it was found that Alan Eagleson had lied to hundreds of hockey players over more than two decades as head of the National Hockey League Players' Association, many players still believe you stay quiet, do what you're told and just assume the powers that be and the hockey world are working in your best interests. Don't step out of line. Don't question tradition. Just accept that's the way it is, because that's the way it's always been done. It's best to keep the questions to a minimum.

That's apparently how Bill's dad feels. For three years, Bill Berg Sr. hasn't spoken to his son, his daughter-in-law Wendy or his grandchildren. Like many family troubles, it's complicated, but it stems from a nasty family argument over the lawsuit and the Berg patriarch's contention that if his grandson is successful, the result will destroy junior hockey in Canada. He worked a blue-collar job at General Motors in St. Catharines, Ontario, for years in order to support his family, and thinks his son and grandson should back off and quit challenging the traditional hockey industry. He found what his grandson is doing to be an embarrassment for him in the community.

Bill Berg Jr., who played junior with the Toronto Marlboros and 546 NHL games for four different teams, remains popular enough with Leafs fans that he still gets fan mail, some of it sent to his parents' house. They'll open it, drive down to Bill's house and put it inside the front door and leave. The family rift has become that distant, that unfriendly. All because of hockey. Bill's father and mother might attend his daughter's hockey game at Brock University, but they will leave before speaking to her or their son. "It's their choice. They chose that they didn't want us around or in their lives," says Berg. "We didn't have to make that choice. They made that choice."

The business of hockey, of the game Bill Berg loved, has created this unhappy division in his family. The game he loves, the game for which he was once willing to do almost anything to be a part of at the highest level, no longer seems to love him back.

LOSING GAME 3 OF the 1993 Clarence Campbell Conference final didn't materially change the situation for the Maple Leafs. They'd already frittered away home-ice advantage, and they knew that to win the series they'd have to win at least one game in California. Toronto head coach Pat Burns knew his team well despite the fact that it was his first season with the Leafs. He'd picked up the pieces left after the team's years of losing, discarded a few of them and hammered the rest into a tight, cohesive team in remarkably short time. They played the game the way he wanted it or they didn't play. There was no confusion as to who made the calls about what this team did or didn't do.

In this case, instead of practising on the day off between Games 3 and 4, he told his players to relax and stay away from the rink. Walk down to the famed Santa Monica pier. Grab a bite with a teammate. Losing a playoff game while giving up two short-handed goals might have prompted many coaches to put their team through a hard, detail-oriented practice, but not Burns. Not on this day. He sensed fatigue. He sensed that seventeen games in thirty-four days had drained his team of the energy they needed to take on a deep, motivated squad like the

Los Angeles Kings. He also had the confidence to do what he believed was right for his team rather than what the outside world might expect.

But one day off was all they had. After Canadian rocker Burton Cummings played the electric organ and sang "O Canada" and "The Star-Spangled Banner," the Leafs got right to work the next day. For Game 4, they had a slightly depleted roster. Dave Andreychuk was back after being ejected from Game 3, but Peter Zezel was unable to play. He'd suffered a concussion in the first round against Detroit, and now a high hit against the end boards in Game 3 from Alexei Zhitnik had sent him back to the infirmary. That's what playoffs do. It's usually not just one spectacular crash but a series of bruises and sprains that wear the athletes down.

Kent Manderville, one of the pieces picked up in the blockbuster Doug Gilmour trade, got the call to replace Zezel on the team's usual checking line between Berg and Mark Osborne. Zezel was an excellent faceoff man and reliable defensively, and he usually killed penalties with Berg. As a unit, the Leafs checking line had been one of the key elements Burns had sewn together during the season to make Toronto a much more difficult team to play against. The trio had a reputation as a group Burns could use during difficult situations or play against the best enemy scorers. They didn't expect power play time, their value wasn't determined by their statistics and they could play their game as well on the road as they did at home. They might even chip in the odd goal, as Berg had done in the third period of Game 1.

Zezel was the general of the group, with Berg and Osborne usually free to roam, forecheck and lay out big bodychecks. So

Zezel's absence left a significant hole in the Toronto lineup. Manderville was twenty-two but still a rookie, and he'd played most of the year in the minors. That meant Berg and Osborne would have to adjust their games to make sure they were covering for the tall youngster out of Cornell University. For defensive zone faceoffs, meanwhile, Burns simply substituted Gilmour for Manderville.

Defenceman Dmitri Mironov sat again, as Burns decided to go with five defencemen and reinserted Mike Foligno and Mike Eastwood. He just didn't have faith in the big Russian. And Manderville, Foligno and Eastwood were all big bodies as well. The Leafs were a more imposing team for Game 4, and Burns hoped they'd have some fresh legs too.

Dave Taylor had scored the key insurance goal in LA's Game 3 triumph, and a turnover by Leafs defenceman Jamie Macoun early in the first period of Game 4 gave him a golden opportunity to score again. But Felix Potvin confidently turned it away. After that, the Leafs took over the period. With just over two minutes gone, Gilmour corralled the puck behind the LA net, a place where he was always dangerous. With Marty McSorley waiting for him in front, Gilmour relied on his superb stickhandling skills and ability to play with his head up to evaluate his options. Andreychuk came cruising in from the side with Kings winger Tomas Sandstrom water-skiing on his back, his stick locked into Andreychuk's body. Andreychuk slogged towards the net anyway and right into McSorley, effectively blocking him like an offensive lineman on a running play. Gilmour seized his chance. He jumped out the other side of the net and tried to jam the puck under Kings goalie Kelly Hrudey. Hrudey made the stop, but the puck bounced into the slot. Wayne Gretzky was in perfect position to clear, but he hadn't noticed that Leafs defenceman Bob Rouse had quietly sneaked past him from his right point position. No one was expecting Rouse to pinch like that. If he was pinching, it meant the leash was off all Leafs defencemen and Burns was looking for more aggressive play. Rouse grabbed the puck and back-handed it through Hrudey's legs, and the Leafs had their first lead since the opening period of Game 2.

LA coach Barry Melrose, with the last change always given to the home team, had decided to play Gretzky head-to-head against Gilmour. Despite the Rouse goal, he stuck with that matchup. Less than four minutes later, with Gretzky out again, Burns managed to change the matchup, calling Gilmour's line to the bench on the fly and quickly getting out the line of Eastwood between Wendel Clark and Rob Pearson. Clark took a big hit from Gary Shuchuk just inside the Leafs zone to move the puck ahead to Eastwood. The Leafs captain had made a similar play early in Game 3, but it hadn't resulted in a goal or a scoring chance. Still, it was the kind of selfless play coaches wanted to see from their leaders.

Eastwood was moving through the neutral zone with speed. Kings defenceman Rob Blake was caught flat-footed. He twice tried to hook Eastwood, but the big centre kept on motoring to create a two-on-one break with Pearson. At the last moment, Eastwood tried to pass the puck to his team-mate, but the puck hit the back of Zhitnik's left skate blade. Hrudey reacted to the pass attempt by stretching to his left with his left pad. That opened up his five-hole, and the puck bounced through his legs and in. The Forum crowd went silent. The announcement of the goal echoed around the arena. The Leafs had a 2–0 lead in a game they had to win to keep their Stanley Cup hopes alive.

THIS WAS BURNS AT HIS BEST. First, the decision to give his players the day off had given them jump for an important game. And he'd shuffled his lineup again, just as all season he'd moved different pieces around, getting contributions from different players. Finally, his ability to play the matchup game and make a quick in-game reaction had paid off handsomely. His best quality as a coach, the quality that ultimately landed him in the Hockey Hall of Fame, was his ability to quickly read the readiness of his players early in a game and make adjustments based on which ones had it that night and which ones didn't.

The Leafs hadn't had a confident, experienced coach like Burns in a long time. The ex-policeman had taken Montreal to the 1989 Stanley Cup final, losing to Cliff Fletcher's Calgary Flames, and won the Jack Adams Award as coach of the year. His reputation and marquee value were even greater than his actual accomplishments in four years of coaching in the NHL. But after the Habs were swept by Boston in the first round of the '92 playoffs, ending Burns's fourth season in Montreal on an extremely sour note, he suddenly became available. Well, first he told media people in Montreal he would never quit. Then he went to Jamaica for a week and came back convinced he couldn't stay on. He pointed his finger at the media, specifically the French-speaking media, as a problem. "I don't consider myself a quitter," he said. "When you're criticized openly, like I've been for the past two weeks, it's tough to take. When the wagons circle and the arrows start, it's tough." Habs GM

Serge Savard said he would stand by Burns if he wanted to stay but wouldn't block his way if he wanted to go because the job had become unbearable. "When he tells me he can't function anymore in Montreal, should we deal with that problem now or in October?" said Savard. "I told him he could talk to anybody he wanted."

The Habs could have demanded compensation, like the Philadelphia Flyers had done when Fred Shero bolted for the Big Apple in 1978. The Rangers coughed up a first-round draft pick to get Shero. Nine years later, New York traded a first round pick to Quebec for the right to hire Michel Bergeron as coach. The Nordiques used that draft pick to select Joe Sakic. Generally speaking, coaches—at least those not named Pat Quinn—didn't walk out on contracts and just go sign with another club unless they'd been fired first. But the Habs wanted to move on from Burns. His agent, Don Meehan, negotiated a settlement for Burns with Montreal, then quickly brokered a new opportunity for him in Toronto.

On May 28, 1992, Burns announced his shocking "resignation" in Montreal, and just hours later he was at a news conference in Toronto being introduced by Fletcher as the new head coach of the Leafs, the proud owner of a freshly signed four-year, $1.7-million contract. Just like that. One moment Burns was the widely criticized coach in Montreal, the next he was a saviour in Toronto, with just enough time in between for lunch and a nap. It was a bit mysterious and certainly unprecedented. Most saw it as a step down. "It's clear that the Leafs wanted a high-profile coach, which is what Burns always had been," wrote legendary *Montreal Gazette* columnist Red Fisher. "He has an uncanny talent for attracting attention, and there's a rich field for it in Toronto. Getting attention is what Burns is very good at." Canadiens forward Brian Skrudland wondered if changing NHL times had caught up with Burns. "When Pat first came [to Montreal] he was the type of coach who played the players he thought would win, it didn't matter if they were making $40 or $1 million," Skrudland told reporters. "But times have changed for every coach in the sense of salary." Montreal newspaper columnist Michael Farber said Burns simply saw the writing on the wall and wanted to move on before he got fired. "Eventually he would end up a chalk outline on the Atwater sidewalk, splattered like the stiffs he used to see in his previous career as a policeman," wrote Farber in the *Gazette*. "There was too much history in Montreal for Burns to continue here. Too many sour players, too many enemies in the media, too many skeletons in the closet and ultimately not enough goals and certainly not enough playoff victories." There were also those rumours of interest from the Kings. "I wasn't interested in going to practice with sandals on," Burns quipped. Gretzky was close with Burns from their days together in Hull, Quebec, when Gretzky owned the major junior team and Burns was his coach. He doesn't know if LA seriously pursued Burns. "I have no idea. Nobody ever said to me, 'Hey, we're going to meet with Pat Burns.' I never heard that," he says.

Fletcher says the Leafs became aware Burns was going to become available long before he quit as Montreal coach. Meehan was a Maple Leafs season ticket holder and close with Fletcher, whose son, Chuck, worked for Meehan's company, Newport Sports. Fletcher didn't pursue any other coach. He says now he was never led to believe the Kings were interested in Burns.

The previous spring, head coach Tom Watt had almost got the Leafs into the playoffs after the blockbuster deal with Calgary, but he'd been reassigned to another job in the organization almost four weeks earlier. Terry Crisp coached the Flames to the Stanley Cup in '89 and might have interested Fletcher, but Tampa Bay had hired him to be that franchise's first coach the month before. "For a while, it felt like all roads were kind of leading to me," says Mike Murphy, an assistant coach under Watt, who had NHL head coaching experience. "I thought I might have a chance of getting the job."

Fletcher's search for a coach lasted less than a month before Burns fell into his lap like manna from heaven. Like Gilmour from Calgary. In less than six months, the Silver Fox had landed a star centre, the first since Darryl Sittler, and a star head coach, the first since Red Kelly in the 1970s. Like Gilmour, Burns brought lots of baggage with him, not to mention a satchel full of superstitions. But in Toronto, a city that hadn't seen a truly competitive hockey team since before the NHL-WHA merger in 1979, all that baggage seemed to evaporate. Nobody seemed bothered by the question of why Burns had left Montreal, or the peculiar circumstances of his departure, or wondered if he would be a good fit in Toronto. The Leafs couldn't win many on the ice, and getting Burns seemed like a victory, just like trading for Gilmour had made the Leafs seem triumphant over Calgary, one of the NHL's strongest franchises. Any sign of progress or indication the Leafs were no longer a laughingstock was greeted positively. That was perfect for Burns. The same gripes and insecurities that had caused him to leave Montreal would eventually resurface in Toronto, but for now he was, like Fletcher, a top hockey man who wanted to work in Toronto. That was enough.

Burns certainly knew how to play the media game, which gave him an advantage over many of his predecessors in Toronto. He could be blustery, he could be grumpy, he could be philosophical. He could be a bully or he could be playful. He could be an invaluable off-the-record source. He might blast his players in a media scrum then defend them the next day. He was superstitious to a fault, down to the ties he wore or the pen he might use before a win. He could complain to a reporter on the side about a player, then bawl out the same reporter the next day for putting the nugget in the paper even when that was exactly what he'd wanted. He could promote his image as a would-be biker and country music guitar player, and the media would lap it up. To say Burns was perfect for Toronto would be to exaggerate the point. He was an outsider, after all. But he was perfect for Toronto in the fall of 1992, when the Leafs needed someone with the confidence to lead. For the first time in more than a decade, here was a coach who could set a course and handle the attention, a coach with a game plan, a coach who could run a dressing room and convince (or force) players to accept certain roles and less playing time, a coach with the ability to make tactical decisions and judge how well a player was going to perform that night on his first shift. Burns had worked with Mike Keenan on Team Canada's staff at the 1991 Canada Cup. He was viewed across the sport as one of the game's elite coaches, and given what he was inheriting with the Leafs, he would need to be.

When Burns arrived, the Leafs hadn't made the playoffs since 1990 and hadn't had a winning record in the regular season since 1979. They had only pieces of a quality team. Both Murphy and Mike Kitchen had served as assistant coaches under Watt the season before, and despite not knowing either of them, Burns decided to keep both. Kitchen had played three seasons at the Gardens as a junior with the Marlies, a team that captured the Memorial Cup, and had an NHL career that lasted 474 games. Four years after retiring, Kitchen proposed to Leafs GM Gord Stellick that he could help coach the organization's minor league team in Newmarket, Ontario, but instead Stellick offered him a position as an assistant coach of the Leafs. He lasted through George Armstrong, Doug Carpenter and Watt, and Burns was officially the fourth Leafs coach he'd worked for.

So Burns had his assistants, and there was Gilmour, who had already demonstrated in forty games under Watt that he could be a number-one centre. Clark was an admired captain, but he had played only 187 games over the previous five seasons because of injuries. Glenn Anderson and goalie Grant Fuhr had been added in a trade with Edmonton the previous season, but they weren't the stars they'd once been. Anderson was happy to join the exodus of players leaving Edmonton for better financial opportunities elsewhere, but he remembers walking into the Gardens dressing room to find a completely different culture than what he had left behind with the Oilers. "The players were beaten down. They had no belief," he says. "It was a shock. I went from the best dressing room in hockey to the worst dressing room. I know things are awry when I can't sleep, and I couldn't sleep at night." Anderson scored twenty-four goals for Watt's team but saw big change coming when Burns took over.

The blueline looked to be the most solid part of the team. Macoun had come over from the Flames with Gilmour, and the Leafs also had Dave Ellett, Bob Rouse and Todd Gill as incumbents on the back end. "Everyone respected [Burns] right away," says Rouse. "You could see the parts they were putting in place. He made everyone accountable." Osborne and Zezel were veteran forwards with an ability to check. Mike Krushelnyski and Foligno had been good offensive players, but they were on the downside of their careers. Pearson was a strapping forward who had been Eric Lindros's winger with the Memorial Cup–winning Oshawa Generals team, and he'd scored fourteen goals in his first NHL season the year before. Eastwood was a hulking centre out of Western Michigan University who didn't play particularly big but could skate. He'd only played nine NHL games. Manderville could skate and had size, but no one was sure of his position or role. Of the team's three top prospects—Potvin, defenceman Drake Berehowsky and centre Brandon Convery—none looked ready to be NHL regulars.

Two Russians, Mironov and winger Nikolai Borschevsky, had been drafted over the previous two years and were known for having been part of the gold-medal-winning "Unified Team"—from the remnants of the old Soviet Union—at the Winter Olympics in Albertville, France six months earlier. Their value as NHL players was unclear. Only a few of the Russians who had come to the NHL over the previous five seasons after hockey authorities in the USSR began allowing players to leave had made an impact. Fletcher had lured one of the first players to come, forward Sergei Priakin, when he was running the Flames, and Priakin had been a total bust.

Another player in that ten-player blockbuster trade with Calgary nine months earlier, defenceman Ric Nattress, had bolted as a free agent to Philadelphia in late August just before training camp. Toronto acquired twenty-four-year-old Sylvain

Lefebvre from Montreal to take his place. He'd played for Burns, but that didn't make him immune to Burns's tough love. "Pat would walk down the bench, say five words [to Lefebvre] in French, and Lefebvre's game changed just like that," says Kitchen, snapping his fingers. Lefebvre gave Burns one player who already understood his coaching methods and objectives.

Fuhr and Mironov both reported to camp heavy and out of shape, hardly the champing-at-the-bit attitude Burns was looking for. Fuhr, the highest paid player on the team at $1.6 million per season, was the biggest disappointment. "He's not in good shape at all. I'm disappointed a bit," said Burns, whose only other option in the crease appeared to be another veteran acquired in the Flames trade, Rick Wamsley. "We expect [Fuhr] to play a lot of games this season and we need him to be in good shape." Fuhr admitted he hadn't been on skates since the Leafs were eliminated from the playoffs the previous spring. "It's more habit than anything," he told reporters. "The bottom line is that I've got to be ready for the first game October 7 and this has worked every other year."

Fuhr, aged thirty, had been a central piece of Edmonton's championship teams, and his dazzling reflexes still made him one of the NHL's best goaltenders when he was healthy. He just wasn't healthy very much of the time. He had a happy, upbeat personality, helpful for a team in a high-pressure market like Toronto, and he seemed to be the Leafs' only real option in net. Wamsley had never been a full-time starter, while Potvin was only twenty-one. Potvin had won top goalie and rookie-of-the-year honours in the American Hockey League the previous season as the St. John's Maple Leafs—the "Baby Leafs"— coached by Marc Crawford, charged all the way to the Calder

Cup final. But he had shared the job with Damian Rhodes most of the season and only had forty-nine professional games under his belt: thirty-four AHL regular season games, eleven playoff games in the minors and four NHL games with the Leafs. Not much to bet on. Fuhr, by contrast, had played 423 NHL regular season games going into the '92–93 season and 112 in the playoffs. He had five Stanley Cup rings and had backstopped Team Canada over the Soviets in the spectacular three-game 1987 Canada Cup final. He was no longer the durable goalie who five years earlier had played seventy-five games for the Oilers, but it still seemed likely he would be Burns's clear choice for his starting goalie that season.

All in all, it was clear that while the Leafs had some good veteran players, they weren't close to being a set team when Burns took over. It was a team with many question marks. The Leafs were winless in three to start the season, but then went on a 5–1–1 run to create a flutter of excitement.

Fuhr's health, however, became an immediate problem. He hurt his knee October 18 in a 5–1 loss to Minnesota and required arthroscopic surgery. With Wamsley also injured, Burns was forced to turn to Potvin. Potvin, nicknamed "The Cat," was making just $145,000 a season. He had appeared in four games the previous season, three in November and one in April, losing two and tying one. "There was not a chance in the world I thought I'd be making the team that year," Potvin says. "I thought I would be going back to St. John's. Unfortunately for Rick, he got hurt, and I came up. Then Grant got hurt. The door just kind of opened for me." Potvin picked up his first NHL victory on October 20 against Ottawa. He made eleven starts before Fuhr returned, winning seven of them. He surrendered seven goals in a loss to Detroit, but otherwise the youngster was rock solid, giving up three or fewer goals in nine of those starts. He had a cool, unflappable demeanour and the same butterfly style that Patrick Roy had used while starring for Burns with the Canadiens.

Potvin grew up in Montreal, but he wasn't coached to play the butterfly. He just started dropping to his knees naturally while stopping shots from his father in the family's driveway. He didn't have specific coaching for playing goal until he reached junior with the Chicoutimi Saguenéens of the Quebec Major Junior Hockey League and long-time trainer Rénald Nepton started giving him tips. At the time, older goalies in the "Q" like Jimmy Waite and Stephane Fiset were starting to use the butterfly, undoubtedly influenced by Roy. Potvin was drafted by the Leafs in 1990, the third goalie taken in the draft behind Trevor Kidd of the Brandon Wheat Kings and Martin Brodeur of the Saint-Hyacinthe Laser. At that time, goalies like Hrudey, Fuhr, Ed Belfour, Mike Richter, Tom Barrasso, Mike Vernon and Bill Ranford were prominent, all playing either the traditional stand-up style or some form of hybrid.

Roy was the outlier, and the Quebec junior goalies were following in his path. "The biggest difference with me was the depth I was playing at. I always played very deep in my net," says Potvin. "That's how I felt comfortable. I could rely on my reflexes." He was six feet tall, big for a goalie at that time. He'd learned passable English while in the minors in Newfoundland, but the Leafs assigned Lefebvre to be his roommate on the road to give him a francophone veteran to talk to. Burns started to get used to the idea Potvin might be able to fill the void if Fuhr couldn't play.

Clark was, as usual, the centre of attention, both for Burns and for NHL rumour mongers. He was the most popular player on the team, displaying a rugged, no-nonsense approach to the sport that had first appealed to Toronto hockey fans at a time when Harold Ballard's destructive ways of running the franchise had left many feeling hopeless. The Leafs had made Clark the first overall pick in 1985 out of the Saskatoon juniors. Michigan State forward Craig Simpson had made it well known he did not want to be drafted by the Leafs, but Clark was happy to come east, endearing him to Leafs fans before he even set foot in Ontario. He had a low-key attitude and avoided inflammatory quotes to the media, but he had a big presence around the hockey club. Even before he officially became captain, succeeding Rob Ramage in 1991, he was the unquestioned leader.

For a franchise run by a blustery owner for years, Clark was a different force, a player who said little but played the game with substance and heart. At times, it almost seemed as if he had been born too late, that his style of play and his unquestioning attitude and loyalty would have been more suited to earlier, simpler times in hockey history. By October 1992, his number 17 still accounted for 50 percent of the team's jersey sales. He was the best-known and most popular athlete in town, even counting stars like Joe Carter and Roberto Alomar from the world champion Blue Jays. He became the natural successor to Johnny Bower, the most beloved Leafs player from the glorious '60s.

Still, by the fall of '92, Clark had never played on a Leafs team with a winning record, and he was damaged goods. Team doctors had told him several years earlier that he should consider quitting hockey because of a serious back problem, and he spent long hours rehabilitating injuries, particularly the troublesome back. The team had become so wary of Clark's availability that all his contracts were based on the number of games he played. He got so much if he played forty-five games, so much for sixty, and so on. For the '92–93 season, his salary would rise from $600,000 to $825,000 if he managed to play sixty-five games. "Every single contract I had, if I didn't get the numbers, I didn't get the cash. Every single one," he says. That hardly inspired confidence for either side of a tricky player-team relationship, no matter how much Clark was admired by the Toronto hockey public for his toughness and loyalty. It was as though he played with a giant question mark attached to his uniform. The team was generally mediocre or worse as the eccentric Ballard failed to spend to develop a quality hockey organization, and the conversation often seemed to revolve around whether things would improve once the injured Clark returned from one of his absences. "I never asked for a trade," Clark says. "I was always just dealing with health issues. Maybe I would have thought differently if I hadn't had health issues. But most of the time, I was just worried about playing the next day."

Clark wasn't a disciplined player, particularly defensively. He'd never had elite coaching as a pro. His helter-skelter style seemed like a poor fit for a team coached by Burns. In those days, with three papers in Toronto responsible for much of the league's trade speculation, other teams were happy to offer tidbits to Toronto sportswriters that might motivate the Leafs to make moves. It had been that way for years. Or perhaps media folks keen on generating interesting rumours put two and two together on their own. Either way, the Clark trade rumours multiplied. Fletcher had already demonstrated a willingness to move out young players who the Leafs had previously acquired high in the NHL entry draft, having dealt Luke Richardson, Vince Damphousse and Scott Thornton to the Oilers to get Fuhr and Anderson, and then Gary Leeman, Jeff Reese and prospect Alexander Godynyuk to Calgary in the Gilmour trade.

It was logical that Clark could be next, and the likeliest destination again appeared to be Edmonton. Winger Joe Murphy was rumoured to be the key piece coming the other way. One scenario had the Leafs offering Clark and Pearson for Murphy and veteran winger Esa Tikkanen, but then there was talk the Oilers wanted Brandon Convery, the Leafs first-round draft choice the previous June. No deal ever happened, and Fletcher insists the rumours were fictional. "The first time Wendel's name ever came up was in a deal for Mats Sundin [in 1994]," Fletcher says now. "He was such an integral part of the team, the heart and soul of the franchise. [Edmonton GM Glen Sather] and I had a history going back to my days in Calgary. We'd made the Fuhr trade. But we weren't exactly close friends."

Clark's fragile relationship with Burns was no rumour. Either Burns didn't like what he was seeing, or he saw the Leafs captain as a useful scapegoat. Right from the start of the '92–93 season, Burns declined to give Clark ice time with Gilmour and instead used him more in a third-line role. He also publicly criticized his captain. When the Leafs dropped their home opener to Washington 6–5, Clark failed to cover Kevin Hatcher on the winning goal. "That's a mental mistake," said Burns. "That's what I call bad-habit hockey. Those are things players maybe have gotten away with all their life, but they won't get away with anymore." When Clark scored his first goal of the season, Burns told reporters, "Anything out of him now would be good." Clark slumped, managing only one goal in sixteen games at one point while getting little power play time. Then he went down with another injury. When Clark went to the Caribbean over the all-star break while still injured, Burns complained that his captain should have been back in Toronto rehabilitating his injuries. The head coach quietly fumed over his captain's various health woes. "Burnsie hated to walk in and see guys lying in the trainer's room with acupuncture needles coming out of them and stuff," says Murphy. "He thought it was bad for the team to see that."

Clark says anti-Burns sentiment often united the team as it searched for an identity. "I was the guy he could pick on," says Clark now. "Everybody rallied around it. No matter who Burns picked on, it was, 'Fuck you, Burnsie.' It was about us. Everybody felt for the other guy who was getting it. That was his coaching style. Those kind of coaches know what they have to do for them to win. They know they're done in three years. Of course, it pissed me off. But as I often explain to people, your players are twenty. Your coach is fifty or whatever. You never see eye to eye. In real life, how many twenty-year-olds hang out with fifty-year-olds? They don't."

Murphy had to talk to players, tell them to shut up, take the verbal abuse and work on their games. "There was a gravitational force among that group against Burnsie, definitely," says Murphy. Gilmour would just "get the look" when he wasn't playing well, but he would support teammates who were getting the full Burns treatment. "Burnsie wanted us to be mad at him. He knew how to pull the strings, who to piss off," said Gilmour. Clark believes Burns knew he could be critical of his captain, knowing Clark would respond with farm-bred sto-icism. "He knew what he was doing. He knew I wouldn't say anything, that I'd just take it," says Clark. "Then, when the next guy was getting heat, he'd think, Clarkie didn't say anything, so I guess I'm not going to say anything. Did he make me a better player? I'd say yes. He's there to win. He might push buttons wrong, but he's there to push buttons. It was the first time I'd played for a coach where the team got coached. Properly. We had more talent in 1986 than we did in 1992. The thing with a coach is he has to get everybody on the same page. Burns did that for our two-year window."

The Leafs sputtered in November, and Fletcher looked elsewhere to try to find players to help Burns and improve the team's depth. After first acquiring centre John Cullen in a deal, Fletcher picked up the twenty-five-year-old Bill Berg on waivers from the Islanders. Cullen was the more high-profile acquisition with the bigger salary, but Berg, despite being picked up for nothing except the waiver fee, would prove to be by far the more influential player. After the blockbuster deals he had made to bring in Gilmour and Fuhr, even Fletcher couldn't have known the significance of the acquisition he had made.

Burns sure wasn't impressed. He grumbled to reporters he wouldn't know Berg "if I drove my truck over him." Berg had been given a termination contract by the Islanders and was thrilled to go to the same city in which he played junior hockey, about an hour from his hometown. He and his wife jumped in their truck and headed north the same day after being picked up by the Leafs, listening as they drove to a radio broadcast of the Leafs losing a game to Chicago, Toronto's fifth defeat in six starts. As they drove along the Gardiner Expressway into downtown

Toronto the next day, Wendy read aloud the newspaper quote from Burns about her husband. Berg shrugged. He was used to not being treated as a very important player. "This was my sixth year pro. You got kicked in the nuts all the time," Berg says.

He showed up to the Gardens and was greeted by an old friend, trainer Brian Papineau. "I knew him as 'Pistol.' His dad had only one arm, but he used to pitch fastball in St. Catharines. I used to run around Lancaster Park, because my dad played fastball too. So I meet with Pistol. The guys start coming in, and I knew some of them who I'd skated with in the summer. So we start with a stretch, and right away somebody chirps, 'Look out, Bergy, don't be in the parking lot in fifteen minutes.' Burnsie comes into the dressing room, looks at me and says, 'Hey, come.' So I go into his office. He said he'd never seen me play. Nothing positive was said. I came to learn the sky is black after a loss with Burnsie." To try and break the ice, Berg tried a little chit-chat. "I said, 'Al Arbour said he knew you.' And he said, 'I don't know Al.' He says, 'Cliff says I shouldn't have said what I said, and I should apologize. . . . So, go get ready for practice.' He never did apologize! But that was Burnsie."

Burns quickly recognized the value of his newest team member, however, and Berg became a reliable "glue" player for the Leafs, a team that surely needed glue. Soon, Burns placed Berg on a line with Zezel and Osborne, and the fit was perfect. On teams in less prominent NHL markets, checkers would barely get noticed. In Toronto, they could be heroes. In a remarkably short time, this new checking line became beloved. "I remember Mike Foligno telling me, 'Don't be surprised if people congratulate you on finally making it to the NHL,'" Berg says. "And it happened!"

He was given number 10, the number once worn by Armstrong, which tells you how the Leafs treated their former stars in those days. Berg had a breezy personality, but on the ice he could be a royal pain in the butt. He loved to trash talk and chirp at opposing players, particularly the tough guys and enforcers. In general, he was a pest, something the Leafs didn't have, and fearless. Zezel was an experienced centre, and Osborne was a big man who could hit and had a heavy shot. For Burns, who liked to match lines, the checking line was a crucial element to add to his team. "I was a good skater, and I could anticipate the play. I could move the puck, although I couldn't score to save my life," says Berg. "Oz was a good skater, and he could score. He'd scored when he was with the Red Wings. Zez was so strong, and he could move the puck. My thing was just to get in there with speed and create havoc."

After six years of never knowing whether he'd be in the NHL the next day, Berg suddenly found himself a regular. "I was shocked how I was used. For the first time in my career, I knew I was going over the boards every shift. I'd never had that. It was incredible." Berg had enjoyed playing for Al Arbour, a four-time Stanley Cup champion. But he saw Burns as just as good a coach. "Burns was so, so good at teaching. He was the best teacher of the game I'd ever come across," he says. "The way Burns taught and the repetition, every day. You knew what you were supposed to do. You knew your role and exactly how we were going to forecheck. He said to me, 'We play different.' He said, 'It's going to take you a couple of weeks, but then it's going to be just like second nature, like you should have been playing that way all of the time.' And he was right. He would say these simple things. Burns would be teaching us how he

Whether you like fighting or hate it, there is no way around the fact that the epic third-period scrap between Wendel Clark and Marty McSorley, the two guys Wayne Gretzky called the "heart and soul" of their respective teams, set the tone for the rest of the series. The Leafs took Game One at home, but the whole hockey world knew that a titanic struggle lay ahead for both teams. (Hans Deryk/CP Photo)

Doug Gilmour served notice in the 1993 playoffs that he was a genuine NHL superstar who could change a game with a single shift. But he didn't do it with the mercurial grace of his opposite number in the series, Wayne Gretzky. He was crafty with the puck, but wasn't afraid to mix it up, or go hard to the net. People called him "Killer" for a reason. Above, that's Alexei Zhitnik, himself a willing combatant in a very physical series, on the business end of a Gilmour hit. (Above: Shaun Best/CP Photo; below: Phill Snel/CP Photo)

The Leafs-Kings series of 1993 was played by guys who would stop at nothing to win. The teams' two owners were willing to cross the line from time to time as well. The maverick, charismatic Bruce McNall changed the face of the league, but ended up in prison for fraud. Steve Stavro worked his way up from a small grocery business to the helm of the storied Maple Leafs, only to see it slip through his fingers. (Above: Reed Saxon/AP Photo; below: *The Globe and Mail*/CP Photo)

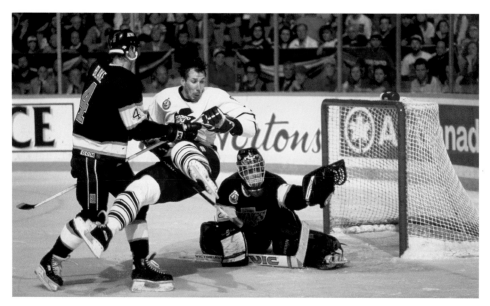

There were times during the series when it seemed that the refs had completely put away their whistles. Rob Blake's work in front of the net was a huge factor in neutralizing usually reliable goal-scorers like Dave Andreychuk (above). But when there was mayhem, Bill Berg (below), who was picked up on waivers that year, was often in the middle of it. (Above: Doug MacLellan/HHOF Images; below: Hans Deryk/AP Photo

The Leafs and the Kings were different in many ways, perhaps none more obvious than their goalies' styles. Felix Potvin, though known as "The Cat" for his reflexes, was in many ways a modern "butterfly" goalie, while Kelly Hrudey was an old-school stand-up goalie who relied on sheer acrobatic athleticism to keep the puck out, as he does here on a one-timer from Peter Zezel. Over the course of the series, though, their numbers were almost identical. (Above: Doug MacLellan/ HHOF Images; below: Doug MacLellan/ HHOF Images)

Kerry Fraser became the most famous, and infamous, referee in NHL history as a result of the most important call he didn't make in Game Six. Twenty-five years later, fans are still wondering exactly what Fraser saw in the opening minutes of overtime, as Doug Gilmour and Wayne Gretzky jousted for a loose puck. There is no doubt what happened moments later: the same stick that had cut the Leafs captain's chin put the puck behind Felix Potvin. (Above: Matthew Manor/HHOF Images; below: Mark J. Terrill/AP Photo)

The final two games of the series turned into a goal-scoring competition between two very different captains. They scored two hat tricks between them, with Clark outscoring Gretzky by a single goal. The difference was that two of Gretzky's were game-winners. Gretzky later called Clark "unstoppable," but in the end it was the Great One who carried the day. (Above: Hans Deryk/ CP Photo; below: Mark J. Terrill/AP Photo)

With each emotional game, the two teams had more and more at stake. The Kings felt a little as though they had already won the Stanley Cup when they emerged victorious from the cauldron of that series. For the Leafs, the loss was bitter, as Mike Foligno's face shows in the dressing room after the game. (Above: Phill Snel/CP Photo; below: Ryan Remiorz/CP Photo)

wanted us to forecheck, and he would say, 'See that forward? He's busier than a one-legged man in an ass-kicking contest.' He'd always have these sayings. And they would stick in your mind! And we would practise them over and over and over. Repetition, repetition, repetition." Berg, like Clark, had to get used to Burns and his acerbic approach. "I didn't like it at the start. And I didn't get it. Al would come in and rip the team, but he very rarely went at individual guys," he says. "Burnsie would go at you in front of everybody else. He didn't have a problem with that. To me, it was shocking. He'd go after any-body. He'd go after Glenn Anderson, who had how many Cups? He'd go after Pearson. He'd go after Manderville." Only Potvin, among the young players, seemed to escape Burns's wrath. When Burns did speak to Potvin, it was in French. "I think he liked to practise his French once in a while. But I didn't have a lot of long conversations with him," says Potvin. "He let goalies do their stuff. I could feel the confidence he had in me without him having to tell me."

Not surprisingly, there was a great deal of grumbling in the dressing room. "There were lots of guys that didn't like Burnsie," says Berg. "But I honestly believe he understood his role, and that was he's gonna call you out if you're not playing good. He was the taskmaster. He understood he had to be that way to get the best out of the guys. And that was the closest team I ever played on. I'd never gotten along with guys that way. It was just great. Oh, we'd go at it in practice. There'd be fights in practice, but that was because Burns would whip the practices up to a fever pitch, and we all loved to compete. But not in the dressing room."

By the winter, Berg was a key member of Burns's Leafs. "Berg was one of the leaders of that team," says Murphy. "He brought the bottom half of the team together. Said the right things, did the right things, practised the right way. People didn't realize what he did for our team."

With the checking line in place, the Leafs became a more difficult team to play against, a team with an edge. The line became as big a part of the team's identity as Gilmour or Clark. Berg loved to get under the skin of opposing players by chirping at them, while Osborne, a born-again Christian, could be more emotional. "So we're playing in Edmonton. The benches are close. We're leaning over the bench and just yakking, just giving it to Dave Manson on their team. 'You're terrible! You're fucking garbage!' Stuff like that," Berg says. "So Oz starts chirping, 'Hey, Manson, you wouldn't even make our team!' And Scott Mellanby from the Oilers bench leans over and says, 'Hey, Oz, that's not very Christian-like.' Oz says, 'You're right,' and sits back down. We're like, 'That's all it takes to shut you down, Oz? Really?'"

That Christianity theme could work both ways. "We were playing St. Louis, and [Osborne] was getting into it with [Garth] Butcher. Butch was dirty. I mean, really dirty," Berg says. "So we've got a faceoff in our own zone. It's to the right of Cat. Butch is giving it to Osborne at the faceoff, saying stuff like, 'You fucking born-again this and that.' Just laying into Oz the whole time. Zez wins the draw, and they ring the puck around the boards to my side. As the puck's coming around, I know Butchie's coming. So I make it look as though I'm watching the puck coming, and at the last moment I just turn and drive my shoulder through him. Just kayoed him. His own stick came up and got him in the face and he was down. Oz skates by, leans over and says, 'See what happens when you mess with the Lord?' and skates away. Zez and I were just killing ourselves laughing."

Around Boxing Day, the Leafs started to roll. They won ten and tied two of their next fifteen games, including an emotional 5–4 triumph in Montreal on Burns's return to the famed Forum. "After Christmas, the group came together," Clark says. "Everybody was playing the way [Burns] wanted them to play. Hardest thing for any coach to do. Everyone playing their role and happy about it. I was the same sort of player but more controlled. When you play on losing teams, it's way harder. A winning team is the easiest team to play on. Just do your piece. On a losing team, every player does that, and a bit more. And a bit more puts you out of position." It was clear this was a very different club. "We were changing the culture of a sports franchise," says Anderson. "That's what made it unique."

Still, Fletcher wanted to improve the roster more. Specifically, he searched for another winger to play with Gilmour. Borschevsky had been a pleasant surprise playing on the right side, but it had been harder to find a left winger. Conveniently, the Buffalo Sabres were looking for a goaltender. The Sabres had lost in the first round of the playoffs for five straight years, three times to Boston and twice to Montreal. Left winger Dave Andreychuk, six foot four with great hands that compensated for his awkward skating style, had scored thirty or more goals for the Sabres seven times. But he had also been criticized as a prolific scorer during the regular season who couldn't find the net in the playoffs. In those five first-round losses, he had contributed only seven goals. Some called him "Andrey-choke" for his spring disappearances. "They were getting frustrated with Andreychuk," recalls Fletcher. So, in another whopper of a trade, the Leafs peddled Fuhr and a fifth-round pick to Buffalo for Andreychuk, backup goalie Daren

Puppa and a first-round pick. "There was a fair bit of risk for us, because that meant we were anointing Potvin as our number-one goalie," says Fletcher. "We didn't know how he'd stand up to the pressures. But Andreychuk sure helped us."

Gilmour had enjoyed success in St. Louis and Calgary with wingers like Mark Hunter, Greg Paslawski and Joe Mullen, and he clicked immediately with Andreychuk, who he had played against in junior hockey. "As soon as we got together, I said, 'Dave, just go to the net,'" recalls Gilmour. "He said, 'That's where I'll be.'" The Leafs now had a strong first line with the addition of Andreychuk, a sturdy checking unit that had added Berg, a rock solid blueline corps and a standout young goalie in Potvin. "No disrespect to Grant, but I was excited when he was traded," says Potvin. "Then you realize you're the goalie for the rest of the year, and you have a chance to stay in the NHL. So that day, I was thrilled." Still, just to be sure, the young goalie continued to rent an apartment behind the Gardens on a month-to-month basis before moving in with Sylvain Lefebvre and his wife when the playoffs began.

The team was close and unified, and an incident in San Francisco in late February demonstrated that. On February 23, two days before a game at the Cow Palace against the San Jose Sharks, the Leafs held their annual rookie dinner. The idea was to go out, have a big meal with lots of expensive drinks, and make the first-year players pay for it. Many teams did something like it. "Our rookie meals with the Islanders were sort of tame," Berg says. "Well, this was a blowout. Guys were throwing food around the room, the drinks are flowing. I'm a lightweight; I cut it out after a while and went back to the hotel." Gilmour went to a pub with a few teammates. Ellett took

Mironov and Borschevsky to a karaoke bar. Sometime after midnight, as the players returned to the Westin St. Francis hotel, spare defenceman Darryl Shannon somehow lost his jacket and money when he was jostled outside the hotel. The details are murky. Shannon was apparently told that a person down an alley had his possessions, and when Todd Gill found him there, he was barely conscious and bleeding after being mugged. He was taken to hospital by ambulance. Clark learned what had happened and set out on the streets around the hotel to retrieve his teammate's wallet to get his identification back, giving out $100 bills to various homeless people.

It must have been a bizarre scene. The captain of the Leafs prowling the alleys of San Francisco like a detective looking for informants. Against the odds, he returned with Shannon's empty wallet. "See, if I put the problems out, then Cliff and Burns don't have to put the problems out," says Clark. "And if Cliff and Burns don't have to put problems out, then we don't have problems. If you can solve things in the dressing room before the GM and coach have to, then the team doesn't get in big shit." Clark had a straightforward philosophy he applied to being captain. "My buddies are the dressing room. It didn't matter what team I played on. That was my circle of friends," he says. "Everybody was looked after. Nobody was ever left out."

The team assembled for practice the next day, and Shannon had to answer questions from the media about his battered face. "Shanns looks like he's been dragged across a parking lot," recalls Berg. "Burnsie comes in, and all he says is, 'Guys, you win and it all goes away.' We went out and kicked the shit out of San Jose, and it all went away." The rest of the regular season, the Leafs were arguably the best team in the NHL. They had come together. They may not all have loved Burns, but they loved winning hockey games.

AFTER STRUGGLING IN Game 3 of the '93 conference final, the Leafs, having earned the early 2–0 lead, were again a strong, unified team in Game 4. The Kings, meanwhile, just didn't look like the confident squad they had been in Game 3. It was that kind of series, back and forth, and would continue to be.

Gretzky tried to get his group going, retrieving a loose puck around the Leafs net during an LA power play and backhanding it high over Potvin at 12:22 of the first period to make it 2–1. It was Gretzky's first goal of the series and the 104th playoff goal of his NHL career. But soon after, Number 99 couldn't clear the puck high in the LA zone, and Gilmour moved it deeper into the zone to Foligno. The former Buffalo captain backhanded a short pass to Krushelnyski and headed to the net with Kurri trying to prevent Foligno from getting there. Kurri couldn't, and Foligno tapped Krushelnyski's return pass home at 14:52 to put the Leafs ahead 3–1. Foligno followed the goal with his characteristic two-footed leap, an enthusiastic post-goal celebration that never failed to get a chuckle from his teammates. The thirty-two-year-old veteran had supplied energy and a goal, vital ingredients Burns had been looking for when he decided to dress Foligno after he had watched the team's listless performance in Game 3 from the press box.

Always a team that played with more confidence when it had the lead, the Leafs settled into a familiar hard-checking pattern in the second period. Burns could match lines more effectively, and he put Berg, Osborne and Manderville out against the LA line of Corey Millen, Mike Donnelly and Tony Granato, a unit that had been causing the Leafs all kinds of problems with its speed. The Leafs checking line could cycle the puck, and they forced the Millen line to play defence rather than attack. Early in the second, Berg picked up a puck behind the LA net, and when no Kings player came after him, he stepped out in front and fired a low shot that Hrudey had to stop. By the third, Melrose was trying to get the Millen line away from Berg and company.

Once more, it was apparent how the NHL game at that time was designed to allow checkers to stop offensive players simply by lassoing them with their sticks. Body position was not as important for defensive players. Using the stick to reel in an attacking player or making him take one hand off the stick was a great equalizer, even for offensive players like Gilmour and Gretzky. It was an ugly style of hockey in many ways, but to be successful a team needed players willing and able to play that way.

While the NHL had been a high-scoring league that season, this style of play could produce a slower game, and it gave a big advantage to teams able to establish a lead. The Leafs, coached by Burns, were that kind of team. Led by players like Berg, Osborne, Foligno and Krushelnyski, they started to grind on the Kings, taking away time and space, retreating and looking for counterpunch opportunities. The Leafs didn't need any more goals; they just wanted the game to turn into a total bore, without the kind of high-scoring play preferred by the Kings, who had averaged almost five goals a game in the first two rounds of the playoffs.

The Leafs got another goal anyway to jump ahead 4–1. It came just after the Kings had a great chance to cut the lead. Pat Conacher's wraparound attempt bounced into the slot, and it appeared McSorley was going to get a point-blank chance. At the last moment, Rouse poked it away, and Lefebvre swatted it out of the zone to send Eastwood on a clean breakaway. Hrudey stopped his shot, and the puck landed just beside the net. Sandstrom had a chance to clear, but he flubbed it, and Pearson jumped on the loose puck and banged it into the open net with Hrudey well out of position.

After that, the game got chippier and bogged down further, just the way the Leafs wanted it. Gretzky set up Blake for a goal with 9:01 left in the third, but that was it for offence from the home team. With four minutes left, the Leafs got one of those classic shifts from their checking line in which the three forwards actually possessed the puck for only a few seconds but killed an entire minute of action. Berg took a run at Zhitnik at the left point, and the puck bounced down the ice. The dedicated Leafs checker doggedly pursued the play and tried to line up Blake in the corner. He missed, but Blake angrily hooked at him. Manderville broke up a Kings rush inside the Toronto blueline, then Berg took a run at McSorley in the neutral zone. Trying to come back against that Leafs team once it had a comfortable lead was like trying to wade through a swamp while being swarmed by mosquitos.

In the final minute, the Kings pulled Hrudey for an extra attacker. Kurri had a chance, but he couldn't settle a bouncing pass from Gretzky. Berg, on his wrong wing deep in the Toronto zone, backhanded the puck to safety. When LA tried to make one more rush, it was the reliable Berg again who cleared the zone. When the final buzzer sounded, the disgruntled Kings fans no doubt felt that they'd just witnessed a boring game and their team had been lifeless. It wasn't pretty, nothing you could celebrate in glorious prose, but Burns loved it, as his troops had totally frustrated the Kings with a nearly perfect road game.

The Leafs had received goals from Rouse, Eastwood, Foligno and Pearson, and the line of Clark, Eastwood and Pearson had given them a second offensive threat. Manderville had filled in capably for Zezel. The Leafs were again a team that was about more than just its star players, more than just the sum of its parts. Home-ice advantage had been recovered by Burns and his squad, with two of the next three games scheduled for Maple Leaf Gardens. Toronto's improbable Stanley Cup dream was alive again.

THE LINE OF ZEZEL, Berg and Osborne became famous that season. They seemed like an unbreakable unit to Leafs fans, like they'd walk together forever. But forever lasted only until May 2009, when the forty-four-year-old Zezel died after years of battling a serious blood disorder, haemolytic anaemia. His health problems left him bloated, no longer the handsome, charming athlete who had once landed a bit part alongside Rob Lowe and Patrick Swayze in the 1986 hockey film *Youngblood*. Zezel's death came as a shock. "He stopped by here one day when he was sick. He was on his way to Niagara Falls, but I didn't believe he was that sick," says Berg. "That was Zez. He let you in, but just a little bit. Always had a kind word. But you never really knew what he was thinking."

Berg and Osborne see each other occasionally. "But once we get together, it's immediately like old times," says Berg. Both have tried a little bit of everything in their post-NHL lives. Osborne did some radio, working on postgame Leafs broadcasts, and became a pro scout in the Los Angeles Kings organization. Berg got his securities licence, owned a bottled water company, worked in media, including radio and television, did some part-time scouting for the Minnesota Wild for six months and coached hockey at a private high school for three years. These days, he and Wendy own two low-rise apartment buildings near Beamsville, Ontario. They have twenty-one tenants and more than a few hair-raising stories about drug addicts and fraudsters. The tenants probably don't realize the guy clearing the snow on a nasty January day used to be on their television set every Saturday night on *Hockey Night in Canada*. "I dabbled around all the hockey stuff," he says. "It's not that easy to stay in the game. Now I enjoy dealing with tenants, doing the fixes, doing the bookwork. It's something different all the time, and I don't have a boss."

Then there are the complications of Sam's controversial lawsuit. It's a worry, and it drags on, but Berg has no doubt he's doing the right thing supporting his son. Sam's story is both simple and complicated. He was drafted in the fourteenth round of the OHL draft in 2012 by the Niagara IceDogs and was also taken in the United States Hockey League draft by Muskegon. Sam went down to Muskegon, Michigan, made the team and was committed to going there until he got a call from IceDogs boss Marty Williamson saying they wanted him. On behalf of his son, Berg demanded four years of guaranteed payment for tuition and books at a Canadian university from the

IceDogs as a condition of leaving Muskegon. He wanted an iron-clad commitment. "My thinking was that it would be like in the NHL when they have to choose between a one-way contract and a two-way contract," says Berg. "They're more committed to the one-way, so it always wins out." The two sides agreed to terms. "I made sure I read the contract carefully. I had just lost twenty-five thousand dollars in a bad real estate deal."

Sam started the season with the IceDogs but soon wasn't playing much. After only one month, the team wanted to send him to St. Catharines Junior B or to another USHL franchise. Ultimately, he reported to the Junior B team then was traded to another club, where he injured his shoulder. After Christmas, he quit. But the OHL said it never officially approved his deal with the IceDogs, and the team refused to honour it. Instead of suing the team, Sam decided to become the lead plaintiff for the class action suit that alleges the Canadian Hockey League "conspired" to force young players into signing contracts that break minimum wage laws. The suit seeks $180 million in outstanding wages, vacation, holiday, overtime pay and employer payroll contributions. "Our position is our players are amateur student-athletes," said CHL president David Branch. "It's important that we defend this, because it could have a huge impact on all amateur sport in this country."

The court battle could go on for years. Berg sees the $50 or $60 a week a junior player receives along with other benefits as just one example of a larger issue. He mentions the US women's hockey team fighting USA Hockey before the 2017 world championships for a living wage and the ongoing debate in the NCAA over the question of paying student-athletes while coaches get multi-million-dollar contracts and lucrative shoe deals. Decades after the death of "amateurism" as an Olympic ideal, some sports organizations and leagues are still trying to keep the concept alive rather than compensate their athletes. "They're all swimming in the same pond," Berg says of so-called amateur athletes.

Berg isn't involved in hockey at all anymore, other than to cheer on his daughter, Annie, when she skates for her university team. Sam no longer plays. Berg admits that his post-hockey career hasn't always been easy after years spent "scratching and clawing every day as a pro, wondering every day which jersey I was going to be putting on." As a civilian, like a lot of former NHL players, he has searched for the keys to a new existence. "Some days, Wendy would think I wasn't happy with her," he says. "I would tell her, 'I just can't get going today.' When I played, there was such meaning to train all summer, to go to camp, to win my spot on the team. After so many years locked into that, to be so intense, so focused, once you got into the wilderness, you wonder where's the meaning." His career ended at age thirty-one. Somewhere along the way, the dream died. "I felt like maybe I could have possibly played a little longer. But I realized my lot in life, at best, was to be a third-line player. Well, I didn't grow up thinking I'd only ever be that."

If he doesn't fit in the hockey business now, he certainly did back in '93. He figured out the hockey life well enough to get drafted into the NHL as a defenceman, switch to forward as a third-year pro and then find a role in the world's best league on its most high-profile team as an irritating, difficult player to skate against. For a time, while he was a Leaf, doing that job made him famous. That's hockey. In Toronto, you could become extremely well-known for doing the same things that wouldn't get noticed on teams that weren't in the same media spotlight. In general, stars always get the most attention, but in hockey, there's always an appreciation for the muckers, the players who do the grunt work. They're often seen as "honest" players, athletes who play the game the right way, and do it with passion and intensity every night.

That was Berg. When he was in hockey, banging bodies, trash-talking his opponent and checking like a fiend, he was in all the way. He personified the hardness of that Leafs team. "I was ready to do anything to get ahead," he recalls. "I wanted it so bad."

ACT FIVE

on't cry. For just once, dammit, don't cry. Kelly Hrudey is intent on getting his message across. He's preparing to speak to an audience of academics at Mount Royal University in Calgary, Alberta, and accept a honorary degree in psychology. Mostly, however, he doesn't want to cry. The president of the university is watching. *C'mon, keep it together.* Hrudey's not intimidated by the situation, per se, although he's never had the opportunity to seek a degree or a diploma at a post-secondary educational institution. Major junior hockey in Canada, particularly when he played, was either openly against players pursuing educational goals or only reluctantly accepting of it. But being in a university setting isn't particularly scary, not to a guy who faced one-hundred-mile-an-hour slapshots in the NHL, or was the winning goalie in a Stanley Cup playoff game that went into four overtime periods. Now that takes nerve. Hrudey is just worried about his well-known penchant for choking up over almost anything. "I've always been one who likes honesty, and I'm not ashamed to say that I'm an emotional guy," he says. "I can cry at the drop of a hat."

This moment is about a lot more than that. Hrudey, at the age of fifty-six, is being honoured by the university for his work in mental health advocacy. It's become part of his life story, the story he shares with his wife, Donna, their youngest daughter, Kaitlin, and the rest of their family. The story of hours spent in the living room trying to help Kaitlin breathe, relax and find "the garden," a mental safe place for Kaitlin to help her deal with anxiety and obsessive-compulsive disorder. Hrudey remembers how naive he felt when he learned of his daughter's challenges. She was just eleven years old. "I didn't know trouble was lurking, that this was already in Kaitlin's brain, this thing that was trying to ruin her," he says. "I didn't know that this already existed. Donna and I admit we both missed all the signs. I'm not ashamed of that. I didn't know I should have been looking. I'm lucky I don't have any guilt with that. Once we made the connection, we were fast to act."

Kaitlin is now twenty-five, working for a video and film production company in Calgary, living her daily battle. She, along with her father, went public in 2013 about her challenges. The two of them speak at countless events together, eager to get the message out about her struggle and how to help others see the warning signs and find help. For Hrudey, it's been almost two decades since he faced a shot in an NHL game. He's gone on to become one of Canada's best-known hockey broadcasters, a fixture on CBC's *Hockey Night in Canada*, and he has been able to use that pulpit to increase public awareness and understanding of mental illness. He personifies a shift in sports culture over the past decade. It's now legitimate and acceptable for athletes to admit to mental health challenges and be active in advocacy, where once it was something to be hidden, to be ashamed of or deny. "As proud as I am of my NHL career or my broadcasting career, the most proud I am is of the work we've done with the mental health initiatives," Hrudey says. On this day at Mount Royal University, he manages to hold it together. Later, he says, "I buckled down. I'm very proud of the fact I didn't cry."

But Hrudey remembers a time, a quarter century ago, when he couldn't stop his tears as he faced his inner demons. A time when he would come home from his job as an NHL starting goalie in a state of frustration and fear that his career might be over. There he was, in the prime of his career, the number-one goalie on the Los Angeles Kings, a flamboyant team that featured Wayne Gretzky and was like a travelling circus, and he could no longer stop the puck.

To most who watched him work his way through the New York Islanders system and then join the Kings, this was strange. A mystery, really. He had always exuded confidence, even cockiness. Hrudey played as if he knew everyone was watching him, with style and creativity. Unlike today's goalies, he was an ordinary sized athlete, about five foot ten, certainly not a physically imposing figure between the pipes. Handsome, though, with a gleaming set of perfect teeth. He wasn't an educated man, but he spoke well, and when it came to hockey he spoke honestly and from the gut. But when it all went wrong, all that confidence and swagger and style vanished. He would come home from the rink, put his head on Donna's lap, and cry. "I thought I was the weakest guy on the planet," he says. "I went from being a pretty good NHL goalie to, without exaggeration, being the worst goalie in the league. The game had me on my knees."

ON MAY 27, FOR THE SECOND time in the '93 Clarence
Campbell Conference final, the two clubs headed across the
continent on the day off between Games 4 and 5, this time back
to Toronto. It made for a long Monday. The miles were starting
to add up, but the Kings believed that, with the help of their
luxurious private plane, they would handle the travel better.

After two games at the Forum, a multi-purpose arena where
many kinds of events occurred only one of which was NHL
hockey, the series was returning to Maple Leaf Gardens, a living,
breathing hockey shrine that only occasionally played host to
other events. It was hockey first at the Gardens. The Leafs draped
blue-and-white bunting around the rink for Game 5, adding to
the festival-like atmosphere, the sense that something important
and memorable was happening. Stanley Cups had once been
lifted by the home team in this arena, the last one twenty-five
years earlier. Elvis had played the Gardens. So had the Beatles,
three times. In 1965, a floor ticket for the Fab Four had cost just
$5.50. Muhammad Ali had fought Canadian boxer George
Chuvalo here. It was a place where history had been made many
times, and most frequently by the hockey team that played here.

Glenn Anderson was born in Vancouver and had spent his
career in Edmonton, only coming to play in Toronto once or
twice a year. Once he became a Leaf, he began to develop his
own relationship with the famous arena, a more intimate relationship. "It had such character. That's why I liked it," he says.
"I would walk around the building, run the steps, stop and look
at the pictures on the walls on a regular basis. Gradually, you
found out the secrets of the building that the average person
doesn't know about. There were hallways underneath, secret
doors, tunnels. It had its own personality."

Game 5 started sluggishly, as if both teams were clearing the cobwebs from their hockey brains before settling in for another taut battle. Peter Zezel returned for the Leafs after the neck injury he suffered early in Game 3, but now Mark Osborne, another member of the Leafs checking line, wasn't available. His wife, Madolyn, was delivering a baby. Kings rookie coach Barry Melrose had grown weary of Jimmy Carson's ineffectiveness and figured his team could use a little edge, so he inserted big winger Jim Thomson for the first time in the series. Thomson meant more muscle for the LA lineup and was as different from Carson as a hockey player could get. Thomson had been a King previously then was lost to Ottawa in the '92 expansion draft. LA got him back for the playoffs in exchange for a good goal-scorer, Bob Kudelski.

Little separated the two teams at this point. In the first four games, neither club had dominated consistently. Gilmour had outplayed Gretzky in the battle of the stars, while the other big scorers—Dave Andreychuk and Nikolai Borschevsky for the Leafs, Jari Kurri and Luc Robitaille for the Kings—hadn't been dangerous at all. Wendel Clark and Marty McSorley had pretty well kept a respectful distance from each other since Game 1. There certainly hadn't been any indication either was interested in another dance. Neither Felix Potvin of the Leafs nor the more experienced Hrudey had stood out, and the first four games hadn't really turned on goaltending. Each team had won once on the road.

The back-and-forth nature of the series mirrored LA's season more than it did Toronto's, which had been a steady, gradual improvement from training camp on. For the Kings, it had been a wild, lurching ride, a soap opera of a season filled with drama and uncertainty. At various points, it seemed the Kings' season might go right off the rails and LA would miss the playoffs for the first time in the Gretzky era. Melrose, a coach with no previous NHL experience, had done a commendable job holding the team together. He'd been hired the previous summer after LA owner Bruce McNall had decided his team needed to replace GM Rogie Vachon, an iconic figure for the franchise from his playing days, and head coach Tom Webster. Losing in six games to the Oilers the previous spring in the first round had been a frustrating defeat, and McNall was tired of coming up short. In four playoff campaigns with Gretzky, the Kings had been unable to get past the second round. So McNall hired Melrose, who had been coaching Detroit's farm club after winning a Memorial Cup in junior hockey with Medicine Hat, and gave the GM's job to Nick Beverley, who had played briefly for the Kings in the 1970s and had been in the organization for twelve years in a variety of roles.

Melrose became the more significant, better known figure. He was a big Saskatchewan farm boy with a big personality and had played against Gretzky in both the NHL and the World Hockey Association. He was actually on hand as a member of the Cincinnati Stingers on January 28, 1979, at Northlands Coliseum in Edmonton when Gretzky signed a twenty-one-year "personal services" contract with the Oilers at centre ice. The Leafs had looked to hire Melrose as head coach in 1989 out of junior hockey, but owner Harold Ballard refused to let GM Gord Stellick replace George Armstrong as head coach. The Kings, by the summer of '92, were looking for ways to at least get out of their division in the postseason, and Melrose seemed to be as good a bet as anybody. "Barry Melrose was a hot coaching prospect, and when I met him, I saw this was a guy who could work with Wayne," says McNall. "And he was an LA kind of guy, where the other guys weren't. Nick Beverley wasn't an LA kind of guy. But he was behind the scenes, so it didn't matter as much."

The hiring of Beverley was evidence of a couple of problematic issues in the LA organization. First, he didn't have the power of other GMs around the league. It was well known that McNall liked to have a significant say in personnel matters and liked to consult with Gretzky, so he wasn't interested in giving any hockey executive full rein over his team. "I felt I knew it enough. I'd never played, of course, but I knew the game pretty well," says McNall. "And I knew this market. I knew what would work and what wouldn't work. Hockey operations, yeah, I was intimately involved. For the bigger transactions, I would make the call."

The Kings lineup had been turned over significantly since McNall had purchased control from Jerry Buss in early 1988. The acquisition of Gretzky that summer had kick-started the overhaul. Gradually, the team acquired players Gretzky was keen on—Hrudey, Tony Granato—or players he had played with in Edmonton, such as Paul Coffey, Kurri and Charlie Huddy. "There was certainly a perception that Wayne ran the show," says McNall. "I'd gotten a lot of players from Edmonton. They were great players, and Wayne knew them and how to work with them. That was important. If Wayne wanted something, I was going to try and listen to him. He was the greatest player in the world, and I was going to listen to him."

That Gretzky was the power behind the throne in LA was accepted NHL wisdom. Until then, few NHL players, even the greatest ones, had influence over a team's personnel moves, but Gretzky did. But then, of course, there had never been a player quite like Gretzky. He'd been in pro hockey for sixteen years. He'd played in the WHA as a teenager and joined the Oilers in the NHL merger in 1979. He had gone on to play for the first three Stanley Cups of the Oilers dynasty. So it wasn't as if he didn't know what he was talking about.

A number of players on those Oilers teams, notably Mark Messier, moved on to other clubs and became just as influential as Gretzky was with the Kings. But the belief that Gretzky was orchestrating moves in LA was something that could be twisted around and held against him.

He was hockey's golden boy, nearly a perfect hockey player and ambassador for the game in many ways, and some people needed to find something about him that wasn't so perfect. Some said he bellyached at officials too much, that he was a crybaby. Others sneered that he was trying to run the Kings. If you believed hockey players should just shut up and play, well, you could hold Gretzky's influence against him. The fact was, however, that all the players that he might have had a say in bringing to Los Angeles were good players.

Gretzky says he had been encouraged to give his opinion in Edmonton under GM Glen Sather. "They always asked my opinion. But I never had final say. In Edmonton, Glen used to have Mark [Messier] and Kevin [Lowe] and me in all the time to ask what we thought," he says. "Ultimately, I was a player. I knew that. For whatever reason, there was always this belief in LA that I was not only playing hockey, I was doing all these things off the ice. Which was so untrue. When they asked my opinion, I gave my opinion. And sometimes they didn't like my opinion. And sometimes they did. But I grew up in a house where you respected authority. And I knew my place. I was a player."

Perception was everything, however, and throughout the organization the perception was that Gretzky had influence. His teammates felt it. "The thing that I was soon to learn about playing on a team with Wayne Gretzky was that people are jealous," says Hrudey. "I saw a lot of really good hockey players become preoccupied with how Wayne was treated, and/or really good players who couldn't play there, because they let that jealousy become greater than it should have been." McSorley, who had come to the Kings with Gretzky, says there was tension in the organization between the Oilers faction and people who were Kings loyalists and had been in the organization for years. People like Vachon (who stayed on as president), Beverley, scout Bob Owen and others. McSorley called the long-time Kings employees part of the "purple-and-gold" tradition that existed before Gretzky arrived and the team went to black-and-silver team colours. "I loved playing for Bruce. The only part I found confusing was that he didn't seem to understand the purple-and-gold problem," says McSorley.

At the press conference to announce the hiring of Melrose and Beverley, journalists asked pointed questions about lines of authority and how much influence Gretzky would have. "It was very complicated, because we were very close friends, and our families were close, and we had business relationships of all sorts," recalls McNall. "Owning the Honus Wagner [baseball] card together, owning horses together, we owned the Argonauts together, all these things we had. So we had a very complicated, interrelated world together. At the same time, in theory, he was a guy who worked for me. I'm not sure who worked for who to tell you the truth! In theory, that was the case. I had to make sure our relationship wasn't so warped or so weird that people couldn't handle it."

None of these things mattered after the first day of the Kings training camp at Lake Arrowhead in the San Bernardino Mountains. A bigger story had taken over: Gretzky was seriously hurt. He'd had pain the previous spring in the playoffs against the Oilers from what seemed to be a rib injury of some kind, which also caused numbness in his hand. On a trip to Hawaii after the season with his wife, Janet, and various teammates, he couldn't even sit to eat dinner. He'd lie on the floor. The pain seemed to subside over July and August, but after skating on the first day of camp it all came back. The thirty-one-year-old Gretzky was in so much pain he couldn't bend over to tie his skates. He immediately went to hospital, and the initial diagnosis was dire. McNall called a few veterans together for a quick meeting and told them it was possible Gretzky's career might be over. "I remember thinking not so much, What's our team going to do? more, What's the game going to do without Wayne?" says Tony Granato. Dr. Robert Watkins diagnosed the problem as a herniated thoracic disc.

Doctors couldn't find many athletes who had suffered the same injury, but one female skier they located who had undergone surgery to correct the problem had subsequently had to quit her sport. Watkins told Gretzky that he would like to try rehabilitation first. "They put me on some sort of anabolic steroid that starting eating away at the issue," Gretzky says. "I went two months without doing anything. It was a hard time emotionally. You don't know where your career is going to be. I put on twenty to twenty-five pounds, partly because of the steroid. I couldn't train, but I had the same appetite." Friends were shocked when they saw the weight gain, adding to speculation he might not be able to come back. For McNall, it was a nightmare scenario. He was juggling his bank loans and trying to put together a deal to sell the Kings. Gate receipts for an LA game, worth $100,000 before Gretzky arrived, were now more than $1 million, and even that wasn't enough to make ends meet. If Gretzky's career was over, McNall's teetering financial empire would suffer a crippling blow. "My money problems were worse without Wayne," he says.

In training camp, the club tried to find some new answers. Melrose persuaded the club to sign speedy Pat Conacher and hardnosed winger Warren Rychel, who had both come to camp without contracts. "I saw we had skill, but not enough will," recalls Melrose. Defenceman Rob Blake was beginning his fourth year, and Melrose decided to go with even more youth on the blueline in twenty-year-old rookie Darryl Sydor and nineteen-year-old freshman Alexei Zhitnik. Both were mobile and had offensive instincts. A popular Hollywood movie that year was *My Cousin Vinny*, starring Joe Pesci as a New York lawyer who goes to a backwater Alabama town to defend a relative accused of murder. Vinny, who speaks with a strong Brooklyn accent, pronounces "two youths" as "two *yoots*." The line got big laughs. Starting in training camp, assistant coach Cap Raeder would refer to Zhitnik and Sydor as those "two *yoots*," which never failed to loosen up the room.

Up front, Melrose moved Kurri to centre, an audacious move given that the classy Finn was thirty-two years old, had scored 497 NHL goals strictly as a right winger to that point in his career and was one of the highest paid Kings at $950,000 a season. "I had no allegiances to anyone," says Melrose. The rookie bench boss also stitched together a new forward line of centre Corey Millen, left winger Mike Donnelly and Tony Granato. The line quickly became LA's most consistent unit and one of the fastest lines in the NHL. "I don't know if there was ever a smaller line in hockey," recalls the five-foot-nine Granato. "I know it was the only line I had played on since bantam hockey where I was the biggest guy." Robitaille was named interim captain, and the season began without Number 99 or knowing if he would return that season. Or ever.

After selling out all forty home games the previous season, the Kings sold out only six of their first eleven home games without Gretzky. McNall, dodging calls from international banks and other creditors, could barely sleep at night. The team got off to a surprisingly good start, but then a major new problem emerged. Hrudey, in his fourteenth professional season and the team's only experienced goaltender, started to have problems stopping the puck. It wasn't physical but more a case of the yips, to borrow a golf expression. When goalies are playing well, they talk about seeing the puck as large as a beach ball. For Hrudey, the puck was a golf ball in a sandstorm.

On Long Island, before he got to the Kings, Hrudey had been carefully groomed by head coach Al Arbour as the successor to Billy Smith. Hrudey was the apprentice goalie who would keep the Islanders at the top of the league after Smith had backstopped them to four Stanley Cups in the early 1980s. Hrudey even pioneered a goaltending technique that would eventually become standard for all goalies at all levels. "It just occurred to me one day that just standing up and being strong on your skates wasn't cutting it anymore. So I started using this paddle-down move, laying the paddle of my goalie stick flat on the ice," he recalls. "Al hated it. He just wanted me to stand up. I tried it a few times in practice, and he came down to my end and gave me shit about using this move. I loved Al, and I would follow him anywhere, but in this case I was pretty stubborn, because I knew I was on to something. First time I ever tried it in a game, I got scored on. But I was convinced it would work. I stuck with it."

Hrudey played with Gretzky at the '87 Canada Cup, and he believes Gretzky suggested to the Kings they should trade for him. In February 1989, LA did, dealing young defenceman Wayne McBean and goalie Mark Fitzpatrick to the Isles for Hrudey, who soon supplanted Glenn Healy as the starter in Los Angeles.

Hrudey was a player with a personality, a goalie who could give a team confidence and swagger. He had just missed out on the dynasty on Long Island and didn't have a Stanley Cup ring or a long history of accomplishments. He was just a good goalie who seemed to carry the attitude of a great goalie. He fit beautifully with the Kings black-and-silver Hollywood look with his long hair, old-style goalie gear and trademark blue bandana. Hrudey averaged fifty games a year once he joined the team. Goalies such as Chicago's Ed Belfour, Detroit's Tim Cheveldae or Bill Ranford of the Edmonton Oilers might play more, but Hrudey was a workhorse and competitive. At $700,000 a season, he was one of the highest paid goalies in the game.

He played with "hate," he says. "It was productive, easy for me to motivate myself to be as charged up as I could be for a game. I played in a high emotional state. I expended a lot of energy. You can't do that unless you manufacture a reason to play at that level. I hated the other team, all those other guys, but for only the duration of the game. The second after a game was over, it totally disappeared."

By the fall of '92, Hrudey was snared in a generation gap between the old style of goaltending and the new butterfly technique popularized by Montreal's Patrick Roy. While goalies like Roy were leading a revolution by starting to go down more, covering up the bottom part of the net and taking away the high percentage scoring areas, Hrudey was still trying to stand up with his pads together, the way he'd been taught. It was too late for him to join the revolution. "I was caught in transition," he says. "I went in my career from trying to be a stand-up to more of a hybrid to a guy who was caught between eras. Guys like me and [Dominik] Hasek were developing this style where we were all over the place, or at least that's what people thought. But it didn't do us justice in the sense there was more rhyme and reason to it than people thought."

Abruptly, after a very good start to the '92–93 season, the confidence that made Hrudey such a good fit in LA started to evaporate. Perhaps it was that nagging sense in the back of his mind that his style of goaltending was no longer in vogue. His problems began on December 1, in a game against Chicago at Milwaukee, a time when the NHL played "neutral site" games as a means of cultivating fans in non-NHL cities. Hrudey stopped forty-four shots, but strange doubts had started to bother him. "The day before, I'd had something weird going on in my head," he says. "I would have a bath most nights on the road the day before a game. A nice warm bath, stretch, read some book, usually some Western Canadian mountain book. To keep my connection with Alberta, I'd read

Canadian explorer books. For some reason, that night I had these doubts enter my head. Things were going well. But I thought, Can I keep this up?"

The Kings, with Hrudey in net, beat Pittsburgh and Hartford at home, then tied Montreal 5–5 in Phoenix in another neutral site game. He allowed five goals on twenty-eight shots, and Patrick Roy allowed five at the other end. "The seeds of doubt were really growing," he says. "Then it went right in the ditch. I went from being doubtful to thinking my career was going to end. It just happened." He went from cocky to dazed and confused in a matter of weeks. After games, he would cry in his wife's lap. "I felt great at the start of every game," he says. "But if anything bad did happen, it all went badly in a hurry."

He let in five goals against Quebec, then five more to Edmonton on thirty-one shots. Rookie Robb Stauber was the backup, a twenty-five-year-old with lots of AHL experience but little in the big leagues. Stauber played a game, then Hrudey returned to face Vancouver and allowed six goals. Stauber started another game against Philly but gave way to Hrudey part way through the game. Hrudey allowed four goals on only sixteen shots. He gave up four more in another start against the Canucks and then five to the Habs on January 2. The NHL was a high-scoring league that year, but these numbers were dreadful. The Kings were reeling. Hrudey was living his hockey nightmare.

Gretzky had survived his scare and was coming back to play. The last thing the Kings needed was for goaltending problems to undermine the return of the game's brightest star. After weeks of workouts, Gretzky skated for the first time on Christmas Day. Twelve days later, on January 6, he played his first game of the season to WELCOME BACK WAYNE placards in the stands.

Melrose, of course, gave Gretzky the captaincy back. Gretzky's mother, Phyllis, flew in for the game, as did his father, Walter, who had suffered a brain aneurysm and had a physical therapist by his side. Gretzky told reporters he didn't want to be a "snail" when he returned. He picked up two assists and had three shots in his first game back, but the Kings lost 6–3 to Tampa. "When I first came back, there was an enthusiasm and an excitement and an adrenalin that you fly off of and flow under, and I had that," says Gretzky. "I thought, Wow, this is pretty good. Then I hit a wall. I was really not a very good player. It was Barry's first year, and I'm sure he thought, Oh my God, this guy's an overrated player." Number 99 had two goals and twelve assists in his first eleven games. Then, in his next seven games, he had no goals and five assists.

Hrudey was just awful again in Gretzky's return game, giving up those six goals to Tampa on just twenty shots. In eight appearances between December 8 and January 7, he allowed forty goals and his save percentage was a dreadful .830. The numbers suggested he was right, that he was the worst goalie in the NHL, and there was no sign the veteran goalie was coming out of it.

On January 17, the Kings were playing the Rangers at home in an afternoon game. Stauber was starting again. A miserable Hrudey was taping his sticks and drinking coffee two hours before the game in his stall next to the door leading to the ice. "The door opens and Barry Melrose walks in, and right behind him is Anthony Robbins," says Hrudey. "It wasn't that unusual, because we had all kinds of Hollywood people and celebrities and stars coming through. Anthony was a big deal at the time. A minute or two later, Barry calls my name and waves me over to where he and Robbins were standing. I was thinking, Why in the world would Tony Robbins want to meet the worst goalie in the league? Barry says, 'I've been working with Tony for a while. I'm wondering if you'd be willing to work with Tony to help you get over this.' The first thing I thought was how great that my coach was going way out on a limb to get me help. In that era, sports psychology wasn't that big. It was, Go figure it out on your own. Slug it out or we'll get somebody new. There was no help. Without any hesitation, I agreed. The only thing Barry asked was would it be okay if he sat in and listened to what I was going through. I had no problem with that. I'm an honest guy, I'll reveal everything about me. It might not be what the head coach needs to hear from his starting goalie, but I needed to get out of this too."

Robbins, an ambitious thirty-two-year-old entrepreneur from North Hollywood, had first gained wide exposure as a "life coach" and self-help guru four years earlier through his *Personal Power* audiotapes. He quickly gained a following and became a bona fide celebrity. His appearance on the Kings scene caused a lot of eye-rolling, lots of it from other teams, and some of it from other Kings players. McSorley thought it was a lot of psychobabble. He was old school, like most of the LA players. Other teams had psychologists, but Robbins was a TV star, and his involvement seemed more about Hollywood than healing. Hrudey, however, was open to anything that might help.

Melrose had seen Robbins on television one night while he was coaching junior hockey and was captivated. "So when I got hired in LA, I called up Tony and we met at the Santa Monica Airport," recalls Melrose. "We had lunch together. He flew in on his helicopter. We had a great talk, spent two or three hours together." After weeks of watching Hrudey struggle and lose confidence, Melrose believed Robbins might be able to help. "You have to be receptive. You have to be open-minded, and you have to be willing to really put yourself out there," says Melrose. "And Kelly was. I just kept waiting for him to get it back, and he never did. So I approached him about sitting down with Anthony."

Hrudey recalls their first session. "I sat in a regular chair, and Anthony stood in front of me. He's six foot seven, so obviously it was on purpose. A position of power. I understood all that. He asked me, 'When you feel really good about yourself, what do you feel like?' It could be a Hollywood character, a cartoon character, anything or anybody. It was really easy for me. The Gulf War was coming to an end, and I loved watching General Norman Schwarzkopf on TV because of his presence. He was a general through and through. He was in charge. He was everything I felt in net when I was playing great." Robbins then asked Hrudey who he felt like when he was playing badly. "I went back to my days growing up in Elmwood, a community in Edmonton," says Hrudey. "If my mom wasn't working, I'd race home from school for lunch and she'd have two fried baloney sandwiches for me. And I'd watch *The Flintstones*. I'd think of Fred Flintstone in Mr. Slate's office getting shit. So I'm telling this to Tony Robbins and Barry Melrose. After every goal I let in, I'd just feel like Fred in the chair, shrinking from Mr. Slate. Talk about being real. I'm laying it all out on the line. We had a good chuckle over it, but it was really scary. I remember looking over at Barry, thinking, What the fuck is my head coach thinking right now?"

Robbins trained Hrudey to change his way of thinking by imagining his positive and negative images of himself as a picture-in-picture scenario. "My big picture was Fred Flintstone;

my little one was Schwarzkopf. I had to turn that around and see Schwarzkopf as the big picture," he says. "I carried a laminated index card with me the rest of my career. It had only four points. The first one was 'Schwarzkopf.' The second was 'picture-in-picture.' The other two were technical things. One was 'toes out,' because I'm naturally pigeon-toed, and sometimes I could get myself caught, and I needed my toes out for balance and manoeuvring. The last one was be at the 'top of the crease.' From that day forward, until the last day I ever played in the NHL, I looked at that card before I went out for warm-up and before the start of every period. I still have it somewhere in storage. Anthony Robbins saved my career. And Barry."

The episode demonstrated something important about Melrose to Hrudey. "Typically, when guys go as low as I was, they go one other place, and that's away. They don't survive in the National Hockey League. They go someplace else," says Hrudey. "I don't want to make it sound like Barry was all fun and giggles. Barry really pushed us, made us all accountable, and he was full throttle. But when a guy is completely broken, most coaches give up on that. They don't have time to focus on one guy when you've got twenty-two other guys trying to pull on the rope." Hrudey's teammates noticed too. Granato says, "I remember thinking, This coach is secure enough to feel comfortable bringing someone else into his locker room that he feels can help us. Other coaches I've been around, or organizations for that matter, would say, No, we're not doing that, it's out of protocol. Great coaches and great organizations look for whatever can help. There's a confidence in that."

Hrudey immediately felt better after meeting with Robbins, but it didn't immediately translate into better goaltending. That took months. The Kings could have made a trade for a goalie. They knew the Leafs were dangling Fuhr, an ex-Oiler who would have fit a transactional pattern for the Kings. But the price was high, and the Leafs were looking specifically for a winger to play with Gilmour. For LA, getting Fuhr would have likely cost them Tomas Sandstrom and Stauber, plus another piece of the future. There were other options for trading goaltenders. Around this time, Washington sent Rick Tabaracci to Winnipeg for Jim Hrivnak and a draft choice.

Instead of making a deal to get a goalie, the Kings stuck with those they had and made a totally different move, one that created more conflict in the organization. The previous season, Paul Coffey had been acquired by the Kings in a massive three-team, seven-player blockbuster with Philadelphia and Pittsburgh. Los Angeles had surrendered a first-round pick in the transaction. Three first-round picks had gone to Edmonton from the Kings in the Gretzky deal, and trading a first-round pick to get another ex-Oiler didn't thrill long-time loyalists in the Kings organization. "Yeah, there was a lot of awkwardness," says McNall. "All the scouts had done a great job. They felt in a way that their jobs were being undermined."

In early January, Kings management had told Coffey they wanted to restructure his $1.1-million contract. "I guess Bruce had some issues. That's all I know. As a player, you just want to do what helps," says Coffey, who had two more years on his deal at $1.3 million and $1.4 million. "So I agreed to defer some money. But I guess that wasn't enough." On January 28, the Kings lost to Calgary 2–1 at home. Coffey, a minus-2 in that game, shared a Manhattan Beach apartment with teammates Jim Hiller and Rychel. "The next day, early in the morning, like six o'clock in the morning, I got a call, and they had traded me to Detroit," says Coffey. It was a six-player trade that also included Hiller, with Carson coming back to California. Carson had scored ninety-two goals in his first two NHL seasons with the Kings but had been moved in the Gretzky deal with Edmonton. Now he was coming back to the Kings, along with minor league forwards Gary Shuchuk and Marc Potvin, both of whom had played for Melrose in the Detroit system. The deal came as a shock to the Kings dressing room. "We had traded Paul Coffey for Jimmy Carson!" says McSorley. "It was hard to believe."

Gretzky was downright angry about the trade and confronted McNall on the team plane. "Barry Melrose did not believe Paul Coffey was a good defensive player," says McNall. "He was an enormously talented offensive defenceman. I had gotten Coffey [from Pittsburgh nine months earlier] because Wayne said, 'He's available. Let's grab him.' But then Barry Melrose is on his case, and we really need a different kind of player for that role. So I said okay, and they went ahead and traded Coffey. Well, Wayne was furious with me. He was mad. He was mad at me because he knew I could stop whatever I wanted to stop. We argued on the plane. It was a heated discussion that everybody around us was listening to. I tried to explain this was what our people wanted to do. He was not happy at all." Coffey was surprised by the move. "I enjoyed Barry Melrose as a coach," he says. "If that's what he thought of me, fine. He coached a real fast, upbeat game, and it was a great bunch of guys. He preached a lot of the same stuff we did in Edmonton. He got a lot out of that team. Barry was good to me. He coached a take-no-prisoners attitude. We had some good young defencemen in Blake, Zhitnik and Darryl Sydor. It was time for those three guys to step up and shine."

Gretzky's influence, seen as all-encompassing outside LA, obviously had its limits. "I don't know if it was a big, loud argument," Gretzky says of his confrontation with McNall. "It was more a question of, you know, I'm just not sure you trade a Hall of Fame defenceman who happens to be, in my mind, one of the great defencemen who ever lived and ever played, one of the most unselfish teammates I've ever had. I was just questioning trading him for two guys in the minors. It had nothing to do with Potvin or Shuchuk. I had a great deal of respect for both of them as teammates, and they were a huge part of our success. But there's only one Paul Coffey. That's what I told Bruce, that's what I told Barry, and Nick. But, as I said to them, 'Hey, it's your team. I'm just a player. I'll do the best I can. But it doesn't mean I can't give my opinion.'" Gretzky all but omits Carson's value, and the truth is the Michigan native was by that point a shadow of the young star who had made such an impact on Southern California. He was only twenty-four, but he was finished as an impact NHL forward. He'd never been a great skater, and his scoring touch had vanished. Other teams thought he was afraid.

A few days later, Gretzky had a meeting with McNall and Melrose in Quebec City. Gretzky was unhappy with his play and suggested perhaps the team would be better off without him. It was unclear exactly what he was suggesting, other than that he thought he was playing so poorly others deserved to be playing ahead of him. At the same time, he felt he wasn't playing enough to get back in the groove. The situation had to change one way or another. Melrose had built a lineup without him and had grown accustomed to giving those players certain minutes and playing them in certain situations. Now, he needed to adjust and start giving those minutes back to Gretzky. "That's when we decided for the rest of the season I was just going to play him twenty-five minutes a night," says Melrose. "He was going to kill penalties. He was going to play. The rest of the year was going to be designed around getting Wayne Gretzky back to being Wayne Gretzky. That is what we tried to do from then on. He got better and better. His endurance got better. You could see the old Gretzky sparkle come back. That got us going into the playoffs."

Neither that meeting nor the Coffey trade fixed much in the short term. By the end of February the Kings were sputtering along at 27-29-7, seemingly going nowhere. On February 27, the Leafs and Gilmour strolled into town and handled the home team easily, 5–2. Hrudey gave up all five goals and didn't appear again in the Los Angeles net for almost three weeks. Gretzky might have been working his way back, but LA still didn't have a goalie.

The Kings tried twenty-two-year-old David Goverde in goal twice. The first time, Goverde gave up five goals in Winnipeg, and on the second try he gave up eight at home to Washington.

The front office was so agitated that they signed thirty-two-year-old minor league journeyman Rick Knickle from the International Hockey League San Diego Gulls. Knickle was actually eleven months older than Hrudey, and they had played against each other as juniors in the Western Hockey League, Knickle with Brandon, Hrudey with Medicine Hat. Knickle had played fourteen years in the minors without getting a single NHL minute and had already given up and retired once. But the Kings gave him a chance for a salary of $68,000 for the rest of the season, as well as a $500 bonus for every win and $2,000 per shutout. He started a February 18 game at Chicago and promptly gave up seven goals in a loss to the Hawks. He then got his first NHL win, on February 22, and cried in the dressing room after. "I thought his dog died," said Melrose.

Knickle became a colourful, inspirational NHL character and a media darling that season. His presence also created tension in the dressing room as Hrudey desperately searched for his game and Stauber demanded more opportunity to play. Stauber, in fact, said he wanted to be traded if he wasn't going to play. Knickle registered five more wins until he played his final NHL game on March 29. By that point, Hrudey was starting to come around with the help of Robbins. Melrose knew he needed one goalie for the playoffs. When he'd won the Memorial Cup in Medicine Hat, it was with Fitzpatrick, the goalie the Kings had traded to get Hrudey, playing most of the games. In his gut, Melrose knew that if the Kings were going anywhere in the postseason, it would have to be with either Hrudey or Stauber. He just didn't know which one, and he wanted Knickle around as insurance.

Stauber got the nod for the final game of the regular season, an indication Melrose was still undecided, but he was terrible, giving up six goals to Vancouver. To start the playoffs against Calgary, Stauber didn't even dress. Melrose started Hrudey in net against the Flames with Knickle as his backup. In the first three games, Hrudey gave up seventeen goals, including nine in Game 2, and the Kings lost twice. By Game 4, Stauber was back in as the starter as the controversial Kings goalie carousel continued to turn. LA won three straight with Stauber and exploded for eighteen goals in the final two games to eliminate the Flames.

Stauber, naturally, started the second-round series against the Canucks. But after LA lost the opener, it was Hrudey's turn again. This time, he didn't give the job up. Stauber saw no more action in the '93 playoffs.

By the time the haphazard Kings season delivered the club to the conference final against the Leafs, Hrudey was back in form, cocky and playing with "hate." He had his mojo back. The sessions with Robbins had helped, as had the refusal of Melrose to write him off. Backstopping the Kings to victory in the second round of the playoffs for the first time in team history gave Hrudey the sense of belief he had lost during the regular season. Despite all the troubles he'd had, his team-mates still viewed him differently than most goalies, who were generally seen as flighty or eccentric. Hrudey was more like one of the other players, and he was combative, which his teammates liked. "Kelly was one of us. You didn't know he was a goalie," says Granato. "He was a huge part of the success of that team. I know it was a roller-coaster year for him. But everybody believed in him, and everybody wanted him to be a big part of it."

The conference final would be Hrudey's series to win or lose. The team and the coach had stuck by him, and he was determined to pay them back.

BY THE SECOND PERIOD of Game 5 after a mundane and scoreless first period, the Hrudey-Potvin matchup had become even more of a focal point as the veteran Hrudey jousted with the rookie Leafs netminder in what became the first goaltending battle of the series.

The Kings took a 1–0 lead at 1:53 of the second period on a two-on-one break with Leafs defenceman Sylvain Lefebvre caught up ice. Andreychuk had tried unsuccessfully to bat the puck out of the air to prevent the break, but Robitaille sped away with Shuchuk on his right. Potvin stopped Robitaille's slapshot and Shuchuk's rebound attempt. But as the Leafs goalie went to cover the puck, Robitaille poked it free and Shuchuk knocked it in for the first goal. The Kings started to dominate the game, and by the five-minute mark of the second were up 14–6 shots as the Gardens crowd grew restless. The Leafs had won Game 4 with a strong, sturdy effort, but now they were back to looking like they had in Game 3, aimless and spiritless.

The Leafs offence, hot and cold through the series, couldn't create much of anything. Their best chance might have been when Todd Gill found himself alone at the right circle, but his rising slapshot hit Hrudey square in the mask, denting his cage. Soon after, Kings blueliner Tim Watters was accidentally hit in the face by teammate McSorley's stick. There was blood all over the ice, along with two of Watters's teeth. He skated off to the dressing room holding a piece of gauze to his bloody mouth, but he would return. Broken teeth had never stopped an NHL player, something consistent throughout the history of the sport and still the case today.

The Kings jumped ahead 2–0 on a goal by Kurri, but by then the score could have been more one-sided if not for Potvin. He was athletic and sturdy, and the Kings needed something special to beat him. First came a pretty four-way passing play, Sandstrom to Zhitnik to Kurri to Rychel. Rychel hammered a slapshot that Potvin stopped, but the puck bounced right back to him. He shot again. Again a rebound that Potvin couldn't control. Kurri, who had continued to play centre even after Gretzky returned in January, buried the loose puck high over Potvin's glove. To that point, LA had a 13–3 advantage in shots for the period and were threatening to run the Leafs out of the Gardens. With five minutes left before the second intermission, the Leafs had only nine shots on goal.

It looked like an easy night at the office for Hrudey, dented cage aside. But Granato was penalized at 15:12 of the second for raking his stick across Bill Berg's face, and the game changed when the Leafs power play cut the LA lead to 2–1. Mike Krushelnyski was standing to Hrudey's left as the puck went back to Rouse at the right point. Normally, a left-handed shooter like Krushelnyski would spin clockwise towards the net and go to tip an incoming shot with his backhand. Instead, Krushelnyski squared up to Rouse, and when the low shot came in, he used his forehand like a pitching wedge to elevate the puck. It was difficult to execute, but he did it perfectly, and the puck went high into the LA net. That seemed to wake the Leafs up. Hrudey needed to make big stops on Wendel Clark and Anderson before the period was over to keep the Kings in the lead to start the third period.

As the third began, Potvin, in his white home jersey with black pads and gloves and a black Koho goalie stick, kept giving his team a chance to win, making quality saves off Robitaille and Gretzky. The Leafs were starting to turn up the pressure on Hrudey, wearing all black save for his white blocker and white goalie stick, wrapped in white tape. Potvin stayed close to his goal line as though attached by a short rope.

Hrudey spent much of his time outside the blue-painted crease, aggressively challenging shooters or playing the puck. He would venture out near the blueline at times. Potvin would go down in the butterfly as though preparing to kneel in prayer, opening up the five-hole between his pads. Hrudey stood upright, his catching mitt held up near his left ear, with his small pads pressed tightly together so as to never open the five-hole. He looked like he was sitting in a straight-back chair. The contrast between the styles and appearance of the two goalies couldn't have been greater. There was an age difference of only eleven years between them, but they seemed like goalies from different centuries. Hrudey looked like he could have played the position wearing a ball cap instead of a mask, like the goalies in the 1920s. He belonged to a dying breed of goaltenders, but he was determined to prove he could still compete with the young whippersnapper at the other end. Visions of Norman Schwarzkopf danced in his head. Fred Flintstone was nowhere to be seen.

At 8:43, the Leafs tied the game 2–2 on a strange goal by Lefebvre, of all people. After breaking up a dangerous looking LA charge, both Lefebvre and Rouse uncharacteristically joined the rush going the other way. It was not how Burns would have drawn it up. He didn't forbid his defencemen from going on offence, but definitely not two at a time. Lefebvre took a drop pass from Gilmour and went to take a slapshot from the left circle. As Lefebvre shot, Sydor lost his balance and slid into Hrudey, knocking the veteran goalie's skates out from under him like a bowling pin as he came out to challenge the shooter. Hrudey still somehow managed to get a piece of the shot, but as Sydor slid into the Kings net, the puck rolled in with him. The

Leafs defenceman was credited with the goal, but surely the Kings defenceman deserved the credit, or at least an assist.

Potvin's excellent goaltending had kept the Leafs in the game, and he'd avoided giving up a killer third goal. Now it was tied. The ice, tilted one way for forty minutes, had begun going the other way. With four minutes left, Gill spotted Gilmour cutting between Blake and Zhitnik and hit him in stride with a pass. Both Kings defencemen hooked at Gilmour and he fell to the ice as the puck rolled harmlessly to Hrudey. Zhitnik went off for hooking, but it could just as easily have been Blake, and just as easily been a penalty shot. The Leafs still had a power play in the dying minutes of regulation time.

Hrudey turned away Ellett's point shot, then stumped Andreychuk in tight. He made another save on a low point shot from Gill through an Andreychuk screen, but the puck squirted loose to a wide-open Gilmour stationed at the right post. The Leafs centre lifted the puck towards the yawning cage, but Hrudey, kneeling on the ice, stretched out his left pad and glove and made a terrific stop. Then it was Andreychuk again, walking out of the left corner without an LA player on him. He drilled a knee-high shot, but Hrudey's stand-up technique meant there was no room between his pads. He squeezed the puck and held it, knowing Andreychuk was looking for a rebound. That made it five saves for Hrudey on the Leafs power play with the game on the line, three of them from fifteen feet or closer.

Unable to get the winning goal past the LA goalie, the Leafs tried another time-honoured hockey technique. They ran him. If you couldn't beat him, soften him up a bit. Zezel's slapshot went wide, but Berg drove hard towards the net with two Kings on his back and rammed into Hrudey, his right elbow crashing into the goalie's head. Maybe the Leafs pest was looking for a rebound, maybe he thought he'd make sure Hrudey wasn't getting too comfortable. The net came off its moorings and Berg landed on top of Hrudey. The puck, however, wasn't in the net. Hrudey was standing his ground, while his teammates hadn't managed a shot for the final seven minutes of the third period.

The overtime period was the first of the series. It was abundantly clear early that referee Bill McCreary, like Dan Marouelli in Game 1, had no intention of calling any penalties regardless of what transpired. The philosophy was "Let the players decide the game," but all the hands-off approach really did was put the skilled players on both teams at a major disadvantage. It allowed the checkers and grinders to decide the game, not the highly paid stars, a peculiar philosophy for a sport trying to sell tickets and attract a major US television network. Hrudey made a spectacular kick save on Anderson, and then Potvin made a good paddle-down save on Millen, precisely the goaltending technique Hrudey had pioneered in the mid-1980s. Lefebvre ran Zhitnik face first into the end glass in the Leafs zone, leaving the Kings defenceman woozy. "He's not sure what rink he's in," chuckled Neale. Zhitnik spent much of the rest of the game sitting on the bench with a towel draped over his head. "He might as well have asked the lady beside him for her scarf," recalls Melrose. "That's how that building was set up. You were in the middle of the fans."

Toronto was now getting more of the chances, and Hrudey was under siege. For the goalies, it was less about form and technique and more about athleticism and being willing to compete with bodies flailing around their creases. Potvin made a save sitting on his goal line. Hrudey blocked a point-blank shot from Mike Foligno and held on.

Potvin was cool and composed in his butterfly stance at his end, while Hrudey was furiously fighting and coming up with different ways to keep the Leafs at bay. He improvised, dropping his stick, grabbing at the puck with his blocker. All around him, players were being tackled or otherwise dragged to the ice. For the second time in the game, Watters, minus two teeth, pushed Clark offside on a Toronto rush with no interference call. Both Gilmour and Andreychuk were hooked rather obviously from behind while on partial breakaways, but still no penalty. "Bill McCreary has his whistle in his wallet," said play-by-play announcer Bob Cole. The Leafs, and Burns, screamed in protest. The ice around the LA net was covered in brown stains from fans pelting the area with soft drinks in paper cups.

As Gardens public announcer Paul Morris tonelessly announced "last minute of play in the period," Leafs defenceman Jamie Macoun shot the puck into the right corner of the LA zone. It was retrieved by Rouse along the right boards, and he shot it around the boards to the far corner. Andreychuk chipped a short pass to Anderson, who made a quick circle coming out of the corner to elude Gretzky's outstretched stick and headed to the net. Anderson's first shot hit Conacher and bounced high in the air into the slot. At the moment it was going to hit the ice, Anderson short-hopped it with a backhand swing of his stick and at 19:20 chopped it under Hrudey as he was leaning to his left to end the game. The Kings goalie toppled over onto his left side then lay his head down once he realized the puck was behind him. McSorley drifted past him in disbelief, like a zombie on skates.

"It was kind of a lucky bounce," says Anderson. "I just kind of slapped at it with my backhand." Coaches and trainers on the Leafs bench high-fived. Potvin skated down the ice into the Kings zone to join the celebration. It was a temporary moment of triumph for Anderson against his old Edmonton teammates, players like Gretzky, McSorley, Huddy and Kurri. "At that point, you just want to prove who's better," says Anderson. "It was like playing your best friend in a game of golf. No way are you giving him a mulligan." Anderson skated off the ice, one arm raised in triumph. It was the only period of the game in which the Leafs, with twelve shots, had outshot the Kings, who had ten on Potvin in the extra session.

Anderson's winner was the thirty-fourth shot of the night for Toronto, and Hrudey had made thirty-one saves. Without his brilliance in the final minutes of regulation, LA wouldn't even have survived until overtime. "That was my best game of the series," he says now. "I played great." Potvin had stopped forty-one Kings shots at the other end, his best game of the series as well. The Kings had blown a 2–0 lead in Game 5, and a 2–1 lead in the series had also evaporated. "Hey, we were playing against a good team," says Gretzky. "One of the great things about Pat Burns is he was one of the best defensive coaches in hockey. I knew it was going to be tough. It wasn't going to be easy, and they had the personnel to be a defensive-minded team."

At least the Kings no longer had to worry about their goal-keeper, who was back to being a consistent, central part of the team. His goaltending style might have been going out of fashion, but his competitiveness was old school and inspiring. Hrudey had survived his personal crisis. He could be the goalie a team could lean on once more.

IT'S TWENTY-FIVE YEARS LATER, and the memories of that difficult time in his career can still cause Hrudey to pause in the middle of a conversation to collect himself. His voice breaks and he chokes up. He's as emotional in his mid-fifties as he ever was, and you realize how shattered he was back in the '92–93 season and how scared about his career. The part he didn't talk about at the time, and never has, was even more frightening. He and his wife, Donna, had established a nice life for themselves in Redondo Beach with their two kids. They'd go to Disneyland often, or get Gretzky to recommend the trendiest restaurants in Los Angeles. They were building a house back in Calgary, with plans to move there one day to live at least part of the time.

They were also expecting the birth of their third child in the middle of all he was going through that season as a professional athlete. Kaitlin was born on January 27, 1993, just after Hrudey had met Tony Robbins and just before the Kings made the Coffey trade. Doctors quickly discovered she had a hole in her heart. Not unusual, but worrisome. Of greater concern was Donna. She had hemorrhaged terribly while giving birth. "She was in serious, serious trouble. She was minutes from passing away," says Hrudey. "She was just bleeding out." Doctors were ultimately able to get the bleeding under control, but it was an awful scare. Hrudey's professional world was a mess, and now he'd come close to losing his wife. He didn't tell a single one of his teammates.

"I never shared it with anybody. I told Barry about Kaitlin's heart issue, but that was it," he says. "Other than my family, nobody knew about Donna. I'd already been weak, and I thought, I can't share something that might make me look weak again in their eyes." He was still part of that culture of male strength in which struggles with problems, particularly mental health or emotional challenges, were kept secret. You might love and trust your teammates, but at that time there was a line athletes didn't dare cross.

Those were hard times for the Hrudey clan, and dealing with Kaitlin's anxiety and OCD over the past fourteen years has been very hard as well. Painful for her, challenging for her family. For five years, Hrudey and Kaitlin have been talking about her fight publicly, and he believes his athletic background has helped him. "In sports, we fight and we battle for everything. You have to dig in, have to find focus," he says. "When I was doing those breathing sessions with Kaitlin, focus was paramount. It was about dropping a lot of other things, and the priority was to get her to 'the garden.' A lot about what I'd learned as an athlete was about perseverance, and I could apply that to this."

The Mount Royal University honorary degree is gratifying for Hrudey as he tries to bring more of his message to the sports world. "Canadian mental health experts say one in five are suffering, but I'd say the number is far greater," he says. "First of all, a lot of people don't like to talk about it. And just from talking to people, I believe it's got to be at least three or four in five that suffer. Every single day, I get emails, texts, phone calls with people telling me about their personal experiences. But let's say one in five is the accurate number. That means if you're a coach on a hockey team and you've got twenty or twenty-three players, you've got to understand you've got four or five people on your team that are going through something." In recent years the NHL has been forced to confront some harsh truths in the wake of the suicide deaths of Derek Boogaard, Rick Rypien and Wade

Belak and players, particularly tough guys, are coming forward more regularly to tell the league and its fans about the strain and the mental cost of the game. Talk to any former NHL player and he'll be able to tell you a sad story about a former teammate who has struggled with depression, alcoholism or drug abuse in his post-hockey career. The good news is that the stories are now being told, not hidden, and former star athletes like Hrudey are making mental health advocacy part of their life's work.

For Kaitlin, the battle continues. "It looks to us like she's finding her sweet spot where her life might be headed down the road," says Hrudey. "She's been so inspirational for so many people sharing her story. But the fact of the matter is it can come and go." Journalist Joe O'Connor was one of the first to write about Kaitlin, in the *National Post* newspaper in 2013. "Joe wrote that it's a life sentence, and he's so right," says Hrudey. "The only reason I kind of hesitate in sharing that is I don't want to scare people who are just starting to learn about themselves or a loved one. They hear that and think, Oh my God, I can't get through today. How am I going to do this for my life?"

That, of course, is where the comparisons end between Hrudey's fight with his inner hockey demons and his daughter's fight. His was contained to a few months in one season of a long, successful career. After the spring of '93, he played another five seasons and another 211 regular season games, although only one more playoff game, which came in his final season with San Jose in 1998. The run with the Kings in '93 was the most successful playoff effort of his career, and the battle with the Leafs among his most treasured memories. "I thought they were a very good team," he says. "But I thought we were the better team."

ACT SIX

A hockey man with deep hockey roots, Kerry Fraser drives through the back roads of suburban New Jersey three days after Christmas, taking his brother-in-law to a traditional Fraser family gathering: a hockey game. This one is at Johnny Gaudreau's long-time home rink in Hollydell Ice Arena in Washington County, where one of Fraser's ten grandchildren, fifteen-year-old Garrison, is scheduled to play for St. Augustine Preparatory School.

With an annual tuition fee in excess of US$18,000, St. Augustine is unlike anything from Fraser's own gritty hockey upbringing in Sarnia, Ontario. There, he skated for three years for the hometown Bees under the watchful coaching eye of his father, Hilton, known by his friends as "Hilt." Fraser's brother, Rick, was on that team as well and soon graduated to the Junior A Oshawa Generals. Kerry, just five foot seven, didn't have the skills or overall package to move on. He played a physical game despite his size and often dropped the gloves to protect his teammates. "My dad was a pretty tough guy," says Fraser. "He had played in Europe, the IHL and

Ontario Senior A Sarnia Sailors. He taught me how to fight in my kitchen, knocked me down a number of times. Ted Garvin, who changed my diapers when I was a baby, later went on to coach the Detroit Red Wings. He once told me that, pound for pound, my dad was the toughest player he ever saw. I was a little guy, but I wasn't afraid. I had fast hands and I was left-handed."

In 1971, Fraser turned to officiating. He was picked out of a tryout camp by long-time NHL referee Frank Udvari, who coincidentally had been involved in an incident years earlier in which Hilt Fraser had punched him during a game. As punishment, the elder Fraser was suspended a game and fined $5. Udvari obviously didn't hold that against the son, and by 1973 Kerry Fraser was already a member of the National Hockey League Officials Association. In 1980, he refereed his first NHL game and went on to officiate 1,904 regular season games and thirteen Stanley Cup finals.

At the age of sixty-five, as he watches his grandson play, his knees ache from five different surgeries. He has another procedure in the offing to fix torn cartilage suffered in his final NHL season. He's also in his third week of taking a chemotherapy pill designed to treat essential thrombocythemia, a rare chronic blood condition with which he had been diagnosed several months earlier. The pill is designed to reduce his platelet count and the risk of heart attack or stroke. Ever since going public with his health issues, Fraser has tried to put a positive spin on his condition, encouraging others to get checked by their doctors. That's his personality. Chipper to the point of seeming a little over the top. Brimming with ideas and stories. Energetic and creative. Still besotted with the game without an ounce of bitterness or regret. He's written one book on his career, and thinks he has enough ideas for another. All those personality traits are now funnelled into his illness. He tells the story of Bill Lochead, a former linemate in Sarnia and NHL first-round pick (ninth overall, 1974) now working as a hockey agent in Germany. "When I was diagnosed, he sent me an email saying three months earlier he had been diagnosed with the same thing while getting a new hip," Fraser says. "It's actually really cool. You end up with a network of reconnections."

For years, he was the NHL's most recognizable referee. He was small, which made him stand out, and he always had perfect hair. Not a strand out of place. His secret was a hair product called Paul Mitchell Freeze and Shine. He remembers walking to the officials' room after a game in Buffalo when he was confronted by a woman. "In a very aggressive tone, she said, 'Kerry, I have a question for you!' I thought, Oh no, she's pissed off because the Sabres lost. So I said, 'Yes, ma'am, how can I help you?' She said, 'Kerry, I have real problem hair, and I can't do a thing with it. You skate around the ice a hundred miles an hour and your hair never moves. What is your secret?'"

He refused to wear a helmet until the last couple of years of his career. Vanity? He says no. "I had developed a sense of awareness similar to the great players in the game," he says. "I felt that heightened awareness was inhibited or restricted by wearing a helmet. Without wearing a helmet, I was cut in the face or head only three times, all by deflected pucks, during those years." By happy coincidence, it also meant no helmet to interfere with his legendary hair.

While he felt he was less likely to be hurt without a helmet, there were other injuries. Lots of them. There was the time in 1982 when he refereed an entire game on a broken ankle after being struck by a Paul Coffey slapshot. "Didn't know until I took my boot off after the game, and the foot just blew up," he says, laughing.

There were thousands and thousands of calls, and hundreds of controversial moments. Like the time Fraser whistled Quebec forward Paul Gillis for interfering with Montreal goalie Brian Hayward during a contentious Battle of Quebec playoff game in 1987, erasing the potential game-winning goal by Alain Cote. Just fourteen seconds after that call, Ryan Walter scored the game-winning goal for the Habs in Game 5 of the series. Afterwards, Fraser heard chatter that a Quebec group was going to launch a lawsuit accusing him of "prejudice" against the Nordiques.

No Fraser call reverberated louder or had a greater impact on his professional legacy than the one he made on May 27, 1993, in Game 6 of the Clarence Campbell Conference final between Toronto and Los Angeles. It's one that can still get hard-core Maple Leafs fans in a hot lather a quarter century later. Kings fans, and players, remember it quite differently, naturally. And Fraser? "The ship went down with me that night," he says. "The country of Canada vilified the referee Kerry Fraser. And I couldn't blame them."

AFTER TORONTO'S THRILLING overtime triumph in Game 5 on Glenn Anderson's winner with forty seconds left in the first overtime, the two clubs made their third plane trip in six days across the continent back to California. It was a gruelling schedule. The Leafs, drained from nineteen games in thirty-eight days, needed one more win to get back to the

Stanley Cup final for the first time since 1967. They had two chances to get it, starting with Game 6 at the Fabulous Forum. The Leafs were weary but confident. "We felt we had momentum," says assistant coach Mike Kitchen. "Wayne had been a non-factor to that point, so we felt good about that. A lot of it was team defence, being aware when he was on ice. And we were really focused on taking away that area behind the net from him." Momentum was a funny thing for hockey players. They felt it in their bones, loved the sense that the wind was at their backs. Some things made hard things easier. At the same time, they were keenly aware it often didn't carry over from game to game, or even period to period. But talking about momentum made them feel more confident, and this was a series that had been filled with players who looked supremely confident at one moment and uncertain the next.

It was certainly true that Gretzky had not had a memorable series. He'd had one goal and four assists in the first five games, and he was starting to draw unusual criticism for it. *Toronto Star* columnist Bob McKenzie had written after Game 5 that Gretzky "looked as though he was skating with a piano on his back." There was criticism in LA as well, suggesting Gretzky had become too "Hollywood" and wasn't as competitive as he once had been. Gretzky heard it all. He had a reputation for being more than aware of things that were said and written about him. Often, he'd responded to criticism with excellent performances. "Gretz had been very quiet," recalls former Leafs GM Cliff Fletcher. "We read the articles and said, 'Shit, we better get ready.'" Other Kings players noticed and thought the criticism was unwarranted and disrespectful. The criticism hadn't come from the Leafs, but LA players still felt they could use the media reports as "bulletin board material," clippings and articles that could be cut out and used to motivate a team. "He was being questioned and doubted by people in the media. Whoever was bringing that up was giving us extra incentive," says Tony Granato. "When someone doubted Wayne, you had an entire city, an entire locker room and entire fan base of Wayne wanting to prove those people wrong. I know I rallied around that. I was almost embarrassed that someone would actually think that or say that."

For his part, Gretzky remembers trying not to be too critical of his own play. He didn't like beating himself up when he was unable to be at his best. "When you're playing in the NHL, you're playing against the best players in the world. And great coaches. If you're an offensive player, they're going to devise a system, and they're going to do things to shut you down. That's the name of the game," he says. "So sometimes, it might take you one game, it might take you three games. You've got to figure out what you can do differently as a player that's going to offset how they're trying to check you or shut you down. Sometimes, it just takes longer than other times."

Gretzky was also carrying a secret. The hockey world knew he had missed the first half of the season with a back problem. He'd come back strongly, playing the final forty-five games of the regular season and registering sixty-five points. What fans and reporters didn't know was that Gretzky was playing against the Leafs with a broken rib. Against Calgary in the opening round, he had been cross-checked by hulking six-foot-four Flames centre Joel Otto after a faceoff. Gretzky's rib cracked. He didn't miss a game, but from that point to the end of the playoffs, he required an injection of freezing before every game and wore a protective flak jacket as well. "Before every game, they'd come in after warm-up and put a needle in my leg," recalls Gretzky. "It didn't really hurt unless I got hit. So in practices, nobody really came near me, because I wasn't frozen. In the games, I didn't really feel the injury. I used to tease the doctor to make sure the freezing goes up, not down, because if my leg falls asleep I'm in trouble. We were able to keep it as quiet as possible."

It hadn't noticeably affected his production, as twenty-three points in twelve games in the first two rounds were excellent by anyone's standards, even his own. "Once they froze it, it was like nothing," Gretzky says. "Nothing to stop me from playing."

It's the perfect example of why teams don't like to disclose injuries at playoff time. If the Leafs had known about the broken rib, they might have targeted him more. That said, even with their star, Doug Gilmour, taking a nightly pounding, they'd shown no interest in subjecting Gretzky to any physical abuse. Certainly nothing like Otto had delivered. So perhaps the broken rib wouldn't have made any difference at all.

Gilmour had enjoyed more success than Gretzky in the series, but all the ice time was starting to wear him down, the Kings were leaning on him every game, and his lean frame had begun to betray him. Intravenous treatments after games were helping, but nothing could keep the weight on, and he dropped to around 160 pounds. His haggard face and dark circles around his eyes made him look like a walking cadaver.

Five other referees had called the first five games of the series. Fraser, rated as one of the top three NHL referees that season, drew Game 6, the first potential series-ending contest. Veteran linesmen Ron "Huck" Finn and Kevin Collins joined him. The series had cooled since the red-hot beginnings of

Game 1, with players conscious of what was at stake, how a foolish error in judgment at the wrong time could cost everything they worked towards over the previous nine months. Many small feuds had festered during the series, but both clubs were laden with veterans who understood how to tuck grievances away for revenge at a more suitable time and what it took to earn a berth in the Stanley Cup final.

The hockey had been vicious and sometimes ugly, with black eyes, broken teeth, nasty cuts and concussions. There weren't the stick-swinging fights of the 1960s or the bench-clearing brawls of the 1970s and 1980s, but there was a meanness to the game and a sense that making a physical sacrifice counted as much as having the skills to score a big goal. "I loved the game. I thought it was pure. You had to have courage to play," Barry Melrose says. "It was fast. It was before the trap, so you didn't have five guys waiting for you in the neutral zone. Skill guys had room to make plays. Defence could join the rush. Goaltending wasn't nearly as good, so more goals were scored. I liked the intensity of the games then. We took care of the problems ourselves. We didn't expect the referees to supply courage. We supplied our own courage."

Fraser had refereed games where he'd let a lot of quasi-legal plays go uncalled, and he'd refereed games where league officials had urged him to crack down, call a lot of penalties and reel in the players. Like most of the better referees of his era, he viewed the rule book as a general guide but gave himself a lot of latitude to interpret it differently on different nights. With only one referee, it was guaranteed things would be missed. The hope of any referee was that he wouldn't miss the crucial stuff, the things that decided games.

Every chance he got, Fraser had been watching the Leafs and the Kings all series. He'd seen Marty McSorley's hit on Gilmour, the subsequent McSorley-Clark fight, the Gilmour head-butt on McSorley, the incessant elbows and cross-checks from players such as Granato and Jamie Macoun. He'd seen Alexei Zhitnik drill Peter Zezel into the boards with a high hit in Game 3, and Zhitnik rammed head first into the end boards by Sylvain Lefebvre and left uncertain what day it was. He'd seen Rob Blake and Dave Andreychuk working on each other with sticks and elbows in front of the Los Angeles net. If a referee were to strictly enforce the rule book, Blake and Andreychuk would have spent entire games in the penalty box. Other than Gretzky, who at times had not been noticeable, it seemed like no player in the series had been spared along the way. Even LA goalie Kelly Hrudey had been run over by Leafs winger Bill Berg in Game 5.

"Oh, yeah, I was aware what had gone on during the series. If you weren't working, you were watching," says Fraser. "I loved being in that situation. The tougher the game, the better I liked it, I welcomed it, I embraced it. For me, it was all about preparation. Staying calm. I found, if you were over-revved, your emotions could run out of control and nervousness would creep in."

After a breezy day of scattered clouds in LA with temperatures around 20°C, the Thursday night atmosphere at the Great Western Forum was tense as local session musician Warren Wiebe, wearing a white Kings home jersey, sang "America the Beautiful" to the celebrity-filled audience of sixteen thousand. It was yet another sellout for a team that a decade earlier had rarely filled the building.

LA owner Bruce McNall sat against the glass alongside actress Goldie Hawn and her family. He hoped his Kings could survive to play one more game. Canadian hockey fans were already feeling closer to the longed-for historic Leafs-Habs matchup after Montreal had dusted off the New York Islanders in five games. Two of the Habs' four wins had come in overtime, giving them seven straight overtime victories in the postseason. They'd already been home resting for three days, waiting patiently for an opponent and more than happy to put their feet up and watch the Leafs and Kings beat the snot out of each other. *Hockey Night in Canada* wanted an all-Canadian final too, and for obvious reasons. That series would be a ratings bonanza. "The Leafs with a chance to go on to the Stanley Cup final against the Montreal Canadiens. On Tuesday at the Montreal Forum," said *Hockey Night in Canada* play-by-play announcer Bob Cole, as Fraser prepared to drop the puck for the opening faceoff.

The Leafs welcomed back winger Mark Osborne, who had missed Game 5 to be present at the birth of his child. Head coach Pat Burns dressed only five defencemen again. It was becoming an increasing burden for those five. The Kings, on the other hand, went with seven defencemen, dressing veteran Mark Hardy for the first time since Game 1. Several of the LA back-liners, notably Zhitnik, were banged up. Veteran Tim Watters, who'd had two teeth knocked out in Game 5, had spent the day off in a dentist chair getting root canals. "Watters was a noble warrior," says Melrose. "He had played for a long time for a chance to win the Stanley Cup. He wasn't going to miss the game." So both Zhitnik and Watters were out there for Game 6, but Hardy gave the Kings some insurance.

Each club was hoping this would be the game when its top forwards would break out. Clark had been a beast in the series, so Melrose wanted his top defensive pair of Zhitnik and Blake out against him as much as possible. It had worked to some degree. Clark had yet to score a goal. But the fact that he hadn't scored wasn't fooling his cousin Melrose. Melrose knew Clark could break out at any moment. On the day of Game 6, however, Clark's chronic bad back flared up on him, and by game time it had become much worse. If it had been a regular season game, he wouldn't have played. Clark had been dealing with back issues for six years, and in 1987 he had been told he probably should quit the game. Instead, he usually did four hours or more of therapy a day just to be able to play. Sometimes, even that wasn't enough. He skated in the warm-up and felt worse than he had in weeks. But like Watters, there was no chance he wouldn't play in a game in which his team was hoping to make history.

On the other bench, Kings winger Luc Robitaille, who had served as LA captain when Gretzky was out for the first half of the regular season and had enjoyed his most productive season ever with sixty-three goals, had also been struggling to find the net. Robitaille had been barely a rumour, mostly drifting on the periphery. But in Game 5, he had generated his best scoring chances of the series and assisted on a goal by Gary Shuchuk. Maybe he was starting to find his game.

THE LEAFS STARTED THE game with Gilmour between Andreychuk and Glenn Anderson. On their very first shift, LA winger Tomas Sandstrom committed a terrible blind giveaway to Gilmour at the left circle in the Kings zone. Gilmour knocked the puck down with his glove and moved it to

Anderson in the slot. Anderson partially whiffed on a one-timer attempt, but the shot hit Zhitnik's skate and slid under Hrudey's left pad with only fifty-seven seconds elapsed, stunning the Kings and the LA crowd. It was an unimaginably good start for the Leafs.

The visitors almost doubled their lead a few minutes later when another Kings veteran, Dave Taylor, also gave the puck away, this time inside the Toronto zone. That created a two-on-one break for Gilmour and Anderson. Anderson, blowing past a back-checking Gretzky, accepted a pretty feed and was in alone against Hrudey, but he didn't get a hard shot off and the Kings goalie made a stick save. The Forum fans exhaled.

The Leafs had a chance on the power play just past the seven-minute mark when Warren Rychel was sent off for high-sticking, but they couldn't score, leaving their extra-strength unit at an anemic 4 for 29 in the series. It had become a big problem, largely because the six-foot-four Andreychuk was struggling to score. In just thirty-one regular season games with the Leafs after arriving in the trade with Buffalo, Andreychuk had scored twelve power play goals and then another four in the first two rounds of the playoffs. If his magical hands were working, the Leafs power play could be deadly.

Against the Kings, however, he had not scored at all, at even strength or otherwise. His specialty was parking himself near the net to look for deflections and loose pucks, and he would work on those skills endlessly at practice. But the size of the Kings defence, notably Blake and McSorley, had rendered him less effective. Normally, Andreychuk had a physical advantage over most NHL defencemen, but not in this series. It seemed like every time he went to the net, Blake or McSorley was standing in the way, and it was difficult to score with Blake wrapping you in a headlock or McSorley cross-checking you in the neck.

Diminutive Russian winger Nikolai Borschevsky, who had joined the Leafs as a twenty-seven-year-old rookie that season, had also been a key power play contributor. He'd scored thirty-four goals in the regular season, twelve of them on the power play. In the first game of the playoffs, he had collided with Vladimir Konstantinov of the Red Wings and suffered a broken orbital bone below his right eye. He'd missed a few games but was back for Game 7 and he tipped home Bob Rouse's point shot in overtime to end the series. It was a dramatic goal that ranked with Lanny McDonald's overtime winner against the New York Islanders fifteen years earlier as postseason highlights for the Leafs during the team's long Stanley Cup drought.

Since that historic moment, however, Borschevsky had been silenced. He looked wary, almost timid. The orbital bone injury had been a severe one, which might have made him shy of contact, and these playoffs had been more vicious than anything he'd experienced before. In the series against the hard-hitting Kings, he had gone from ineffective to rarely used. With Andreychuk and Borschevsky both unproductive, the power play had become a liability for the Leafs. In Game 3, they had surrendered two goals to the Kings with LA short-handed.

The Leafs still had a 1–0 lead. But *Hockey Night in Canada* analyst Harry Neale detected one promising development for the home team, something that would have worried Leafs fans. "In my opinion, Gretzky is moving better tonight than in any of the previous five games," said Neale, who noticed Melrose was double-shifting Gretzky early in the game. "He's taken quite a bit of abuse in the LA press for his lack of productivity.

If Wayne Gretzky ever comes up with a vintage performance, it's either because he's nearing a record or has something to prove. Maybe tonight."

Right from the start it was clear the game was going to be a challenge for any referee to call, particularly with the style of play in the NHL at that time, filled with interference, hooking and holding. "There were only so many things the hierarchy wanted called, especially in the playoffs, when everything was ramped up," Fraser says now. "You wanted to provide an entertaining flow. Successful referees were the ones who could get the players to play on their terms without actually having to put the hammer down and call so many penalties. That was our objective." Game 5, particularly the third period and overtime, had at times resembled a football game with players being tackled around the opposition net, and it seemed likely Game 6 would be similar. The challenge for Fraser, or any referee under that style of officiating, was to be able—and willing—to make an important late call if necessary after letting so much go earlier in the game.

LA tied the game at 10:32 of the first period on a goal that should have been disallowed. During a delayed penalty call on Rouse for hauling down LA forward Mike Donnelly, Kings rookie defenceman Darryl Sydor found himself behind the Leafs net with the puck. He tried to centre it, but the puck hit his teammate Corey Millen, who was falling to the ice. The puck bounced back to Sydor, who again tried to get the puck to the front of the net. At the same moment, Granato, a thorn in Toronto's side all series, drove directly towards the net from the slot. "I was small. I was somebody who had to play bigger and act bigger and tougher than I really was," says Granato.

"That was part of why I was able to play and able to have some success." He drove his shoulder into Rouse, then fell into Potvin at the precise moment Sydor's centring effort was getting into the blue paint of the goal crease. The Leafs goalie was kneeling on his goal line when Granato crashed into him, and the puck crossed the goal line. Fraser called it a goal, and then the play went to replay review.

The Forum didn't have a traditional hockey press box. The media occupied about a dozen rows halfway up the darkened stands, as did league officials. The replay review officials were essentially stationed in the middle of the crowd with access to two monitors. They were at the mercy of whatever replays the television broadcaster could provide. At times, home broadcasters would even deny access to incriminating footage of their team simply by saying they couldn't find it. In the case of the Granato play, the two league officials looked at the play and also ruled it was a good goal. Maybe that's what they saw. Maybe that's all they could see in the dark. Maybe that's what their interpretation was in the middle of a raucous, impatient LA crowd. The game was tied, and the Kings had benefited from what would be the first in a long list of controversial calls. The Leafs and their fans were right to feel the call had been wrong and the review unjust. The best they could hope for, like all teams, was that the calls would even out. Either way, it was 1–1.

As the series had worn on, Blake had become an increasingly significant presence. Of the three young Kings defencemen, Sydor and Zhitnik were very effective, but Blake, a fourth year player, stood out as a tower of strength, particularly in a physical way. In Game 6, he made big hits all over the ice, some legal, some not so legal, some during the play, some after the whistle. It was the beginning of a Hall of Fame career that would see him win the Norris Trophy five years later, and he was clearly not intimidated in any way by the challenges and pressures of the Stanley Cup playoffs. The three young LA blueliners had gone on the road in the playoffs to hockey-mad Canadian cities, first Calgary, then Vancouver and then Toronto. By Game 6, they weren't kids anymore. They'd proven to themselves they could perform on the big stages of the sport. "Had we got Toronto in the first round, it might have been a different lot of younger guys," says Gretzky. "By the time we got to the third round, they'd lost that deer-in-the-headlights look."

The final minutes of the first period got a bit crazy. Potvin made a spectacular save on Rychel. Gilmour was flattened into the side boards by Shuchuk and responded by charging across the ice to hit the LA forward. Shuchuk had shown a willingness to make Gilmour pay a price and distract him, as Granato, Rychel and McSorley had done earlier in the series. The hits on Gilmour just kept on coming.

Rouse, a player who played a more physical brand of hockey in the postseason when the stakes were higher, went off with McSorley for roughing at 18:39. But with ten seconds remaining before intermission, Blake made another big play. Berg and Macoun found themselves on a two-on-one break against the LA defenceman with a chance to give the Leafs the lead again. Blake waited and waited, then executed a perfect sweep-check, knocking the puck to safety. "Blake was unbelievable," Melrose says. "He really came into his own."

The Kings outshot the Leafs 13–8 in the first period, but then ran head first into the freight train they'd managed to dodge for five games: Wendel Clark. He finally scored his first goal of the series. Leafs defenceman Dave Ellett just chipped the puck out to centre to clear the zone. Toronto forward Mike Krushelnyski got his stick on it and banged the puck to teammate Mike Foligno, who stretched and directed the puck forward into the Kings zone down the middle of the ice.

Clark took over from there. It was a foot race between him and LA defenceman Charlie Huddy, and Clark had more speed. He got to the puck first, and with Huddy harassing him from his left, the left-shooting Clark used his leg to shield the puck while he moved it to his backhand, not his preferred offensive weapon. He had a big slapshot and a terrific wrist shot that could bruise an NHL goalie or beat him from forty feet, but the Leafs captain hardly even practised his backhand. Huddy dove to dislodge the puck at the last moment but couldn't reach around Clark's body as the Leafs captain steadied himself, then lifted a backhand over Hrudey's glove at 3:57 of the second. The Leafs were ahead again, and their gritty captain was finally on the scoreboard. With a 3–2 series edge and the lead in Game 6, that date with Montreal the following Tuesday beckoned.

But instead of inspiring the visitors, Clark's goal seemed to make them sag. Even worse, their veterans started making bad decisions. Just as it seemed Fraser had tucked his whistle away for good, he started sending a parade of Leafs to the penalty box, and in quick succession three LA power play goals were on the board. The Kings, and their stars, demonstrated to the Leafs what a crucial element an opportunistic power play could be in a tense playoff series.

It all started with Blake getting behind Macoun to accept a perfect lead pass from Gretzky for a breakaway on Potvin.

At the last second, Macoun dove. He might have got a piece of the puck, but he certainly took Blake's legs out from under him. Fraser's arm, however, stayed down. At the least, it should have been a penalty, and quite probably a penalty shot. But the veteran referee was unmoved despite the outrage of the Kings and their fans. Chants of "Fraser sucks! Fraser sucks!" filled the Fabulous Forum.

Soon after, Foligno was whistled for interfering with Taylor, and the LA power play pounced. Robitaille moved the puck to Sandstrom behind the goal line. Sandstrom spun and put a perfect pass onto McSorley's stick in the slot. The big blueliner had managed to sneak in unnoticed from the point—Gilmour was the nearest Leaf—and he pounded home a high shot in one motion to tie the game 2–2. The Forum no longer felt that "Fraser sucks."

Macoun took a stupid slashing penalty at 10:05 when he retaliated after being bumped by Rychel. Just seventeen seconds later, Sydor swiped at the puck from forty-five feet along the boards, producing a fluttering, dipping shot. Potvin saw it all the way but missed it, a rare bad goal for the young netminder in the '93 playoffs.

Five minutes after that, it was Foligno taking another retaliation penalty, this time for whacking Shuchuk across the back of the helmet after a hard hit against the boards. LA had a third straight power play. Potvin made several huge saves, keeping the Leafs close, including one on a rising Kurri blast. But at 16:27, the pressure paid off, and this time it was Robitaille finally finding the net.

Robitaille been a King since the 1986–87 season, when he, Jimmy Carson and defenceman Steve Duchesne had taken Los

Angeles by storm with impressive rookie seasons in the year Pat Quinn started the season as LA's head coach and Mike Murphy, now the Leafs assistant, finished it. Robitaille, like Clark with the Leafs, had stayed through all the changes. He'd been extremely important to the Kings that season, particularly in the first half, when Gretzky was out. "We learned not just to count on Wayne all the time," says Robitaille. "We learned to play as a team. We had to survive without Wayne for half the season."

Robitaille's relationship with Melrose during the season had at times been contentious. Back on March 28, the Kings were leading a game at Winnipeg in the third period until Jets centre Alexei Zhamnov tied it late. Afterwards, LA media reported an audible shouting match between Melrose and Robitaille from inside the visitors dressing room that could be heard in the halls of the Winnipeg Arena. "You're a selfish player," said Melrose. "No, I'm not," said Robitaille. "You are too!" shouted Melrose.

Melrose later played down the incident to reporters, saying he and Robitaille were "discussing fishing spots in Northern Quebec." Today, he admits it was a nasty fight, one that surprised even Cap Raeder, his assistant coach. "Cap said, 'Wow, haven't heard one like that in a while,'" says Melrose. "I demanded a lot from Luc. He was a leader, and I needed more from him. That's what happened. I challenged him to be a better leader. It got pretty heated. But it was never mentioned after. If you have the right type of relationship with players, you can do something like that." Robitaille had never had a coach he could argue back and forth with. "He let me vent. He had a little smirk on his face while I was doing it," recalls Robitaille. "I think Barry liked it. He wanted guys to stand up for themselves. He wanted guys to fight for the right to play."

It had taken Robitaille more than five games against the Leafs to do what he did best: score. But he finally did. The play started with Zezel in control of the puck in the Toronto zone, but he couldn't clear it past Blake at right point. The LA defenceman hammered a shot towards the net that hit Robitaille in the hip and dropped right at his feet. In one quick motion, the high-scoring winger dunked his first of the series into the open side. For Robitaille, the goal was a massive relief, and LA had suddenly opened a two-goal lead, 4–2. LA was destroying Toronto with its extra-strength unit. The Forum crowd had been waiting for Robitaille to get involved, and it exploded with joy when he finally did.

Game 6 was turning out to be a classic—wild and very physical, with lead changes, great goaltending and big goals— and the Inglewood crowd was loving every minute. All the storylines first introduced in Game 1 were now being brought to a boil like sap from a Canadian maple. It was not a game for the faint of heart. With five seconds left in the second period, Granato cruised across the ice and hit Krushelnyski square in the numbers, sending the Leafs forward headfirst into the boards. Granato received a minor penalty. He didn't care that it was a dirty play. "I didn't worry about what people thought of me. I knew if they liked me, I probably wasn't doing my job or what I was supposed to do. I'm not proud of the fact some of the things I had to do weren't some of the nicest things, but that's what my job was." The Kings took their two-goal lead to the dressing room for the second intermission.

By the start of the third period, Gretzky had still not been a major presence on seventeen shifts, skating fourteen minutes and fifteen seconds of playing time. Sure, the Kings were winning, but what was he waiting for? He almost seemed to be holding back. Gretzky says the broken rib was annoying but it wasn't hindering his game. He just couldn't find the openings. He was, however, a master at biding his time. "In Edmonton, John Muckler used to say to me all the time in the playoffs, 'Gretz, we'd love you to get three or four goals, but we need you to get big goals. We need a big goal, we need a big play. That's what we need out of you,'" recalls Gretzky. "Guys like Gordie Howe did that, and Bobby Orr. I always remembered that when I played."

The Leafs fought back in the third, forcing Hrudey to make a brilliant diving glove save on Anderson, and then an acrobatic left foot save on Foligno. Still two goals behind. Clark, a stone-faced, smoldering presence all series, was the player the Leafs were looking to, the player who could pounce on the right counterattack opportunity. For years, when he was healthy enough to do it, he had always been a player who could lift the Leafs, even when they were awful. He was more than willing to take the lead. He didn't need to wait for others.

At 11:08 of the third period, the Leafs captain got his second goal of the night to cut the Los Angeles lead to 4–3. Clark took a lead pass from Rouse. With only McSorley between him and Hrudey, Clark cut inside and snapped a hard, low rocket past Hrudey's left foot from thirty feet, using that glorious, penetrating wrist shot that was the envy of NHL forwards. Hrudey was at least ten feet out at the top of his crease, and still he couldn't handle the velocity of the shot. "Our best player was Wendel Clark," says Anderson. "It was like he was shot out of a cannon. He did it all."

The Kings, still leading by a goal, tried desperately to add another as insurance. Gretzky and Sandstrom had a two-on-one break but couldn't connect. Gretzky, starting to make more of an impact, then set up Granato with a perfect lead pass with less than two minutes to go in regulation. Granato beat Ellett to the outside, but Ellett turned and hauled him down with a hook to the chest. No call from Fraser. The Leafs had got away with one. The Kings weren't at the finish line yet.

Toronto roared the other way, and Potvin charged out of his net to the Leafs bench. Leafs defenceman Todd Gill moved the puck to Gilmour in the corner to the right of Hrudey. Millions watched as the Leafs' most skilled player cradled the puck and surveyed the possibilities. All eyes were on him. The Kings were drawn to him magnetically, desperate to smother this final threat. Then, out of nowhere, their worst nightmare materialized. They were watching the wrong Leaf. When Potvin had arrived at the Leafs bench, Clark had vaulted over the boards. Now he was roaring down the ice and into the LA zone. Unmarked.

Gilmour saucered a slick pass into the slot, with the puck landing perfectly flat. The kind of pass great playmakers make. Clark took the pass and in one motion ripped another of his patented wrist shots. The puck rose in a straight line over Hrudey's catching glove and into the top of the net to tie the game with 1:21 remaining.

The crowd, on its feet thinking victory was at hand, was silenced. Players on the Leafs bench jumped up and down, pounding each other on the back. It was Clark's third goal of the game. It was one man against the Kings, and now the contest was deadlocked. It also may have been the greatest game of Clark's career. "The puck just seemed to follow me that game," he says. "That must be what Wayne feels like every night!"

It seemed all those bad penalties in the second, that terrible penalty killing and the punchless power play, weren't going to stop the Leafs after all. But as the clock ticked down, Blake was fighting with Gilmour for the puck behind the LA net. As Blake turned, Anderson charged in and hit the LA rearguard squarely in the back with his right shoulder, knocking him headfirst into the boards. The Kings defenceman lay on the ice for several moments. It was similar to the hit on Krushelnyski that Granato had been penalized for in the second period. But everyone knew that what was a penalty in the second wasn't usually a penalty in the third.

And yet it was. Fraser called Anderson for boarding. "Never should have been called," says Clark. "[Blake] got up." There were just twelve seconds left in regulation time, which meant the Kings would have 1:48 of power play at the start of over-time. Anderson had a reputation for being reckless, usually with his stick. He was famous for his "excuse me" slashes after being hit. But he insists he just "bumped" Blake and that the defence-man took a dive. "He totally embellished it," says Anderson. "I barely touched him. With twelve seconds to go in the game? Are you kidding me? With how that series had gone and the way the game was played back then?" He was wrong in that it was more than a bump. He hit Blake hard, and dangerously. But in terms of how penalties were assessed in the NHL at that time, he wasn't wrong. Players in this very series had got away with worse. The emotion for the Leafs was similar to Game 1, when they won the game but saw McSorley alter the atmo-sphere with his hit on Gilmour. This time, Clark's heroics had pumped up the Leafs, only for the team to find they would start overtime short-handed.

Then, in the first minute of overtime, came The Call.

As overtime started, Zhitnik shot the puck into the Leafs zone, and Gretzky snared it in the corner. He worked his way back up the boards, absorbed a two-handed slash to the hands from Macoun and moved the puck back to Blake at the right point.

Fraser was positioned on the far side of the ice. Blake returned the puck to Number 99 just above the hash marks along the right boards. Gretzky waited, and when Gilmour, the nearest penalty killer, didn't move towards him, he stepped towards the net, wound up and fired a slapshot. The puck hit Macoun in the leg and bounced directly to Gilmour. The two stars, Gretzky and Gilmour, converged on the puck. As the Leafs centre leaned over to play it, Gretzky tried to lift his stick and instead pitchforked Gilmour on the chin with a barely detectable flick of his stick. With thirty-seven seconds elapsed in overtime, Gilmour fell to the ice like he'd been shot.

It had all happened so quickly. Gretzky's shot, Macoun's block, the bouncing puck, the flick of the stick by the quickest hands ever to play the sport.

Fraser had a clean line of sight on the play but appeared to be either looking at the net or searching for the puck. From where he was standing, the net was at eleven o'clock, Gilmour was at one o'clock. "I did not see it. If I didn't see something, I didn't want to guess. But something didn't smell right. It's just an instinct you develop," Fraser says.

Gilmour was cut. He wasn't spurting blood, but he was cut on the chin. "When I went to Gilmour, I said, 'Doug, tell me what happened?' He said, 'Wayne shot the puck and the follow-through hit me in the chin.' I said, 'That's not a penalty, then.' He said, 'Okay.'" Following through on your shot and hitting an opponent was not a penalty. But it had all happened so quickly even Gilmour didn't have it right. It hadn't been Gretzky's follow-through. Television replays clearly showed he had jabbed Gilmour's chin with his stick when both were reaching for the loose puck.

Gretzky sheepishly circled far away from the referee, which seemed suspicious to Fraser, who was used to Gretzky trying to argue calls. "He always wanted to sell or tell," says Fraser. Gretzky knew what he'd done, but obviously confessing was out of the question. Fraser called the linesmen together to confer. Millions watching on TV knew what had happened even if the referee didn't. "Wouldn't this be something if Gretzky was thrown out for a high stick!" said Neale on the *Hockey Night in Canada* broadcast.

It wasn't just up to Fraser. Either Collins or Finn could have called a penalty. Linesmen had that power, but they also knew that if they did report that they'd seen a high stick, Gretzky would be booted out of the game. You couldn't blame an official for not wanting to be part of that ugly scene. "Neither linesman was sure. So I had to eat it," says Fraser. Three officials on the ice, and not one of them saw the high stick? It seemed dubious. "Clearly, as the replays showed, Gretzky should have been penalized," says Fraser. "There's nothing worse, believe me, than the helplessness of feeling something happened and you didn't see it."

Clark argued briefly with Fraser. But the Leafs captain had never been one for long-drawn-out beef sessions. He'd say his piece then accept the verdict with the stoicism of a farmer. He knew there was no changing Fraser's mind. The game went on.

With less than ten seconds left in the power play, the visitors had defended effectively, not giving up a chance. It looked like the Anderson penalty would expire and the two clubs would get back to playing at even strength. But then Rouse, Zezel and Ellett all ventured below the goal line behind Potvin to battle for the puck with Robitaille and Sandstrom. Three Leafs, two Kings.

The odds were on the visitors coming up with the puck. But it was Robitaille who burst out of the pack with possession. He circled out and looked for a teammate. Gretzky had started at the far boards, waiting for the right moment, staying away from the play, drawing no attention. It was his David Copperfield moment. He'd scored 871 goals in the NHL to that point, including regular season and playoff competition. He'd won nine Hart Trophies as league MVP. Yet somehow he'd managed to make himself disappear in overtime of an elimination Stanley Cup playoff game.

Gretzky waited until Robitaille circled out of the corner with the puck before breaking for the net. Berg, the fourth Leafs penalty killer and one of Toronto's most conscientious forwards, didn't notice him, and he also didn't shift down closer to his own net to protect against a goalmouth pass. Why would he? He didn't think a Kings player was around.

Gretzky slid into the open spot by the Leafs post unchecked. Robitaille's pass was perfect, and Gretzky redirected it in one motion. The puck headed towards the middle of the net and hit Potvin's right knee, but then it bounced high into the net at 1:41 of overtime. In a wild, controversial finish, the Kings had a 5–4 victory, and the series was going back to Toronto for Game 7.

The Call quickly became the focal point of the game and the series. Leafs fans felt they'd been robbed, that Gretzky had got away with the flagrant high stick just because he was

Gretzky. The postgame scene was chaotic. Both teams quickly began to pack their gear and prepare to head back to Toronto.

Celebrities milled about. Cindy Melrose, Barry's wife, carried a sign in the hallway between the two dressing rooms—just forty feet apart—that read KINGS CHEER WHILE CHERRY WINES and noisily taunted *Hockey Night in Canada* personality Don Cherry for his pointed criticisms of her husband. She'd become a regular on a popular LA morning radio show during the playoffs and wasn't afraid to make her opinions known. Loudly. "She was a cheerleader for the Cincinnati Stingers when I first met her back in 1978," recalls Melrose. "She's no shrinking violet."

In the Leafs dressing room, things were a little ugly. "A lot of the guys looked like they were down and out. Things were said that pissed me off, things that, to be a championship team, you just don't say," Anderson says. "It would have never happened in a different room. It was just guys frustrated. Maybe they didn't play as much as they wanted to. But the timing was wrong in my opinion." The veteran winger felt some of his teammates were pointing the finger at him for his penalty late in regulation. "I know they were blaming me. They were looking for an excuse," he says. "I just kind of let it slide. I didn't want to stand up and say, 'Shut the fuck up and get ready for the next game.' The game was over."

Anderson's penalty had been a major mistake, and it had cost the Leafs. At the same time, he had been one of the best Leafs forwards all series. And he was right: good teams pick up their teammates when mistakes are made. If the goalie whiffs on one, it is up to his teammates to pick him up. That's the mentality good teams have to have. The problem was the Leafs had only been a good team for a matter of months. They didn't have the scar tissue from years of being in the heat of playoff competition. "We should have been oozing with confidence because we'd already won two Game 7s in the playoffs," says Anderson. "One penalty should not be able to beat you."

Referee-in-chief Bryan Lewis went in to confer with Fraser, Finn and Collins afterwards. "He shook our hands and said, 'Good job, boys,'" says Fraser. "He told us there was a report that *Hockey Night in Canada* may have a replay showing that Gretzky high-sticked Gilmour. We explained our perspective. I hadn't seen it, the two linesmen couldn't help. And I told him what Gilmour had said, that it was a follow-through of the shot."

The next day, Fraser flew back home to southern New Jersey, and called his father, who for years had recorded all the NHL games his son officiated. "My dad said, 'Well, we had a little excitement here last night,'" says Fraser. His father had fallen asleep in his favourite chair, and at about 3:30 A.M. had woken to a commotion outside. He had a little motor home parked out back, and he looked out the window to see a car ramming into the trailer hitch of the vehicle. The car then backed up and rammed the motor home again.

Dressed only in his underwear, Hilt Fraser whipped open the patio door, grabbed an axe he had at the back door for splitting wood and chased the car down the street, delivering a few solid blows before the car drove off into the night. On hearing his father's story, Fraser called NHL security, and a few days later he got a call from league security boss Al Wiseman. "They'd found the car in a body shop in Kitchener [Ontario] getting repairs for damage from an axe," he says. "They questioned the man. He was a Leafs fan from Kitchener, and he was pissed off at my call and had gone to my hometown looking for my family home."

It didn't stop there. Fraser's mother, Barbara, kept getting obscene phone calls from irate Leafs fans. "My mom was probably tougher than my dad. She was a real hockey mom," says Fraser. "So I gave her one of my whistles, and like a good hockey mom, she tied it onto a skate lace and hung it on a hook by the phone. As soon as an obscene phone call came in, she had the whistle, and she would blast it into the phone. So the obscene phone calls stopped." Almost two decades later, long after Hilton Fraser had passed, Barbara began to suffer from dementia and moved into a senior's residence. When her sons went to clean up the family home so it could be sold, they saw some things remained unchanged. "By the phone in the house, the whistle was still on the skate lace," says Fraser.

A QUARTER CENTURY LATER, the Call is still being hotly debated. Members of the Kings dismiss it as meaningless, certainly not the moment that decided anything. "Yes, Gretzky high-sticked Gilmour," says Hrudey. "But so what? To me, it was a non-issue. They still had Game 7 at home." McSorley points to all the other calls that weren't made in the game, like Blake being hauled down by Macoun on a partial breakaway. "When it was all over, there had been seven games, and we could talk about several instances that could have changed the series," he says. "Gilmour head-butted me. No call. With that [Gretzky] high stick, people in Toronto are not looking at anything in context."

Gilmour doesn't blame Fraser. "I don't think Kerry saw it. I think one of the linesmen did. All they had to do was say to

Kerry, 'Say you saw it,' and give him two minutes, or a double minor. Otherwise, the way the rules were in those days, if the linesman called it, he would have been out of the game," says Gilmour, who needed eight stitches to close his cut that night. "At the time, it was heated. People still talk about it. But do I have any remorse or regret? No. Who wants that job of being a referee? And look, I wasn't a clean player. You know that. I'd cut your eye out if I was playing against you."

The truth is that it was a crazy, wild, entertaining, nasty game. A game people still talk about, still agonize over. Still get angry over. A number of obvious fouls in the game weren't called, many of them committed by the Leafs, including one by Ellett on Granato that allowed Clark to tie the game. It really was a night of a thousand crimes, and a few were called. The Call, however, occupies a central place in Leafs mythology. If Fraser had made the right decision, Gretzky would have been in the Kings dressing room and never would have been on the ice to score the winning goal. That's just a fact. A high stick that drew blood wasn't a subjective call, like tripping, boarding or holding. If detected, it was an automatic penalty. In this case, the Leafs would have been on the power play, with a chance to win the game and advance to play Montreal in the Stanley Cup final.

So The Call cuts right to the core of being a Leafs fan, and being a fan in general, that belief you carry in your heart at the beginning of every season that this is going to be a good one. It's not based on logic. It's based on emotion. To some, the emotion of that moment is as powerful as when your first child is born, or seeing that child walk down the aisle one day. For Leafs fans, their team, such a doormat for so long, was tantalizingly close to getting to play for the Cup again. You couldn't blame them for feeling aggrieved, for feeling that a terrible injustice had been done. You still can't.

From a more detached point of view, The Call didn't decide the series. Fraser didn't miss it out of mendacity. He just missed it, like Bill Buckner booted the ball in the '86 World Series. Like Steve Smith put the puck in his own net. Like Jim Marshall ran the wrong way. Fraser whiffed. He missed the call and burned the biggest fan base of any team in hockey. That made the error seem so much worse. Still, the Leafs lost Game 6 because they took thoughtless penalties, and the LA power play scored four times. In losing Game 6, they didn't lose the series. That's also a fact.

Clark delivered a heroic performance, and he'd done it while gritting his teeth through awful back pain. "You could probably say it was one of the best games of my career if we had won," says Clark. "But we didn't, so it didn't matter." Potvin made brilliant saves, but so did Hrudey, and the Kings got more from more players. Robitaille finally scored, and he set up Gretzky for the game-winning goal. Gretzky finally made a big play. LA didn't win because of an edge in play or technical superiority but through the will and personalities of a group of individually great players. On a chaotic night, they handled the chaos just a little better. The talents of two future Hall-of-Famers, Gretzky and Robitaille, shone through, although neither had played particularly well in the series. How could Gretzky have been left alone to win the game? That was part of his genius. In a violent sport filled with violent men, he never seemed to get hit. And when it was time to make the difference, it was as though he had his own cloaking device.

Fraser, for his part, doesn't mind chatting about the Call, telling his side of the story. That's good, because he's been reminded of it constantly ever since by media and hockey fans. That incident, and his hair, are his NHL legacy even more than the record number of NHL games he officiated. When he announced in 2017 that he had cancer, many of the media reports noted he was best known for the non-call on Gretzky in '93. "Hey, I'm part of hockey history, and a big part of Leafs history," he says. "I'm a big boy. I wear big boy pants. It was the worst call that I never made, one that I would want back."

Fraser had faced harsh criticism many times. He remembers a checking-from-behind call he made on Calgary's Mark Hunter for a hit on Montreal's Shayne Corson in Game 5 of the 1989 Stanley Cup final that led to the winning goal by the Canadiens. "It had to be a penalty. Otherwise, I might as well go into the dressing room and watch the game on TV," he says. "I got ridiculed by the media, by Don Cherry. But my MO was that I wasn't afraid to make the tough call." In this case, however, it was a call he hadn't made, and it was easy for his critics to read a lack of courage into his decision. Unfair, but easy.

It's not as if he was a lousy ref. He was one of the best in NHL history. In a 2005 poll, Fraser was named the NHL's most consistent referee. Some fans saw him as a pretty boy with pretty hair who had never felt the pointy end of an elbow to the face, but the truth was Fraser was a hockey man from a hardnosed hockey family. Nobody pushed Hilt Fraser's kid around. He understood the game and its roots, respected the tough guys, understood the traditions and the history of the game, loved the personalities of the sport and wasn't reluctant to be one himself. Yet there are still some, mostly Leafs fans, who believe it came down to fear, that Fraser was afraid to make the tough call on Gretzky, afraid to give one of hockey's greatest players a penalty at such a critical moment of an elimination playoff game. A generation later, people remember the game and definitely remember the referee.

Fraser blames himself for not seeing Gretzky's high stick. "I replayed it and replayed it, over and over. I should've moved my feet better," he says. "I think I stayed focused on Macoun when he blocked the shot and didn't refocus back to where the puck went. It happened so quickly. But even Killer didn't fully understand what had happened. He got it as wrong as I did."

ACT SEVEN

Even now, the crowds are there. The expectations and the crowds. It's more than forty years, maybe even forty-five, since they first started to gather. Wayne Gretzky never chose the crowds any more than he chose to have sublime mental and physical talents that made him perfect to play the sport of hockey. He accepted both, one a blessing, the other a duty. He instinctively understands what others want from him and has almost always delivered. So there have never been stories out there about Gretzky snubbing a kid, or behaving badly in public, or sticking a hand in a cameraman's lens. He sees dealing with his public as his responsibility, almost like a royal. He gives back to the game. He doesn't complain, at least not within earshot of anyone but family and close confidantes. He always says the right thing. The one time he didn't, thirty years ago, when he called the New Jersey Devils a "Mickey Mouse organization," it followed him like a bad smell for years. He has never made that mistake again. The next time he created a storm of controversy with his public remarks, at the 2002 Winter Olympics when he cited "American propaganda" and said the hockey world "hates Canada," it was an intentional effort designed to divert attention from the troubles of the Team Canada squad he had put together as executive director.

When Gretzky arrives, he does so quietly. Bobby Orr can light up a room, make everyone feel special with his jokes and smiles and back slaps. You know he's there. Gretzky is just Gretzky. Unassuming. If he picks you out in a crowd, steps away from a press conference and walks over and asks you a personal question or gives you a snippet of his insight, it feels more like he's being considerate, bringing you into his confidence, his circle. He's always been just as comfortable stepping back and observing while somebody else is speaking. He'll always wait his turn. He accepts the spotlight and the crowds, but has never seemed to need either.

But these crowds he's anticipating are different. This week, he's outside his element. He's a golfer at one of the world's most famous courses, Pebble Beach, in California. The crowds haven't come to see him. Not exactly. But a crowd is a crowd, right? And in golf, you can't get lost within a team. When you step to the tee, the focus is on you. This is the prestigious AT&T Pebble Beach Pro-Am, an event that attracts the stars of the PGA and celebrities from all walks of life, and he's playing alongside his famous son-in-law Dustin Johnson, who is married to his oldest daughter, Paulina. Gretzky's a better than average golfer. His drives still require a walk of 250 yards or more before hitting his second on a good day. That leaves him just 100 yards behind Johnson. "The crowds are hard for me, because first of all, I'm not that great. The expectation of people is because you're an athlete, you're supposed to be a really good player," he says. "That makes it tough. But I've played enough with Dustin that I know if I hit a bad shot, or if I'm out of the hole, I can pick up my ball. It's not going to affect anything for him. I know, no matter what I do out there, it's not going to affect what he does or how he plays." These crowds are even bigger than usual, as the Gretzky-Johnson tandem is paired with Jordan Spieth and country music star Jake Owen. You want pressure? Try being one of the greatest hockey players of all time standing on the tee at number 8 at Pebble Beach, with the waves of the Pacific Ocean crashing into the spectacular jagged rocks on your right, just begging you to lash your drive there, as three or four thousand people watch along with your pro golfer son-in-law. That's pressure. "I'm a legitimate twelve or thirteen handicap, so I can hit some good shots, I can hit some bad shots," says Gretzky. "But Owen is a two handicap, so I'm the fourth best player in the group. We've played enough times you learn to battle through it." You get the sense that after being the best, Gretzky doesn't mind being less than that. Just one of the guys. It would be perfect if it were just the guys. No crowds. But duty calls.

Golf is his game now, although he dabbles in tennis with his youngest daughter, fourteen-year-old Emma. She's an aspiring young player who is coached by former Canadian Davis Cup team member Philip Bester. But it's mostly golf he plays, and definitely never hockey, which can make the old back woes roar to life again. He admires his son-in-law's deep love for the sport. "He really has a passion for it, you know? The year he lost in the U.S. Open in Seattle [2015], when he missed that putt to win, we were all going to Idaho as a family for a while," Gretzky says. "They came for three weeks, and he played golf every single day for twenty-one days. You either have it in you,

you either love it, or you don't. I couldn't imagine losing Game 7 of the Stanley Cup final and getting up the next day and playing shinny hockey with a bunch of buddies. Just couldn't have done it. But he played every day for twenty-one straight days." Maybe he couldn't imagine losing a Game 7. He could certainly imagine that kind of dedication to a sport. That was him a long, long time ago.

It's 2018, and twenty-five winters have passed since the last major peak in his career, the 1993 Stanley Cup playoffs with the Los Angeles Kings. Most of those winters have been spent under the palm trees enjoying the warm temperatures of La-La Land, very different from his early days in Brantford, when he would be the one spending hour after hour, day after day, learning to play hockey in frigid temperatures on a backyard rink, dedicating himself to the pursuit of excellence in his sport.

Hockey, at least as a player, exists in his past, not his present. But he loves being a time traveller. He gets asked about many of his exploits in the game, including that series against the Maple Leafs in the '93 Clarence Campbell Conference final. He never seems to tire of the stories, either his own or those of the players and coaches he played with. His memory is excellent, and he tells the stories with gusto, not as if by rote. He's got opinions, some strong ones, but never speaks ill of the game. He particularly enjoys telling stories that give credit to others. Like Orr, and the late Gordie Howe, there's always a humbleness about him, an absence of the kind of ego you might expect and accept from an athlete who scaled the heights Gretzky did.

Gretzky chats for an hour about the Leafs series, then texts a couple of other memories, then calls back to add a little more. He talks enthusiastically about what it was like to play at Maple

Leaf Gardens, where he'd first gone as a six-year-old with his grandmother. It was a twenty-six-year journey from that point to Game 7 against the Leafs, about the same amount of time that has elapsed since. Draw a timeline of Gretzky's extraordinary life in hockey, and Game 7 against the Leafs at the Gardens comes almost smack dab in the middle. "I remember Game 7 from the night before to the morning of," he says. "I remember everything about it."

IT WAS CLOSING NIGHT. All the main characters had assembled for the dramatic conclusion of the series between the Leafs and Kings. If it was an Agatha Christie novel, Hercule Poirot would have been there, prepared to name the murderer. No matter how good the overall performance would be, and it would surely have to be something to top the previous game, this was closing night. All that was known for sure was it had to come to an end, one way or another.

Bruce McNall sat up high in what passed for a "luxury" suite at aging Maple Leaf Gardens, close to the spotlight he craved, joined by Hollywood celebrities John Candy, Peter Guber, Goldie Hawn and Kurt Russell. McNall had become a Kings fan in the 1970s when nobody else had been, and now he was on the verge of getting to the Stanley Cup final as owner of the team. For a few hours, none of the things that had happened in between mattered. Not on closing night.

He could just cheer for the Kings.

His Leafs counterpart, Steve Stavro, was there in the directors box behind the penalty benches with his key lieutenants. Stavro thought of himself as a great Canadian, and here he was,

running the Leafs as they attempted to return to the Cup final
for the first time since 1967. The Greek immigrant had made
it to the inner sanctum of Toronto the Good. Cliff Fletcher,
the man Stavro wanted to fire, who had orchestrated the building of this Toronto team, was in the press box. He'd brought in
Doug Gilmour and Pat Burns, both of whom had been front
and centre in the series since Game 1, since Gilmour got
whacked by Marty McSorley, and since Burns had charged
across the aisle to get at LA coach Barry Melrose. Kelly Hrudey
and Felix Potvin, goalies from different generations, were again
set to backstop their respective teams. Hrudey's mid-season
problems were all behind him. He'd been just a bit better than
Potvin in Game 6.

Bill Berg and his mates on the Leafs checking line, Peter
Zezel and Mark Osborne, were prepared to try and shut down
the star-studded LA attack for one more game. Burns might
not have known Berg at all just a few months earlier, but now
he was a key Leaf. McSorley, his black jersey so oversized it
looked like it should belong to a three-hundred-pound man,
prowled around the Gardens ice, itching to get going.

Then there was Gretzky. All but silent for five games, he
had scored the winning goal in overtime of Game 6 on a perfect pass from Luc Robitaille. He seemed to be finding openings that hadn't been available to him earlier in the series.
Number 99 hadn't been in a Cup final since leaving Edmonton
five years earlier, since scoring the Cup-winning goal at 9:44
of the second period at Northlands Coliseum to sweep the
Boston Bruins four straight. The Oilers had won without him
in 1990, and now this was his chance to show he could win
without the Oilers.

A few blocks away from the Gardens, the acclaimed musi-cal *Miss Saigon* had opened a few days earlier at the new Princess of Wales Theatre on King Street to the largest box office advance in Canadian theatrical history. But there was only one show in town this night. "I remember going out for warm-up in Game 7 and thinking, This is one of those events that is going to be big in the history of the NHL," says LA winger Mike Donnelly.

It was the seventieth Game 7 contest in NHL playoff his-tory, but curiously only the fourth at the famed Gardens. Previously at the Gardens, there had been Game 7s in the '42 Cup final, the '64 Cup final and the second round of these 1993 playoffs against St. Louis. The Leafs had won all three of those Game 7s by a combined 13–1 score. In fact, Ottawa-born Syd Howe of the Detroit Red Wings had the distinction of being the only visiting player ever to have scored a goal in a Game 7 at the Gardens. Howe scored the opening goal in the '42 final, but the Leafs scored the next three to complete a magnificent comeback from being down 3–0 in the historic Cup final.

The narrative between the Leafs and Kings had been build-ing for thirteen days. Game 1 had the dramatic fight between McSorley and Clark. Game 2, the Kings bounced back. Game 3, thirty-seven-year-old Dave Taylor scored a key short-handed goal to give Los Angeles a 2–1 series lead. In Game 4, the Leafs reclaimed home-ice advantage. The fifth game at the Gardens was ended by Anderson's dramatic overtime winner, concluding a terrific goaltending battle between Hrudey and Potvin. Game 6, arguably the most thrilling game of the series, would always be remembered for The Call by referee Kerry Fraser, the decision not to penalize Gretzky in overtime.

Now it was time for Game 7. The Montreal Canadiens were waiting to battle the winner. They'd been waiting for five days. *Hockey Night in Canada* had already held planning meetings about how they might best approach a Toronto-Montreal final, a matchup that would surely grab the attention of the entire nation. The weather had cooled since hitting 25°C mid-month, and now it was a comfortable 17°C. Nice and dry, too, for fans parking their cars or walking along Carlton Street with tickets in their hands. As the two exhausted teams prepared for one final joust, beer sales were brisk in the Gardens, and scalpers demanded ten times the face value of tickets and even more.

Gretzky arrived hours before game time, just like another NHL superstar had once mentored him. "Guy Lafleur taught me when I was younger—and I guess Bobby Orr taught Flower—that the sooner you get to the locker room, the sooner you can focus on the actual game," says Gretzky. "Nobody can call you, nobody can talk to you. I left for the Gardens about five hours before the game. I get there, have a coffee with the trainers. In those days, it was more of a locker room, not like a lounge. Just a training table and a little TV. You'd sit there for a few hours. I do remember I was scrambling around trying to get tickets. Friends had wanted seats, and friends of my family wanted seats. I knew the scalper out front, who'd been there forever. The clubhouse boy would go out and say, 'What do you need for four tickets?' And I'd trade three signed sticks and a jersey and maybe a pair of gloves so I'd get what I needed." The training staff knew Gretzky liked to have four sticks ready for every game, each with sticky black tape lightly covered in talcum powder. He used two-piece Easton aluminum sticks, which took a little longer to prepare.

If the game itself didn't have enough significance, Gretzky knew his beloved father, Walter, would be on hand. Walter Gretzky had suffered a near-fatal brain aneurysm in 1991, just five days after his fifty-third birthday. It was only a year and a half later, and he was still very much in recovery mode. "It was a hard time for my entire family," says Gretzky. "At that time, he wasn't that aware what was going on, because they had him on a medication that was really a downer, protective against a heart attack. So we knew we wouldn't get a true reading of where he was at until we started weaning him off of this drug that kept him a little comatose, for lack of a better word. But we knew he was making progress. We also knew we had time on our hands and where he was at wasn't the final result. It was a blessing he was there."

Gretzky was still wearing the flak jacket and getting a pregame painkilling injection for the broken rib suffered in the first round of the playoffs. But given that nine months earlier there had been fears his career was over, the rib seemed like nothing. "By the time we got into the playoffs, I was feeling like a young kid again, energetic and excited," he says. "Those forty games I missed were probably important in my career in that it showed me how much you miss the game when you can't have it."

Friends and family of Kings players and coaches were girding for a hostile welcome at the Gardens. It had been that way since the ugliness of Game 1. For Game 7, Donnelly's father, Mike Sr., courageously decided to wear an LA Kings jacket to sit in the middle of an arena filled with Leafs fans. He sat beside Dave Taylor's wife and the wife of Kings broadcaster Jim Fox and decided the easiest way to calm the Leafs fans sitting around them would be to play bartender. He started buying beers, making friends and easing the tension before the opening faceoff.

In the Toronto dressing room, the Leafs were trying to get their collective energy up for a game they wouldn't have dreamed they'd be playing back at training camp the previous September. They'd won a pair of Game 7s to get here, beating Detroit in overtime in the first round of the playoffs, then whipping the Blues to end a hard-fought series. They needed one more Game 7 victory to get to the Cup final, but they were running on fumes. Gilmour had continued to get intravenous fluids after every game. Potvin was losing six to eight pounds every game in the heat of the Gardens and the Forum and spent most of his time on the off-days trying to eat and drink as much as possible.

The Game 6 loss been deflating. Berg was still blaming himself for not rotating down to take Gretzky on the overtime winner. Clark had played the greatest game of his career and it was still not enough. Potvin had got his pad on Gretzky's winner but just failed to keep it out. Anderson had felt like his teammates blamed him for his late-game penalty in Game 6 and was trying to shake it off. Among all the Leafs forwards, he had the most significant reputation as a clutch playoff scorer. He had eighty-seven goals in 164 playoff games going into Game 7, two more than the great Islanders winger Mike Bossy and fewer than only his three former Oiler teammates Mark Messier, Jari Kurri and Gretzky.

The Toronto defence, in particular, looked worn out. Burns had used only five defencemen most of the series, while the Kings had rotated six, sometimes seven, as they would again in Game 7.

In particular, Burns had leaned heavily on twenty-nine-year-old veteran Dave Ellett, his best all-around defender. Ellett—born in Cleveland near the end of the long minor league hockey career of his father, Bob—was tall, good-looking and talented. His teammates called him "Roy," as in Roy Hobbs, the hero played by Robert Redford in the baseball film *The Natural.*

Advancing to the Cup final seemed like it would be the next step in a natural progression for Ellett. He'd been part of an NCAA championship team in 1984 with Bowling Green University, a title won in quadruple overtime over Minnesota-Duluth at the Olympic Center in Lake Placid. He'd graduated to the NHL and the Winnipeg Jets, and soon scored twenty-two goals as a flashy offensive defenceman with a big shot. He'd already known defeat at the NHL level. His power play goal against Edmonton in the 1990 playoffs had given the Jets a 3–1 series lead. The Oilers had roared back to win the series, but Ellett's goal was still regarded as the biggest postseason goal in the team's history. Like his close buddy Clark, he had been around and had paid his dues. This seemed like his time, per-haps his chance to play hero again. "Ellett wasn't an emotional player on the ice, but he was an emotional voice in the room," said assistant coach Mike Kitchen. "He supported Clarkie. He made everyone accountable. He took on so much ice time for us in those playoffs."

Since Gretzky and Gilmour had faced off in Game 1 to start the series, 1,381 minutes and one second of action had taken place. Each team had three wins. Each team had won once in overtime. Each team had won once on the road. The Leafs had scored nineteen goals, the Kings had scored seven-teen. It had been as close and hard-fought a series as a series could be. Gretzky had two goals and four assists in the first six games, while Gilmour had accumulated four goals and six assists. So far, Number 93 had out-produced Number 99 in the '93 conference final.

Anderson had scored four of the Leafs goals and Clark had three, which meant the three Leafs—Gilmour, Anderson and Clark—had combined for more than half of Toronto's offence in the series. The Kings hadn't received more than two goals from any one player, and thirteen different LA players had scored. The Leafs had received two goals from their defence-men, while the Kings had five from their blueliners. The numbers didn't lie: for six games, LA had been getting more offence from more players and using more defencemen to share the burden, while the Leafs were relying on a smaller group to carry them to the next round. "At that point, it's really about mental endurance, the strength you hope you have as a team," recalls Leafs assistant coach Mike Murphy. "Well, the Kings had chipped away at a little bit of ours."

LA's victory in Game 6 had buoyed the Kings. Both teams carried the weight of their respective history, and a deciding game like this came with intense pressure for both clubs and all the players involved. Hockey players, by habit, liked to feel more of the pressure was on the other team, that they could just play free and loose without the same consequences. It eased their angst and pre-game jitters. It didn't matter what was actu-ally true. It mattered what players believed. "By the time we got on the ice, we honestly felt the pressure wasn't as much on us as it was on them," says Gretzky. "Everyone was hoping for a Toronto-Montreal final. That was the talk of the country."

Both teams needed to be better. Toronto's power play had

gone south, and they'd given up four LA power play goals in Game 6. The Kings, meanwhile, had blown two-goal leads in Games 5 and 6. They were making things unnecessarily difficult for themselves by not being sound defensively.

As the fans filed into the Gardens, many were wondering if Dave Andreychuk or Nik Borschevsky would ever score again. They'd both been reliable scorers all season but had come up dry against the Kings. For the fans, it had been so long since the Leafs progressed this far in the NHL postseason it was hard to have any expectations. This playoff run had been a surprise, a pleasure, but now that it was coming to an end, Toronto supporters didn't know whether they should be thrilled at what had been accomplished so far or hungry for more. It all seemed a little unreal.

THE LEAFS STARTED GILMOUR between Clark and Anderson, and they immediately sped away on the attack but were then whistled for offside. Seconds later, Leafs defenceman Jamie Macoun, who had taken two slashing minors in Game 6 to put LA on the power play, was penalized for cross-checking. With only fifty-nine seconds gone, the Kings already had the man advantage again. The line of Gretzky between Tomas Sandstrom and Luc Robitaille, and Corey Millen between Tony Granato and Mike Donnelly, both generated excellent chances. The Kings top skill players had lots of open ice early, and they were flying.

Granato suffered a nasty cut to his face while being driven into the end boards as part of a four-man pileup involving himself, Donnelly, Bob Rouse and Sylvain Lefebvre. "Lefebvre had a chance to get me back after something I'd probably done to him," says Granato. "I expected that." Donnelly says it was actually his stick that cut his teammate as he tried to take a hard run at Lefebvre. Regardless, Granato was bleeding profusely from the jagged cut to his upper lip and cheek. "I was trying to stop my upper lip from hitting my nose as I skated," he recalls. Trainer Peter Demers just taped the cut together and Granato returned to the fray, re-taping the ugly wound after every shift.

Soon after, Mike Foligno jumped to try and get his glove on a puck flipped high through the neutral zone. Like a defensive back cutting down a receiver, Tim Watters low-bridged the Leafs veteran, who landed on his head. Foligno wore a bowl-like Northland "dome" helmet, one of the ugliest buckets in the history of the game. But it might have saved him from serious injury on that occasion. He crouched in pain on the Leafs bench as trainers Chris Broadhurst and Brent Smith attended to him. As he rose to his feet, three fans squeezed by, trying to leave their seats for the concession stands. The Gardens was that intimate, and the players were afforded that little room on the benches. Foligno didn't even look surprised or irritated that he had to make room for the fans to pass.

At 8:45 of the first, the Kings were caught with too many players on the ice, the kind of dumb mistake that tends to be costly in big games. As McSorley was trying to get off the ice and Rob Blake was trying to get on, Alexei Zhitnik touched the puck in front of the LA bench. After a series in which so much ugliness had gone unpunished, it seemed like a minor offence.

But it was the visitors and not the home team, that capitalized. McSorley had danced around Macoun for a good chance earlier in the period, and even though the Kings were short-handed, McSorley jumped into the play again. "Barry kept telling us, 'You can't be afraid to play,'" says McSorley. Not that McSorley had ever been afraid. But after arriving in the NHL as an enforcer-in-training he had become a versatile rearguard capable of playing at both ends of the ice. He could play offence with the most skilled players in the world.

Leafs defenceman Dmitri Mironov, who had reported to camp nine months earlier out of shape and had been in and out of the Burns doghouse all season, was back in the Toronto lineup after being scratched the previous three games. It was a signal Burns knew his defence corps was dangerously tired, but he didn't trust Mironov much. For the power play, however, Burns decided he would give the big Russian a shift. There shouldn't have been as much risk with the Leafs holding a man advantage. But there was.

Gilmour turned the puck over to Kurri just inside the LA blueline and the Kings took off on the rush. Todd Gill hit Kurri hard into the Leafs bench, but Gretzky was following the play and grabbed the loose puck. McSorley joined the rush, giving the Kings a two-on-one break, with Mironov back. It was exactly the same scenario as Game 3, when Mironov had faced McSorley and Kurri on a break, and he played it just as badly.

Mironov positioned himself between Gretzky and McSorley, taking away neither the shot nor the pass. Gretzky slipped the puck across to McSorley who, instead of firing it into the yawning net, passed it back to Gretzky. Mironov, spinning like a top, didn't cut that off either.

McSorley's pass wasn't a good one. It was behind Gretzky and into his skates. Most players in that tight to the net couldn't have made the play. Gretzky, of course, wasn't most players.

He deftly turned his right skate out, redirected the puck to his stick and coolly shot it into the Leafs net at 9:48 of the first period with Potvin sitting on his rump at the far post. It was classic Gretzky, a difficult play he made look routine. Only a few players could make it. "No other player in the world could react that quickly," says Hrudey. The Kings had killed the Leafs with their power play in Game 6, scoring four times, and now they'd scored a short-handed goal to get the all-important first goal of the game. Gretzky, assisted by former Oiler teammates Kurri and McSorley, became only the second visiting player in NHL history to score in a Game 7 at the Gardens.

It was the third short-handed goal of the series for the Kings, and short-handed goals tended to have more impact than any other kind. Teams on the power play were never supposed to surrender a goal. Ever. When they did, it was a massive breakdown. The Leafs liked to use Gilmour short-handed to create that opportunity. The Kings often sent out Kurri and Gretzky, two of the greatest scorers in NHL history, knowing they might score short-handed and deal a demoralizing blow to the opponent.

With three minutes left in the period, the line of Gilmour between Andreychuk and Borschevsky, so important in Toronto's second-half success that season, had a terrific shift, creating several chances in the LA zone. The puck skittered into the corner, and then the Kings broke out of their zone with an emboldened McSorley again leading the rush down the middle of the ice.

McSorley moved the puck to Gretzky on his right, and the LA superstar found Sandstrom alone in the slot. Sandstrom fired a low shot past Potvin's blocker and the Kings had a 2–0 lead.

The Gardens was in shock, as were the Leafs. "I thought we were heavy. Things weren't coming easy," recalls Anderson. "It felt like we were still on the plane, and we weren't bouncing the way we should. We had the momentum going into Game 6, but it was taken away and we didn't know how to get it back." McSorley's offensive aggressiveness was paying off, and Gretzky had more room to make plays than he'd had in the whole series.

The Leafs, however, had become a hard, tough team since first assembling as a mishmash of veterans and unproven youngsters the previous fall. Just as they had in Game 6 while trailing 4–2, they fought back with all they had. On the power play to start the second period, they got off the mat and delivered a heavy blow of their own.

Andreychuk attacked on the right wing, not his usual left, and drove around Watters, who sprawled to the ice. Not known as a playmaker, Andreychuk normally would have either taken the puck to the net or shot, and Blake came across to try and thwart either play. Instead, the big winger drove around the net, his head up the whole time. Nobody noticed Clark cruising into the slot. Andreychuk put a pass right on the stick of Clark, who buried it past Hrudey to make it 2–1 at 1:25 of the second. The Leafs were on the board, and the game started to pick up speed.

Ellett went to retrieve the puck behind the Toronto net and Shuchuk tripped him, causing Ellett's left knee to bang hard into the boards. He took a few moments to get up, and the Leafs were on the power play again. The Kings killed that off, but they had to spend more time in their own zone to do it, adding to the sense the rink was tilted. Off a faceoff in the Los Angeles zone, Gilmour ended up with the puck in the corner and Corey Millen holding him with both arms, having dropped his stick. The Leafs centre kept his feet moving, squirming loose. Anderson, reading the play, bolted for the open ice between Donnelly and Watters, and Gilmour found him with a perfectly timed pass. Anderson barely touched the puck before shooting it off the post and in, tying the game 2–2 at 7:36. It was his eighty-eighth career play-off goal. Game 7, like Game 6, was turning into a contest in which the Kings could build leads but couldn't protect them. Mike Krushelnyski almost scored a minute later on a pass from Borschevsky, and suddenly it was the Kings who appeared to be tiring. Melrose called a timeout, desperate to get his team to re-group and regain its composure.

Still, the Leafs pressed furiously. Osborne hammered McSorley with a heavy hit along the boards in the Kings zone, sending the LA tough guy flailing to the ice. Manderville, the Leafs rookie, jumped on the ice with Zezel and Osborne, spell-ing Berg. Burns was trying to find more bodies to help the cause. Melrose, seeing inexperience on the ice, spotted his opening. He sent Gretzky over the boards. Sandstrom carried the puck down the right boards over the Leafs blueline ahead of Gretzky, who was trailing the play.

One of Burns's key defensive tenets was to always check for the trailing player on the rush. Leafs assistant coach Mike Murphy shouted at Manderville from the bench to do just that as the play moved down the ice. Lefebvre had Sandstrom, Rouse was close enough to Robitaille to check him and Manderville's job was to come across and take Gretzky, the trailer. The Leafs were in perfect defensive position.

But when Sandstrom made the drop pass, Manderville tried to sweep it away with one hand and missed it. Gretzky grabbed the puck, stepped inside and took a slapshot from twenty-five feet, beating Potvin clearly on the glove side. It was a mistake by Manderville. Then again, it was also a mistake by Burns, who had a rookie out against the greatest scorer in league history. "That goal was just vintage Wayne Gretzky," says Robitaille. "I felt we were going to win when he scored that." The Kings had absorbed a second-period haymaker from the Leafs, and not only had they kept standing, they had jumped ahead again, 3–2, with Gretzky suddenly the most dominant LA player on the ice with two of the three goals and an assist on the other. "We were climbing a mountain, and it seemed like there was a lot of sand at the top," says Anderson.

The two clubs adjourned to their respective dressing rooms after forty minutes, unsure if they had one more period to play in Game 7 or if the series, for a third straight game, would go to overtime. The visiting dressing room at that time was incredibly small, an L-shaped room with one urinal and one toilet stall. Hrudey had his routine between every period of taking enough of his gear off so he could urinate. He went to do so only to find his way blocked. "John Candy and Mike Myers were around a lot," Hrudey recalls. "So I had to wait, because they were using the toilets. I remember thinking, How absurd is this?"

The third period began with the Leafs behind 3–2, but once again they tied it, and once again it was Gilmour and Clark doing the work. Clark was hacked to the ice in the Kings zone and for a moment lay stretched flat out, spinning on the newly cleaned Gardens ice surface. But he jumped to his feet as Gilmour retrieved the puck behind the LA net. Watters tried to get to Gilmour but caught his leg on the side of the Kings net. Gilmour delivered a pass nearly as perfect as that with which he had found Anderson in the second period, and Clark drilled home his fifth goal in two games to again tie the game, 3–3, at 1:25 of the third. There was bedlam at the Gardens. The Leafs simply wouldn't go down and stay down, and it seemed like the two clubs were determined to produce an even higher level of entertainment than they had in the classic Game 6 contest. The intensity and passion the Leafs and Kings had brought to the competition was off the charts.

Neither team wanted victory more than the other. Neither appeared to be decisively better than the other. There were plenty of potential heroes on both sides, plenty of players toughened by years of playoff experience. But only one team could advance to the Cup final.

After six goals had been scored in less than forty-two minutes, suddenly the well dried up for both clubs. The game stayed tied 3–3 for five minutes, then ten minutes, then twelve minutes. An agonizing eternity. Waiting. Wondering. Overtime loomed again.

With just over ten minutes left, Berg shrugged off an LA checker at the left boards and took the puck hard to the LA net. He went flying over a diving Kings defender, but the puck stayed out. Zezel stole the puck outside the Kings zone with eight minutes and stepped into a slapshot, but Hrudey came fifteen feet out of his crease to stop the shot. Andreychuk took a pass from Gilmour but shot the puck over the net. Gilmour was knocked down from behind, then Blake knocked him down again.

The Kings line of Millen, Donnelly and Granato raced back the other way. Granato crossed the Leafs line with the puck and moved it across the ice to Zhitnik as Donnelly headed for the net. Donnelly, a native of Livonia, Michigan, had come out of Michigan State University as an undrafted player despite having scored fifty-nine goals in forty-four games in his senior year, out-duelling Brett Hull of Minnesota-Duluth for the NCAA goal-scoring crown. He'd also scored the winning goal against Harvard in the 1986 NCAA championship game. As an NHLer, first with the New York Rangers, then the Buffalo Sabres and now the Kings, he'd never been put in an offensive role. "I was always driven to score," he says. "I wanted to score. I knew I could score more in the NHL than I had."

Zhitnik lost control of the puck for an instant, then slapped it towards the net. It hit the leg of Rouse and glanced directly through the slot, past Lefebvre, to Donnelly at the right post. Potvin had no chance whatsoever as Donnelly swept the puck into the open side to give the Kings their third lead of the game, 4–3. "I'll never forget it," says Donnelly. "It was just a broken play, and the puck came right to my stick. There was no chance I was going to miss that one. It was the biggest goal I ever scored in my life." Donnelly raised both arms in celebration, then jumped into the arms of McSorley and both Kings crashed to the ice. After fourteen minutes and forty-four seconds, the tie had been broken. It was the third goal scored against Gilmour and his line. But with 3:51 left, there was still time for more heroics from the Leafs.

Still time to change history.

On the next shift, Melrose sent out Pat Conacher and Dave Taylor, who he liked to use to start games on the road immediately after a goal had been scored by either team. Seeing the night Gretzky was having, Melrose sent him out as well. "That's one of the things I learned when I played with great players, guys like Borje Salming and Darryl Sittler in Toronto," says

Melrose, a Leaf from 1980 to 1983. "They never played enough. I had no problem with Gretz going out with the fourth line. He was smart. He didn't expend a lot of energy all the time." The Leafs countered with the unusual threesome of Anderson, Krushelnyski and Borschevsky. It was almost a random selection of players. No Gilmour, no checking line.

Four Kings defended, while Gretzky lingered just outside the visiting team's blueline. Taylor, falling to the ice, chipped the puck past Ellett to Gretzky, who reached behind him with his right hand on his stick and pulled the puck forward to himself. Hounded by Gill, Gretzky skated down the right side, around the right corner of the Leafs zone and behind the net. He was alone, not a teammate in sight. Ellett, Borschevsky, Anderson and Krushelnyski had skated back hard and were in position. The rest of the Kings were changing.

Ellett, confident Gill had Gretzky under control, turned counter-clockwise away from the Kings superstar, looking for any other LA players. There were none. Gretzky flipped a back-hand pass to the front of the Toronto net. "One of the things that Barry had drilled into everybody's head all year long was one guy high and one guy go to the net hard, especially when an offensive guy has the puck," says Gretzky. "I was just throwing it to the front of the net. Fortunately for me, and unfortunately for them, it just ricocheted off [Ellett's] skate and went in. Did I do it on purpose? No. One hundred percent, no."

There wasn't an LA player in sight as the puck hit Ellett's right skate and rolled just inside the right post at 16:46, the second Kings goal in thirty-seven seconds. "That one hurt," says Potvin, who tried to kick at the puck before it crossed the goal line. "I just remember looking around, knowing Gretzky was by himself. I didn't want to give him a wraparound chance. He threw it in front, and there was no time to react. I've looked at it many times. You don't see another LA player around." Melrose still isn't so sure it wasn't an intentional play. "People say he was lucky," he says. "How can one man have that much luck in his life?"

Gretzky was elated. From the bench, he looked across the rink at his father, confident that despite Walter's groggy condition he would still understand the moment, and pumped his right glove. "I wish I hadn't noticed it, but I noticed Wayne gesturing to his dad," says Hrudey. "I thought, Oh my God, I just caught an incredible moment. Right away, I wished I hadn't. I was distracted."

Just before the announcement that only one minute remained in the third period, Andreychuk's shot was blocked by Blake in the LA zone. The puck bounced to Ellett, who buried it past the distracted Hrudey inside the right post with sixty-seven seconds left. It was 5–4. "The Leafs are not quite dead," said commentator Harry Neale on the *Hockey Night in Canada* broadcast. "But they're not breathing very hard."

Burns called a timeout. The Leafs coach put his arm around Clark's shoulder as he talked, and he tapped Anderson to tell him he'd be going on for Potvin once the way was clear to pull the goalie. Over on the Kings bench, Melrose told Gretzky to go over the boards and was surprised at the response he received. "That was the only time in my career when a coach said go, and I said no, it's not the right thing," recalls Gretzky. "I wasn't ready. We had to do everything not to allow a goal. I felt like if they tied it up, we were going to be in trouble."

All season long, knowing Gretzky would often start to take off his equipment on the bench in the dying minutes in order to get out of it quickly after the game and deal with his media responsibilities, it had been a standing joke on the LA bench that Melrose would tell him to go on the ice anyway. "He'd say, 'Gretz, you're up.' And I'd say, 'Yeah, yeah, good one Barry,'" recalls Gretzky. This time, however, Melrose wasn't kidding. And neither was Gretzky. "I was surprised," says Melrose. "I'd never seen him turn down ice time. It was like a drunk turning down cold beer." Conacher and Taylor were going on the ice for sure, along with McSorley and Huddy. Instead of Gretzky, Melrose sent Kurri, one of the best defensive forwards of his era. So it was four former Oilers and the former captain of the Kings assigned to defend the one-goal lead.

The Leafs shot the puck into the Kings zone and Potvin scrambled to the Toronto bench for Anderson to come on. Kurri made a weak attempt to flip the puck out of the zone, and it was intercepted by Gilmour. The Leafs tried to get one clean shot. Anderson made like a goalie with an incredible kick save at the blueline to keep the puck in the zone. With fifteen seconds left, Ellett moved the puck to Gilmour behind the net, the same place from where Gilmour had scored his memorable overtime goal against St. Louis the round before. Gilmour, for a moment, had control of the puck and space to make a play. Rouse pinched down from his blueline post and cross-checked Huddy from behind, sending him sprawling into Gilmour. That forced the Leafs centre to skate out from behind the net, and he lost the puck, defusing the opportunity. The puck was cleared to centre, and moments later the horn sounded to end the game. It was over.

Gretzky jumped on the ice with his teammates, then turned back to the bench, skated over and locked in a warm embrace with Melrose. Three months after meeting with his coach in Quebec City and demanding more ice time, Gretzky had repaid Melrose's faith in him with a spectacular three-goal, one-assist performance that pushed the Kings into the Stanley Cup final for the first time in team history. "The greatest player in the world just took over," says Robitaille. "I remember saying, 'We're going to play hockey in June!' I had never done that before." The Leafs had contained Gretzky for more than six games, but he'd killed them in the end. "We let the gorilla out of his cage," says Anderson.

In the postgame handshake line, Gretzky paused for a moment with Burns to tell the Leafs coach, "I just couldn't let you win," as he grasped his hand. They'd known each other since their junior days in Hull, with Gretzky the owner and Burns the ex-cop and aspiring coach. "Pat and I were really good friends. In a lot of ways, he reminded me of my dad," says Gretzky. "Not their personalities, but their work ethic, and their work habits. So it was like trying to please your father sort of thing. I remember thinking in the [handshake] line, gosh, I felt so proud. Because I knew we had beaten a good team, and I knew we'd beaten a good coach."

On the ice, in a memorable interview with *Hockey Night in Canada*'s Ron MacLean, Hrudey spoke defiantly about his trying season. "I can't help but think back to January, February and March, when I was being pelted with all the criticism. Believe me, this is awfully sweet. I'm not vindictive, but it's awfully sweet. I was sick of answering all the questions and sick of all the negative talk, but I didn't believe it. I knew at times I wasn't playing very well, but I knew that, in me, I had it. It was just a matter of trying to concentrate and get through it. I had some real dog days. I think around the beginning of March, I started to feel real good. I guess my biggest obstacle was trying to get the respect back of my teammates and their confidence, and I did that."

The Leafs retreated to their dressing room stunned. The coaching staff sat in their office, trying to understand how it had gone wrong. "Whether it was the intrigue of Gretzky, the pressure of the seventh game, the national audience, all the games we had played, I don't know," says Murphy. "All those things had worn on us to the point, maybe, we didn't have that usual strength of character. There probably was some doubt in our team, and the Kings put it there." Hockey in general, and the NHL in particular, was a far less technical sport then. There were no analytics, no Corsi, no possession stats. There were fewer coaches per team. The games were less systematic, and often people in the sport read victory as a vindication of the inner determination of the players as much as evidence of superiority of skill or speed. That fed myths and hockey stories.

After a while, the coaches' wives joined the Leafs coaches, and they all sat there, some drinking a beer. Told that the streets outside the Gardens were jammed with unhappy Leafs fans, they stayed there for two and a half hours, trying to focus on how much they had accomplished. "We didn't have a lot of regrets, because the team played hard," says Mike Kitchen. "It was just unfortunate we couldn't get to the next stage. But weird things happen in Game 7s. That's why you try not to let it get to that point."

A few Leafs players braved the crowds to retreat to their usual haunt, P.M. Toronto. Gilmour was escorted through the mob back to his apartment. Unhappy fans, many angry, drunk and still resentful that Fraser hadn't kicked Gretzky out of

Game 6 for high-sticking Gilmour, banged their fists on the Kings bus. There was less than ten feet between the Gardens door and the LA bus, but Robitaille was still hit in the head with an egg when he tried to board.

Brian Cooper, who worked for Gretzky, McNall and Candy as president of the CFL Argonauts, had his tan Mercedes 300E parked underneath the Gardens. Gretzky, his suit sweat-soaked after doing interviews in the tiny visitors dressing room, was bleary-eyed and exhausted from the game. He got into the front seat and put the Campbell Conference trophy between his legs. They drove up the steep ramp to leave the Gardens, and at the top, the car had to stop. Fans saw Gretzky and began to rock the car. "Wayne said, 'This is getting dangerous,'" says Cooper. They escaped, and drove to Gretzky's restaurant in downtown Toronto, where he joined up with his teammates to celebrate. They were going to the Stanley Cup final starting in Montreal in three days.

FOR TWENTY-FIVE YEARS, many players on both sides who played in that famous Game 7 contest between the Leafs and Kings, and many fans in Toronto, have clung stubbornly to the belief that what made the difference was that Gretzky was motivated by all the criticism he had received during the series, particularly in the Toronto media. "It lit him up like a Roman candle," says Anderson. "He read everything. He knew every- thing that was said. It one hundred percent motivated him." For his part, Gretzky says that's nonsense. "Those kind of things were things they'd bring to me in the locker room. They would try to fire me up," he says. "Was that the difference in the series? Absolutely not. Did I stand there and hand out the article and put it on my fridge? Absolutely not. It was one of those things where I knew I had to play better. That was the motivation."

In the end, his five goals and four assists in seven games wasn't his best Stanley Cup final series ever, but in each of the final two games he had scored the winning goal. Once again, the Gardens had brought out the best in him, bringing his career totals to thirty goals and thirty-nine assists in twenty-eight appearances at the Carlton Street Cashbox. More than just goals and assists, Gretzky had supplied the moments his team needed to win. It wasn't how many goals he'd scored but when he had scored them that made the difference. Gilmour and Clark had done much the same for their team. But Gretzky had conjured up the deciding plays. It didn't matter what he'd done in the first five games anymore. It only mattered what he'd done in the final two.

It had been a spectacular series, start to finish, packed with emotion, colour, characters, nasty hockey and spectacular, unforgettable moments that Gretzky still cherishes. So much has happened since. Another Art Ross Trophy. His father's return to health. The World Cup disappointment of 1996, followed two years later by the shootout loss to the Czechs in the Olympics. There was the wonderful goodbye tour leading into his retirement, an Olympic gold medal in 2002 as executive director of Team Canada, four unsuccessful seasons as head coach of the Phoenix Coyotes. Financial complications as a part-owner of the Coyotes pushed him away from the game, but he returned in 2017 to become vice-chair of the Oilers Entertainment Group in Edmonton.

Gretzky's been in the game for five decades, and still relishes the chance to go over his hockey memories. To him, '93, and the series with the Leafs, was a special time. "When Wendel and Marty fought, that was a man's fight. When Wendel scored those three goals to tie it up in Game 6, that's a man, that's a superstar, that's a guy bringing it to the table. The best players were doing something every game to excite the fans and motivate the fans to cheer for their team. That's what made it exciting," he says. "It was such an emotional series because of how good the hockey was. It's like the '72 series and the '87 [Canada Cup]. In my mind, and in a lot of ways, Toronto might have given Montreal a better series than we did. I'm not saying they could have beaten the Canadiens, but a Toronto-Montreal matchup might have been better for Toronto than it was for us.

"You can't sit here and say the Kings should have won the series in five games, or that Toronto should have won that series in five. If we played Game 7 again ten more times, they might have won five and we might have won five. That's how close it was."

EPILOGUE

THE SUN SPLASHED ACROSS Vancouver Harbour on a glorious, warm spring day. It was May 23rd, 1994. Snow-peaked Grouse Mountain beckoned in the distance as sea planes landed and took off over the harbour. Ships cruised lazily under Lions Gate Bridge. At the cushy Westin Bayshore hotel on the edge of Stanley Park, members of the Toronto Maple Leafs had a perfect view of the vista as they stretched out on cushioned chaise lounge chairs, catching a few rays. Or catching their breath. They were down three games to one against the Vancouver Canucks in the 1994 Clarence Campbell Conference final, with Game 5 the next night. They'd played seventeen games in thirty-four days, including three in the Central Time Zone and five in the Pacific. The travel had been endless. Including a pre-season trek to England for a two-game exhibition series with the New York Rangers, the Leafs had played 103 games over the previous nine months. They were running on fumes.

Head coach Pat Burns convened an impromptu meeting over a poolside lunch with the two longest-serving Leafs, captain Wendel Clark and defenceman Todd Gill, plus star centre Doug Gilmour. They knew the situation was bleak. Just like the 1993 playoffs, the trip to this point had been long and exhausting. The Leafs had beaten Chicago in six games, then needed seven games to vanquish the surprising and stubborn San Jose Sharks. Vancouver, however, had proven to be like running into a brick wall.

Back then, teams with home-ice advantage in a series could choose a two-three-two game format against teams from certain time zones. The Leafs had used that choice effectively to win Games 6 and 7 at home against the Sharks, but against the Canucks, the ploy had backfired. The Canucks, the seventh best team in the conference, had split the first two games in Toronto, then won the first two at Pacific Coliseum. The weary Leafs were on the ropes.

Toronto had been shut out in Games 3 and 4 and were in desperate need of help. A boost. An injection of energy. Something. But the magic of '93 was gone. That had been a joyous, raucous, surprising ride. By comparison, this had been a grinding uphill slog. The team had won an NHL record ten straight games to start the '93–94 season, seemingly shaking off the disappointment of losing to Wayne Gretzky and the Los Angeles Kings in the previous year's conference final. That early streak seemed to serve notice that it might be the year the Leafs returned to the top for the first time since 1967, that they were ready to take the next step.

After that spectacular start, however, the season had bogged down. In the final seventy-four games, the Leafs had won thirty-three, finishing second in their division. Gilmour had led the team in scoring. Dave Andreychuk had become the first

Leaf ever to score fifty goals—he ended up with fifty-three—and Clark had been right behind him with forty-six of his own. But the team just wasn't quite the same as the group that had suffered that painful Game 7 loss to the Kings twelve months earlier. Not as close, not as unified, not as able to produce extraordinary moments.

Some players, set to be free agents, were already eying the door. Sitting around a pool basking in the sun felt like surrender. It wasn't the image hockey players traditionally wanted to create while the season was still alive. Like getting caught on a golf course. As Burns huddled with his leading players at the Westin Bayshore pool, munching on fries, club sandwiches and burgers, he already knew it was over. His team was out of gas and he was out of answers. Gilmour had gone public two weeks earlier with the news he had received death threats from an unidentified stalker earlier in the season, and now he was hobbling on a badly injured ankle. He'd played 204 regular season and playoff games over the previous two NHL campaigns, most of them while skating in excess of twenty minutes a game. He barely could lace his skates, let alone bear the painkilling injections before each game.

Still, the Leafs players tried to lighten the mood as they wore sunglasses to darken the bright sun. Gill and Gilmour joked about getting their heads shaved for Game 5. Clark, wearing jeans and a black t-shirt over his muscular torso, playfully distended his belly, as if to show how he planned to look in retirement. He was also dealing with tough questions about his play. After being a nearly unstoppable force in the '93 conference final against the Kings, Clark had been that same player for the first two rounds of the '94 playoffs, scoring eight goals against the Blackhawks and Sharks. But against the Canucks, like the rest of the team, he was ineffective. He didn't have a single point. Vancouver fans taunted him with the "Wen-dy, WEN-DEE" chant that had started in Detroit the year before when an anonymous Red Wings player said he was "Wendel at home and Wendy on the road." Mean-spirited, nasty stuff. We often hear that hockey is a family and that players respect opponents who play the right way. But this was just an anonymous slur against an honourable player who had finally been given a chance to show what he could do in the playoffs on a good team, and had delivered exemplary performances.

The Canucks put the Leafs out of their misery the following night, but not before subjecting the easterners to one final dose of humiliation. The Leafs led Game 5 by a 3–0 score, but gradually frittered it away, and then lost in double overtime on a rebound goal by Greg Adams. Four straight losses. Felix Potvin, after being unable to stop Adams, slumped, then fell backwards into his net, expressing the exhaustion and disappointment of a team that believed it was destined for greater things that spring.

The beloved underdogs of the year before had given way to a contender that never seemed comfortable in the role of favourite. The Leafs had gone back to the well with basically the same team, minus Glenn Anderson, who had been traded to the Rangers for Mike Gartner. But they had ended up even further away from the Cup, while Anderson ended up getting another ring when the Blueshirts beat Vancouver in the final. "We just can't get over the hump," said Burns after the final loss to the Canucks. "We tried two years in a row and we just can't."

Two days later, Burns was talking even more negatively. He

spoke of the need for an overhaul of the roster. It was an entirely different feel from the loss to LA the previous year in the conference. That felt like the beginning of something. This felt like an end. The Leafs coach was making it plain that the roster GM Cliff Fletcher had given him wasn't good enough. Plus, he wanted the final two years of his contract ripped up, replaced with a new deal and a big raise. He was more than well aware that two straight visits to the Final Four had given the franchise twenty lucrative home dates over the previous two years, representing millions of dollars in revenue. That was more playoff home games than the Leafs had played in the previous decade before Burns arrived. His general unhappiness with the status quo also meant the gnawing insecurity that had driven Burns out of Montreal two years earlier was back. "If management is satisfied with me and the work I do, then we have to change the club," he said. "If they want to stay with the team they've got, then maybe it's time for me to move." To Burns, the Leafs had already become "they," no longer "us."

Burns got his raise and stayed, but it was over for the Leafs, for the group of Leafs players who had come so close in '93. A month later, Clark was finally traded after all those years of rumours, sent to Quebec City along with defenceman Sylvain Lefebvre in a blockbuster deal for Mats Sundin, another multiplayer Fletcher special. The stoic Clark cried, and a city mourned. Underrated Bob Rouse bolted to Detroit via free agency for a big pay increase. Mike Foligno was sold to Florida. The Leafs tried to build a new team around Gilmour as captain and Sundin as the new star, but it didn't quite mesh. Eventually, the other stalwarts of the '93 playoff run—Gilmour, Andreychuk, Dave Ellett—were all traded. Fletcher eventually fired Burns after a loss in Denver. Owner Steve Stavro finally fired Fletcher, which he had wanted to do the moment the Silver Fox was hired. Eventually, Stavro lost control of the Leafs, and lost his business empire along the way.

That gritty '93 team had promised so much, but after losing Game 7 to the Kings, really didn't deliver anymore. At the time, it seemed Gilmour and Clark would be Leafs forever. It seemed Potvin would stop pucks in Toronto for the rest of his career, en route to the Hall of Fame. It seemed the Leafs had finally figured out how to be a competitive NHL club and sustain it. But those promises turned out to be empty. Three years after the '93 play-offs, Toronto was once again one of hockey's worst teams.

For the Kings, the fall was even more precipitous, even uglier. After the exhilaration of riding Gretzky's magical night to the Game 7 win over the Leafs, LA lost the '93 Stanley Cup final in a dispiriting five games to Montreal. Marty McSorley, such a force against the Leafs, was caught using an illegal stick in Game 2—penalized by Kerry Fraser, no less—and it proved to be the turning point in the series.

On the way home from Montreal after losing the final game, McSorley argued on the plane with a team scout who felt all the former Edmonton Oilers on the team had cost the team the Cup, that it meant the team was divided into cliques rather than unified. By July, McSorley signed in Pittsburgh as a free agent, with Kings management deciding to give the younger Warren Rychel a new contract instead. McSorley had been everything to LA, both a blood-and-guts performer and a dangerous offensive player. But the Kings just let him go. Corey Millen, a key player against the Leafs, was quickly dealt to New Jersey. It was all more evidence that Bruce McNall's empire was crumbling and he couldn't hide that fact from prying eyes any longer.

McNall defaulted on a $90-million bank loan six months later, and by May, 1994, as the Leafs were playing the Canucks, McNall had been forced to sell controlling interest in the team and was out as chairman of the NHL's board of governors. Just one year after being in a box at Maple Leaf Gardens celebrating with his Hollywood friends, McNall was headed down a path that led to prison.

While the Leafs made it to the '94 conference final against Vancouver, the Kings didn't even make the playoffs. Dave Taylor retired, while Gretzky lasted only two more years with the Kings before being traded to St. Louis. LA didn't make it back to the Stanley Cup playoffs until 1998. "It was heart-wrenching," recalls Mike Donnelly, who was eventually traded to Dallas. "The way our team dissolved was brutal."

Looking back, it's clear that the thrilling Leafs-Kings series of May, 1993, was a spectacular peak for both teams. It was as special as it was fleeting. It was about a specific time and place, although players on both teams genuinely felt they were part of something that was going to last for more than one shining spring.

Maybe the Leafs and Kings knocked the heck out of each other, and left each other broken, like Muhammad Ali and Joe Frazier after the Thriller in Manila in 1975. The Leafs and Kings certainly brought out the best in each other, delivering all-or-nothing performances. Both clubs were heavily laden with veterans, and you could certainly argue that many of them were either at the top of their careers or never played as well as they did in that seven game set, either before or after. Both owners had used questionable or outright illegal means to become NHL proprietors, and when their empires started to crumble, their hockey teams did too. In an event of pure irony, Steve Stavro could have signed Gretzky as a free agent in '96, but didn't have the money. Perhaps McNall, had he not been on his way to prison by then, could have helped Stavro negotiate a bank loan to pay for Number 99.

The inability of both teams to take the next step makes their extraordinary '93 clash that much more meaningful in retrospect. At the time, it was a rollicking, entertaining hockey series, one that seemed to sidestep a date with history when the Leafs lost and didn't get to meet Montreal in the final. But a quarter century later, it's as if those fourteen days of heated playoff competition now appear larger in the review mirror. Rather than fading with time, that series has been enhanced as the years have passed. "I kinda get goosebumps when I think about our team," says Donnelly. "When I look back at that year, I don't look at Montreal series, at the final. It was that series against Toronto that was unbelievable."

The Kings survived all kinds of problems that year, from a back injury that threatened to end Gretzky's career to goalie Kelly Hrudey's in-season crisis of confidence to internal problems linked to McNall's fraudulent business practices. It forged a unique bond between players on that team. "What was it like to sit on the bench next to Wayne, and Dave Taylor and those guys?" asks Tony Granato. "Those were guys that if they called me up today and said we're challenging that old Leafs team to a best of seven series, can you be ready? I'd do it in one second. Just because I'd want to have the opportunity to compete with those guys again."

For the Leafs, obviously, the series left painful scars. Bill Berg still agonizes over failing to curl down in the defensive zone far enough to thwart Gretzky's power play winner in Game 6. He has never watched a replay of Game 7. "That was the best playoffs ever. I loved that time," he says now. "But I don't want to watch it because the hockey gods were against us." Dave Ellett, the victim of Gretzky's infamous bank shot in Game 7, the series winner, prefers not to even discuss the series. Twenty-five years have passed, and still the wound is fresh. "As of today, I am not interested in commenting on your book," he politely explained in an email. "This was, and still is, one of the most devastating losses in my career, and personally there is no joy in re-living it. Sorry."

Other Leafs don't want to forget. Potvin has a copy of a video of the '93 Leafs playoff run called *The Passion Returns*, the creation of Mark Askin, then a senior producer with Molstar Sports and Entertainment. Every once in a while, Potvin pulls out the video, pops it in to an old VCR player and watches the memories. He grimaces over getting his knee on Gretzky's winning shot in Game 6 but not being able to keep it out, and then giving up a hat trick to The Great One in the deciding game. "Having Wayne score three goals on me is not one of the great souvenirs I have from my career," he says.

There remains for all the Leafs the satisfaction of being part of a team that was so tight, so close, and a team that erased the negativity surrounding the Leafs and replaced it with, at least for a time, an exciting, winning culture. "Whenever I see those guys it's like I'm transported right back to Maple Leaf Gardens," says Berg. There was a formal team reunion before Burns died of cancer in 2010. "It confirmed a lot of things to me," says Berg. "To me, Burnsie was all about roles. His role on that team was to be the taskmaster, to get the best out of us. That meant not being the nicest guy. The last time I saw him at the Air Canada Centre, I walked into the luxury box where we were sitting. Burnsie came over and gave me a big hug. I couldn't have imagined him doing that when I was playing for him. But it gave me perspective."

Gretzky's four-point, Game 7 performance seemed nearly poetic. He was the kid from Ontario who was recruited to sell hockey in Hollywood, then returned home as a conquering hero. Ironic how, back in the Original Six days, Toronto would have once had playing rights to Gretzky simply by the fact that he was born in Ontario. When Gretzky led the Kings to victory over the Leafs, it was another symbol of the inability of the Toronto franchise to succeed and win in the more complicated post-expansion NHL when the Leafs were no longer granted those preferential territorial advantages.

Gretzky played in 208 Stanley Cup playoff games and four Stanley Cup finals, as well as four Canada Cups, one World Cup and the 1998 Winter Olympics in Nagano, Japan. Still, he says playing against the Leafs in '93 and winning that series stands up to any of those competitions in terms of his personal satisfaction. "It was one of the best series I've ever been a part of," he says. "It just went on and on. It was incredible how hard everybody played, and what they brought to the table, and the energy and the emotion."

That series was also his last hurrah, as it turns out, arguably his last burst of truly magnificent play. He was only thirty-two years old. He did win the NHL scoring championship in the '93–94 season even though the Kings missed the playoffs. But after that, as scoring dried up across the NHL, he never scored more than twenty-five goals or one hundred points in a season again. He played another seven seasons, but was unable to get another serious sniff at a fourth Stanley Cup ring. Canadian hockey fans will always remember him sitting forlornly on the Team Canada bench at the '98 Olympics when head coach Marc Crawford didn't pick him to take part in the critical shootout against the Czech Republic.

Gretzky played seven full seasons in LA and most of an eighth, but the only time the Kings got past the second round with him in the lineup was in the '93 playoffs. He believes personnel decisions by management cost LA a better chance at a championship during his time there, particularly the trade of Mike Krushelnyski to the Leafs in November, 1990, and the deal that sent Paul Coffey to Detroit during the 1992–93 season. "Had Mike Krushelnyski been on our team in the '93 playoffs, he would have been a difference-maker in the final series against Montreal," says Gretzky. "He was strong, he could play left wing, centre, right wing. He was a good faceoff guy, a great teammate. From my point of view, that was a trade that maybe cost us a Stanley Cup. At the time when they made the trade, I understood they wanted to get younger. Michael was a little bit older, they traded him for John McIntyre. Ultimately, had Mike been part of our team in that final, it could have been a different outcome. There's no question in my mind. If we could go back in time I wished they hadn't made that deal."

On the Coffey transaction, Gretzky acknowledges that Gary Shuchuk, one of the players acquired from the Red Wings, played a significant role for the Kings in the '93 playoffs. "He was that guy that brought that energy and toughness that maybe we lacked. But Paul Coffey would have been pretty nice heading into the Stanley Cup final. I'm biased because I have a great deal of respect for guys who win. Both Paul and Mike had won a lot."

On the Toronto side of the ledger, both Gilmour and Clark played the best hockey of their careers in that series. They went from Leaf stars to Leaf legends. Gilmour equalled Gretzky's 1.67 points-per-game average in the '93 playoffs, and after years of competing against Number 99 while a member of St. Louis and Calgary, he was finally vaulted into a position of being on equal competitive terms with Gretzky in that series. Gilmour only played four full seasons and parts of three others in Toronto—he came back in 2003 and played one game before suffering a career-ending injury—but that series and his gutsy performance still made him one of the most popular Leafs of the post-expansion era.

Gilmour succeeded Clark as Leafs captain after the trade with Quebec. But Clark one-upped Gilmour by returning to the Leafs not just once, but twice. Less than two years after being dealt to Quebec in 1994, Clark was re-acquired in a deal with the New York Islanders. On March 15, 1996, he made his triumphant return at Maple Leaf Gardens against the Dallas Stars. The Leafs were in desperate shape. Burns had been fired weeks earlier, and scout Nick Beverley—the Kings general manager in '93—had been thrust behind the Toronto bench. Only six players remained from the roster that had clashed with the Kings and Fletcher was desperate to do something to dramatically improve his team, whatever the cost.

Clark, wearing noticeably bulkier shoulder pads, scored in his return and the Leafs beat Dallas that night. But it's what happened late in third period during a lull in play that people remember. Clark was on the ice, waiting for the next faceoff. The Gardens seemed to grow oddly quiet, and then organist Jimmy Holmstrom popped in a CD. The very familiar lyrics from the popular sitcom *Welcome Back, Kotter* filled the Gardens. Just as the song says, the names had all changed, but the dreams had remained. It was a brilliant, emotional moment, and the Gardens crowd rose as one. The officials leaned against the boards, drinking it in with the fans. Clark seemed to briefly tear up. It was an expression of how Toronto fans already longed for those special feelings of just three years earlier when their Leafs came so close against the Kings, and Clark was their beloved leader. It was about him, but it was also about then.

In 2000, as his career wound down, Clark was released by Chicago. He returned to the Leafs one more time. Clark was used sparingly, and was a healthy scratch for seventeen of thirty-seven regular season games. In the first round of the playoffs against Ottawa, he dressed for only two of six games. But when the second round began against New Jersey, Clark was in the lineup at Toronto's new home, the Air Canada Centre. The Leafs were up 2–1 in the third period, and Clark roared through the neutral zone, crossed the Devils blueline and released one of his patented wrist shots that had so often thrilled Leafs fans. The shot beat Martin Brodeur in the New Jersey net, but struck the post and stayed out. The Toronto fans reacted as if Clark had scored. The whistle blew moments later, and the fans stood for an extended ovation that lasted more than a minute. All for hitting the post. "It was as though the fans knew I was done playing before I did," wrote Clark in his book *Bleeding Blue*. He never played another game, and the Leafs have never been as good as when he captained the team.

Clark is one of fourteen Leafs who are part of "Legend's Row," a series of bronze statues outside the Air Canada Centre. The young man who came to Toronto off the farm from Kelvington, Saskatchewan, to save the Leafs with his scoring and fighting is a unique character in Leafs history. In his mind, he played at a time when characters and personalities were embraced more than today. "Today if you have a personality, you're suspended," he says, only half-jokingly. "You started losing personality with the game the era before me. The time when there were no helmets. You got to know everybody by their face, their hair. You know, Motor City Smitty's choppy skating style, one hand on the stick. Because you could see faces and hair and everything, you got personality. You could really identify with a player. Today, everybody's a robot. Kids grow up with mouthguards, neckguards, face guards, helmets. You've taken away the personality because of all the equipment and how the game is."

Clark's right. But if hockey started losing personality in the era before he played, as he contends, the process accelerated after the '93 playoffs. It was then that the hockey industry began to change dramatically under the leadership of Gary Bettman and new players' union boss Bob Goodenow, and the game itself also began to change dramatically. Uniformity, not individuality, became the goal of the NHL head office, which certainly made sense from a business perspective. Hockey began to see the growth of a more homogenous NHL with a more homogenous style of play. New gimmicks flourished. When the Fox Network bought rights to broadcast NHL games, it introduced "FoxTrax," which came to be known as the "glowing puck," and talked about re-organizing hockey into a four-period sport.

Player salaries escalated wildly, erasing the myth of hockey players who loved the sport so much they would play for nothing. Rob Blake, for example, was making $165,000 during that series with the Leafs. By 1995, his salary had jumped to $2.25 million, and by 2001 he was making more than $9 million per season, more than the entire payroll of the Leafs team he had faced in that '93 playoff series. Over the course of twenty seasons, Blake made more than $80 million. By comparison, his teammate Dave Taylor, at one time a member of the highest scoring line in the NHL, never made more than $1 million in any of his seventeen seasons and made about one-tenth of Blake's career earnings. That's how much the money in the NHL changed in a generation. In '93, millionaire players were stars, and still fairly rare. A decade later, they were the fourth-line checkers making less than the NHL average wage. By the turn of the century, making the NHL was no longer just about fulfilling a dream. It was about becoming impossibly rich.

With this escalation of salaries came a new militant attitude from the NHLPA, and led to a series of owner-imposed lockouts. What began with a ten-day walkout from the players in the spring of 1992, the first in NHL history, grew into open warfare between owners and players. Teams in Quebec City and Winnipeg couldn't keep up with the costs of the game and were squeezed out. They were vibrant, enthusiastic hockey markets in the 1992–93 season, but soon after moved south to new US homes, as it seemed the league no longer cared about protecting the heartland of the game if larger, more lucrative US markets wanted a team.

Along with more money and more focus on profits gradually came greater walls between the media and players, coaches and executives, and between the public and those same figures. The days when Gilmour or Clark would walk out of the east doors of the Gardens onto Church Street and sign a few autographs before walking home or jumping in their car were over.

The '93 playoffs also marked the end of wooden sticks and goalies wearing equipment that approximated their physical size. New composite sticks gradually came into the game allowing just about anyone to absolutely rip the puck. That, however, didn't produce a more offensive game. Instead, offence began to wither. Goalies gradually became the most dominant force in the game, using lighter and larger equipment to take up more of the net. As well, the butterfly technique, little used in the early 1990s, gradually became the only accepted goaltending style. Save percentages jumped from around an average of .880 in '92–93 to .910 by the turn of the century. Along with that came greater use of video by coaches, along with larger coaching staffs and strategies like the neutral zone trap. Analytics invaded the game eventually, and by the 2017–18 season, a new version of the sport had emerged based on speed and possession. The pokecheck—an "active stick"—became more important than the bodycheck. The slapshot as a means of scoring had come close to disappearing.

Comparing eras in the NHL has always been difficult. Technology has played a major role, particularly in the last twenty years. All we can really say is the NHL in 2018 is a far different game than that which the Kings and Leafs used to burn an indelible mark in the memory of hockey fans twenty-five years earlier.

From that series, a basic hockey question remains: why, in the end, did LA beat Toronto? After all, the Leafs were the better team in regular season, won the series opener easily, led the series 3–2 at one point and had Game 7 on home ice. Their best players played well, usually a recipe for success. With all those factors in their favour, the odds were with them. The debate continues to this day as to why the Kings prevailed, although more from the Leaf side of the equation where Fraser's Game 6 call still endures as a primary point of complaint. The problem with that reasoning, of course, is that the Leafs still had Game 7 at Maple Leaf Gardens after that call, and as a team that had already won two seventh games in those playoffs, they should have been a team more confident of victory. The Fraser call extended the series, perhaps, but it didn't decide the series.

From the LA point of view, many believe McSorley's hit on Gilmour in Game 1, and his resulting bout with Clark, was actually the decisive sequence, robbing the Leafs of the momentum that should have been theirs after a resounding, series opening victory. "It was the pivotal moment of the series," says Hrudey. McSorley was one of the most influential players at both ends of the ice with his skills and his fists. "Marty was a beast in that series," says Berg. "Everybody talks about Gretz and all that. But the guy who killed us in that series was Marty."

Toronto was primarily a defensive team that relied on a few players to generate offence, while LA was primarily an offensive team that, with the biggest payroll in the game, had several good scorers along with Gretzky, perhaps the greatest offensive player in the history of the game. As the '93 conference final wore on, and as the two teams grew increasingly weary and bruised, it became more of an offensive series. In the final two games, eighteen goals were scored, ten by the Kings. It was wildly entertaining, and a style of play that favoured the high-scoring Kings.

Neither Dave Andreychuk nor Nikolai Borschevsky, who had combined to score fifty-nine goals for the Leafs during the regular season, scored at all against the Kings. Andreychuk, a right-handed shot playing left wing, was nullified almost completely by the right side of the LA defence, particularly McSorley and Blake. They had the requisite size and nastiness to deal with him. Toronto was more effective than LA at even strength, but the Kings power play was better, scoring four times in Game 6 alone. Even more decisive was the fact that LA scored four short-handed goals in the series to none for the Leafs, and won two of the three games in which they scored while Toronto was on the power play. Gilmour, Clark and Anderson combined for more than 60 percent of Toronto's goals, while the Kings had a more balanced attack and got goals from thirteen different players. Goaltending wasn't a deciding factor. Hrudey was marginally better in the final two games, stopping fifty-three of sixty-one shots while Potvin saved fifty-one of an identical sixty-one LA drives.

One of the aspects of the series that hasn't received a great deal of focus over the years is why Burns and the Leafs coaching staff didn't devise a specific plan to stop Gretzky, and force other LA players to beat them. In the first round against Detroit that year, Wings forward Dino Ciccarelli had been a major problem for the Leafs early in the series, but Toronto came up with a new game plan in Game 3 to make Ciccarelli less of a factor in front of the net and it worked brilliantly. But no similar adjustments were made to stop Gretzky as he heated up in the LA series. Burns seemed to either discount the fact that Gretzky alone could beat him, or he decided matching against him was too difficult, and he needed to be able to play various groups against him. Maybe Gretzky lulled the Leafs into a false sense of security by being relatively ineffective in the first five games of the series. Whatever the reason, the Leafs simply rotated defencemen against Number 99, rather than assigning a specific pair, and used a variety of forwards, rather than assigning a player or a line to check the game's most prolific player.

In Game 7, the Leafs, who had the last change on home ice, were caught with rookie Kent Manderville assigned to check Gretzky with the game tied 2–2. Not surprisingly, Gretzky won that matchup, and scored to put his team ahead 3–2. Defenceman Bob Rouse is still bothered by the fact the Leafs didn't have a specific game plan for Gretzky. "He got better and better. I just don't think we paid enough attention to him," says Rouse today. "We had no game plan trying to stop Wayne Gretzky. That may have been a bit of a blunder. I just never felt there was an emphasis on that." To be fair, few teams had ever had much success shadowing Gretzky, and he was difficult to track, often jumping on with different linemates or even seeming to play left wing or right wing.

Most hockey analysts would have given the Leafs the coaching edge before the series. Melrose was a raw rookie as an NHL head coach, while Burns was one of the most high-profile coaches in the game and had been to a Stanley Cup final. As it turned out, Melrose was more than up to the task of coaching against Burns. He shuffled his lines more, using Gretzky on eight separate lines in Game 1 alone. He got more from fourth-line players like Conacher and Dave Taylor than the Leafs did from similar players on their rosters. His players rallied around him, appreciated his style and liked the way he helped players like Hrudey when they struggled. Leafs players, meanwhile, appreciated Burns's ability to teach, but feared him. Some loathed him, and that dislike was a unifying factor for the players. This much is true: most expected Burns to thoroughly outcoach Melrose, and that didn't happen. It was a saw-off at worst, which was essentially a victory for the California side.

Melrose lasted only a season and a half more with the Kings and never had any further success as an NHL coach. In fact, the Tampa Bay Lightning was the only other NHL team to hire him, and they fired him after just sixteen games. Burns, on the other hand, coached another 418 NHL games after Toronto with Boston and New Jersey, and won the Stanley Cup with the Devils in 2003. He's in the Hockey Hall of Fame. Burns was, compared to Melrose, by far the more celebrated and successful NHL coach. They weren't equals before or after that series, but for seven games in the '93 playoffs, they were.

There was also the unpredictable element of what folks in the industry might call puck luck. Alexei Zhitnik's slapshot ricocheted off Rouse's leg directly to Donnelly with Game 7 tied 3–3, and gave Donnelly an open net to score. Only thirty-seven seconds later, Gretzky got an even better bounce off Ellett's skate for another LA goal. To what can such fortuitous bounces be attributed? Probably nothing more than the natural unpredictability of a sport played on slippery ice by players moving very quickly on razor sharp blades chasing a piece of vulcanized rubber. That's hockey.

A generation later, the memories probably linger more in

Toronto where the fans still wait for another Stanley Cup, and where hockey is more part of the daily conversation. In LA, two Cups won by the Kings in 2012 and 2014 have written the most successful chapter in team history. For many, beating the Leafs in '93 has been surpassed by defeating the Devils and the Rangers to lift the greatest trophy in sports.

But Toronto sure remembers '93, the heightened sense of drama and the extraordinary competition. For the most part, the players who competed love to relive the games, the moments. It was a spectacular, interesting time to be a hockey fan. It was a time when the game seemed just a little bit out of control, both on and off the ice, because it was. A time when the value of a player was defined more by his ability than his contract and the salary cap space his pay cheque represented.

For fourteen days in May, 1993, the Leafs and Kings captivated the hockey world at a time when passions seemed to run a little higher, burn a little brighter.

It's easy to miss what the sport had then that it doesn't have now.

ACKNOWLEDGMENTS

This book sat on my brain for a long, long time. It always seemed like a good idea, but the time never seemed right. In 2017, my friend and Sportsnet colleague Brad Fay loaned me a book called *The Anatomy of a Song*, the central thesis of which was that music couldn't be considered iconic until at least twenty-five years after it was written. A generation to fully appreciate the quality, in other words. Well, it's been twenty-five years since the Leafs and Kings played for the right to compete for the 1993 Stanley Cup. It was pretty clear the time was right to get this book off my brain.

So here we are.

My friend Phil Bingley, the editor at *The Toronto Star* who asked me to move from the general assignment pool to take over the Maple Leafs beat in 1989, was encouraging from the moment I brought this idea to him. He pitched in with some really useful research. Another colleague from *The Star*, awarding-winner writer Bill Schiller, was relentlessly positive, taking time to talk writing even when it took away from his own book project. When somebody that talented thinks you're on to something, you stick with it. Sportsnet's Rob Purchase went out of his way to track down the recordings of those seven games in May, 1993, not as easy to do as you might think. My friend Bob Borgen, well-known in Kings circles, took time to explain L.A. to me, and to give me a tour. My editor at Penguin, Nick Garrison, refused to let this project die, and rescued it from the disabled list several times. More important, he just kept demanding more. More from the story. More from me.

I owe a debt to those from those two teams who took time out to talk with me and share their memories and insights, particularly Marty McSorley, Bruce McNall, Doug Gilmour, Bill Berg, Wendel Clark, Kelly Hrudey, Barry Melrose, Kerry Fraser, Cliff Fletcher and Wayne Gretzky. Mike Murphy, the man with a foot in both camps, met with me countless times for coffee at his favourite morning hangout as I asked him every question under the sun.

Finally, my wonderful wife, Vicki White, never complained when I went into that book haze or took over the dining room table, and continues to insist against all available evidence that her husband is a skilled typist. My four children—Meghann, Delaney, Dawson and Leagh—once again all showed the unique skill to work around dad when he's lost in thought. Or just a little lost.

All these people helped me write the book I long wanted to write, helped me try to do justice to a truly memorable sports story. For that, I will forever be grateful.

Damien Cox
June, 2018

INDEX